Islamic Art & Patronage

This publication was conceived five years ago to serve both as a catalogue of an exhibition of more than one hundred objects chosen from the al-Sabah Collection in Kuwait as well as a group of essays tracing the evolution of Islamic art and patronage.

A few days after the objects left Kuwait for the first venue of the tour, Kuwait was invaded.

Despite the national and personal losses that resulted from the tragic turn of events, the owners of the collection decided to proceed with the project as a testament of their dedication to the preservation of Islamic culture and unfaltering support of the arts. In doing so, they have demonstrated the essence of true patronage.

E.A.

Islamic Art & Patronage

TREASURES FROM KUWAIT

Edited by
Esin Atıl

PUBLISHED ON THE OCCASION OF
A LOAN EXHIBITION FROM THE AL-SABAH COLLECTION

ORGANIZED AND CIRCULATED BY
THE TRUST FOR MUSEUM EXHIBITIONS, WASHINGTON, D.C.

THE AL-SABAH COLLECTION

Published on the occasion of the exhibition
Islamic Art and Patronage: Treasures from Kuwait
A loan exhibition from the al-Sabah Collection

EXHIBITION ITINERARY:
The State Hermitage Museum, St Petersburg
The Walters Art Gallery, Baltimore
Kimball Art Museum, Fort Worth
Emory University Museum of Art & Archeology, Atlanta
Scottsdale Art Center, Scottsdale
The Virginia Museum of Fine Arts, Richmond
St Louis Museum of Art, St Louis
Canadian Museum of Civilization, Hull
New Orleans Museum of Art, New Orleans
Institut du Monde Arabe, Paris
Haags Gemeentemuseum, The Hague
Palazzo Vecchio, Florence
Fitzwilliam Museum, Cambridge

First published by Rizzoli International Publications, Inc.
300 Park Avenue South, New York, New York 10010

Copyedited by Kathleen Preciado
Designed by Alex Castro, CASTRO/ARTS, Baltimore
Photography o objects from the al-Sabah Collection by Gordon H. Roberton
Calligraphic design by Mohamed U. Zakariya
Typeset by Monotype Composition Company, Baltimore
Printed by Amilcare Pizzi, Milan

ISBN 0-8478-1366-5
Library of Congress Cataloging-in-Publication Number: 90 28571

Page 4: Detail of **66**
Cover photograph: Gordon H. Roberton

Contents

Foreword

Historically, the two major forms of art collections have been the religious and the princely, often in combination with one another. The more stable and constant of such collections—ancient Egyptian tombs, Hindu temples, Byzantine churches, or Cairene mosques—have formed a natural locus, a place of assemblage and preservation of artistic work, consisting of both the objects and the buildings that house them.

Whatever the functions of these collections, neither the artifacts nor their repositories could have existed without the patron and the artist. Both exercised their natural gifts and cultivated skills toward one purpose—the embellishment and enrichment of the world around them. What neither could fully anticipate at the time of the commissioning and execution of such works was the influence of their acts, which would spread beyond their own milieu to a wider circle of appreciators.

In most countries the transformation and augmentation of private collections to become public institutions have been very much aided by the force of law—by state-controlled excavations or nationalization of religious properties and private holdings—or through more subtle means—by exemptions from taxes for works of art or monies donated to public museums. Very rarely have such collections been formed as the result of purely philanthropic deeds.

Detail of **62**

The case of Dar al-Athar al-Islamiyyah is distinctly outside these parameters. It shares with other museums the purpose of caring for and displaying its collections while educating the public, through exhibitions and special programs such as conferences, lectures, tours, and classes. The formation and growth of the al-Sabah Collection and its realization as a public museum, Dar al-Athar al-Islamiyyah, have been prompted by a purely cultural conviction, underlined by a profound sense of commitment toward Arab and Islamic civilizations. To make this private collection

9

available as part of the Kuwait National Museum is not a philanthropic gesture but rather an act of gratitude toward the State of Kuwait.

It is this larger context of the patronization of its subjects by the government of Kuwait that provides the framework within which Dar al-Athar al-Islamiyyah operates. Under the aegis of the Ministry of Information, the State of Kuwait has made Dar al-Athar al-Islamiyyah part of an all-encompassing program of social services, including subsidized health care, education, and public housing. Due to special and fortunate circumstances, the Kuwaiti government is able to carry out such massive public patronage, just as it is due to special and fortunate circumstances that such a collection could be formed through private means. The awareness of the responsibility that such good fortune brings is precisely what has created and sustains Dar al-Athar al-Islamiyyah and made possible this exhibition and publication.

It is hoped that the individuals and institutions that have contributed to the realization of this project will be rewarded by the results of their efforts, by the expanded appreciation of the breadth and beauty of Islamic art among the visitors to the exhibition and readers of the publication. Without fully realizing it, they themselves have become patrons.

Hussah Sabah al-Salem al-Sabah
Director, Dar al-Athar al-Islamiyyah
Kuwait National Museum

Preface

Patronage has always been a most significant impetus for the development of the arts. All great moments in cultural history bear the impact and stimulus of outstanding patrons who demanded excellence in production and innovation in expression. This demand instigated competition and even bitter rivalry among artists and forced them to excel in their metier to reap the benefits of recognition, thus creating new modes and movements.

Patronage of art and architecture could be undertaken by individuals as well as established families, imperial courts, foundations, government agencies, and religious institutions. Patrons evolved from diverse social levels and ranged from powerful emperors and kings, ambitious princes and governors to affluent officials and merchants. All patrons shared the desire to own or sponsor beautiful and precious objects or grand and impressive buildings reflecting their cultural and political aspirations and achievements.

Communities also benefited from benevolent patronage since the patrons' interest frequently extended from owning and sponsoring items and structures for personal pleasure to endowing architectural complexes that provided religious, charitable, educational, and commercial activities and facilities. In addition, works commissioned by patrons set standards or established trends that promoted the production of similar art and architecture of more humble proportions.

The most influential patrons in the Islamic world were the enlightened caliphs and sultans who ruled over vast and rich lands. These patrons manifested the superiority of their states through the splendor of their courts and attempted to impress and awe both local residents and foreign observers by commissioning magnificent objects and buildings. The protection of artists and sponsorship of art and architecture were considered prerogatives of great rulers. Their status was represented not only by the political prestige of their domains and economic affluence of their societies but also by the wealth of their courts and scope of their royal studios. These courts attracted the intellectual elite of the age, including celebrated artists and scholars. Here the diverse traditions brought by those of differing backgrounds fused together to create vibrant and unique styles and themes that came to identify the artistic characteristics of a region or period.

A second level of patronage, at times even more important for establishing new trends and artistic movements, was provided by aspiring princes and amirs. The members of this group were highly competitive and tried to attract and employ the most renowned artists. The products of the princely workshops also reflected the patron's taste and aesthetics in contrast to the more hierarchic expression of grandeur that prevailed in the imperial courts.

Great patrons of art were also great collectors. The desire to own rare and precious items promoted the establishment of imperial or princely treasuries in which unusual and expensive items were collected together with those considered aesthetically and technically superior. Emperors and princes sought after unique and splendid pieces, whether produced locally or made in foreign lands. Collecting itself was a form of art, and the range of items included in a given collection reflected the extent of the patron's interests, knowledge, and connoisseurship.

In recent times many collections assembled by Asian and European monarchs and princes were donated to the public and became the core of national museums, including those of the Hapsburgs in Vienna (Kunsthistorisches Museum), Romanovs in Leningrad (State Hermitage Museum), Ottomans in İstanbul (Topkapı Palace Museum), Qing emperors in Beijing (Palace Museum), and Medici in Florence (Galleria degli Uffizi). Similar collections amassed by religious organizations, such as the Shosoin in Nara and the Papacy in the Vatican, have become accessible to the public as well.

Donating private collections to public institutions is also an American tradition, as exemplified by the national museums founded on the collections of Andrew W. Mellon and Charles Freer in Washington, D.C. (National Gallery of Art and Freer Gallery of Art), the latter a part of the Smithsonian Institution, which itself was initiated by the collection and endowment of an individual—James Smithson. Other major American museums named after their benefactors include the Phillips Collection in Washington, D.C., the Frick Collection in New York, and the Walters Art Gallery in Baltimore. Belonging to this group of great collectors and benefactors are Sheikh Nasir and Sheikha Hussah al-Sabah of Kuwait.

Patrons of Islamic art not only supported artists and encouraged their work but also amassed vast collections. As patron-collectors, Nasir and Hussah al-Sabah have fulfilled the traditional Islamic role of sponsoring scholarly and educational activities and facilities by making their collection accessible to the public. This exhibition and its publication are yet other manifestations of their patronage and generosity.

When the possibility of introducing the al-Sabah Collection to the United States was being considered, the theme of the exhibition became immediately apparent to me. The exhibition was conceived to concentrate on objects that reflect the development of the artistic traditions in the world of Islam, represent diverse periods and regions, and highlight unique techniques and styles, united by the theme of patronage. The importance of patronage in Islamic culture had not been thoroughly studied, although the influence of certain rulers or dynasties on the promotion of the arts had been the focus of recent exhibitions. This project provided the opportunity to investigate the impact of individual patrons on the historical development of Islamic art.

The objects chosen for the exhibition fell naturally into four major historical periods. The chronological division was particularly appropriate for the discussion of patronage, beginning with early Islam, when the first great empires—those of the Umayyads and Abbasids—were established. During its formative years Islamic art selectively adopted certain themes and motifs from the pre-existing traditions and formulated its own vocabulary. The following period, classical Islam, witnessed a change in patronage with the rise and fall of numerous states and amirates, each of which attempted to display its newly established—and often short-lived—power through an active and deliberate sponsorship of art and architecture, promoting an exuberant and dynamic artistic environment extending from Spain to India. This was the age of diversified patronage, with wealthy individuals competing with the rulers by purchasing and commissioning works of art. In the postclassical period patronage continued to be a major activity in the courts of sultans and princes with the centers of production dispersed throughout the world of Islam. During the late Islamic period artistic activities became centralized, with the royal workshops of renowned emperors—Ottomans, Safavids, and Mughals—becoming the source of creativity, the styles and themes developing there radiating to all corners of the empires and influencing the traditions of neighboring states.

I am grateful for the enthusiasm of my friends and colleagues who contributed to this publication: Oleg Grabar, who authored the overview of Islamic art and patronage; Estelle Whelan, Jonathan M. Bloom, Sheila S. Blair, and Walter B. Denny, who wrote the introductory essays to the four sections; Marilyn Jenkins, who described the establishment of Dar al-Athar al-Islamiyyah; and Ghada H. Qaddumi and Manuel Keene, who provided the entries, the latter writing on his specialty, jewelry and precious objects (**16, 43–44, 69,** and **96–102**). Three contributors—Jenkins, Keene, and Qaddumi—have been or still are involved with the al-Sabah Collection, Jenkins was instrumental in preparing the inaugural exhibition in 1983, Keene was visiting curator at Dar al-Athar al-Islamiyyah between 1982 and 1984, and Qaddumi has been the curator of the collection since 1984.

My task as guest curator of the exhibition and editor of the publication could not have been accomplished had it not been for the encouragement and support of Sheikha Hussah al-Sabah, director of Dar al-Athar al-Islamiyyah. She made her collection available for research and selection and graciously consented to every whim and wish of all those involved with the project.

ESIN ATIL

The European tour of this exhibition was greatly assisted by the generous support of:

Ministry of Information, Kuwait
Ministry of Oil, Kuwait
Ministry of Awqaf and Islamic Affairs, Kuwait
Kuwait Airways Corporation
Kuwaiti Banks Committee
Al-Futtooh Investments Co. WLL

Islamic Art & Patronage at The Fitzwilliam Museum

The Fitzwilliam Museum, itself founded in 1816 by a noble act of patronage, counts it a signal privilege to present the only British showing of *Islamic Art & Patronage*. This exhibition's title is applicable not only to the original patronage involved in the production of such a range and variety of works of art from the Islamic world, but also to the enlightened patronage of Sheikh Nasser Sabah al-Ahmad al-Sabah and his wife, Sheikha Hussah Sabah al-Salem al-Sabah, in assembling their superb collection, and in making these treasures available for the education and delight of our visitors.

The Fitwilliam Museum's own collections of Islamic art are high in quality but limited in quantity and range, compared with those held by the British Museum and the Victoria & Albert Museum. The presence in Cambridge of *Islamic Art & Patronage* will thus open the eyes of many to the extraordinary level of artistry and craftsmanship achieved in the Islamic world. As a university museum concerned with, in our Founder's words, "the Increase of Learning", the Fitzwilliam Museum is particularly pleased to show *Islamic Art & Patronage* at a time when interest in Islamic art and its history is burgeoning. We hope indeed that the exhibition will give a fillip to Islamic scholarship in Cambridge.

We are grateful first and foremost to Sheikh Nasser al-Sabah of Kuwait and his wife Sheikha Hussah, who have given every possible encouragement and assistance to the Cambridge showing of their exhibition. We are also grateful to Dr Esin Atil, the curator of the exhibition, who was also responsible for editing its splendid catalogue. In Britain our thanks are due to Katie Marsh, who has co-ordinated arrangements, which, at the Fitzwilliam Museum, have been in the hands of my colleague Robin Crighton.

SIMON JERVIS
Director and Marlay Curator
Fitzwilliam Museum
University of Cambridge

Note to the Reader

It is not possible to use a standardized transliteration system when dealing with the entire world of Islam. Therefore, the preferred Arabic system of transliteration is used for Arabic words, Persian for those of Persian origin, and modern Turkish for Ottoman Turkish terms. Diacritical marks are not used in the transliteration of Arabic and Persian words and names. Words not found in *Webster's Unabridged Dictionary*, third edition, appear in italics. Unfamiliar terms are defined parenthetically at first reference. English spelling has been followed, except when variant usage is preferred, as in Madinah (Medina), Makka (Mecca), and Quran (Koran).

Islamic dynasties and their dates are listed in the Dynastic Tables, both in geographic and chronological groupings and in alphabetical sequence. Dates for individuals, particularly their reigns, are cited parenthetically at first reference. All dates are given in the Christian calendar, except when quoting from inscriptions, in which case the Islamic year appears as A.H. (indicating the Hijra year, based on the lunar cycle), followed by the A.D. date. When a year in the Islamic calendar falls between two consecutive years in the Christian calendar, the dates are rendered with a slash, as in 946 A.H. (1539/40). Furthermore, if a monument or work of art was completed during a span of years, then a dash is used, as in 1539–40.

Numbers in **boldface** refer to catalogue entries.

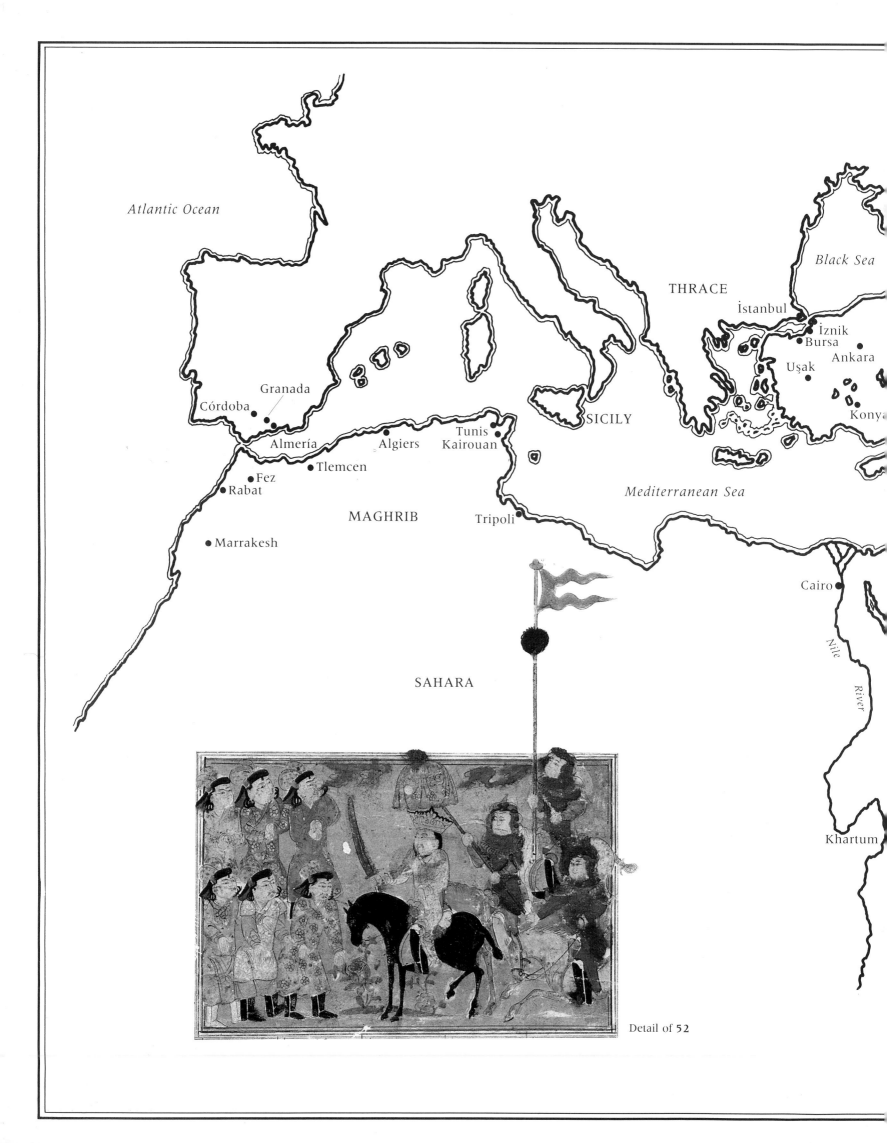

Atlantic Ocean

Black Sea

THRACE

İstanbul

İznik
Bursa

Ankara
Uşak

Konya

Granada

Córdoba

SICILY

Almería   Algiers   Tunis
                        Kairouan

Mediterranean Sea

Tlemcen

Fez
Rabat

MAGHRIB   Tripoli

Cairo

Marrakesh

Nile

River

SAHARA

Khartum

Detail of **52**

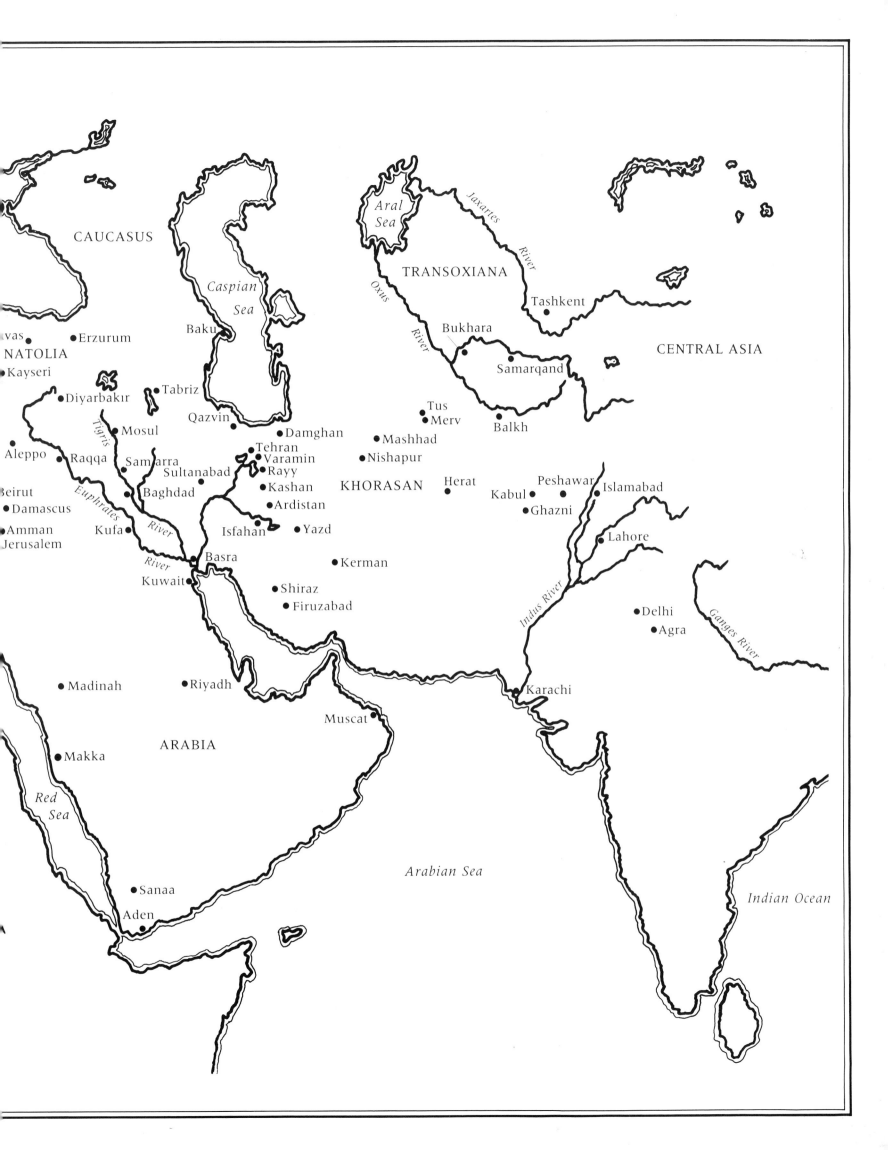

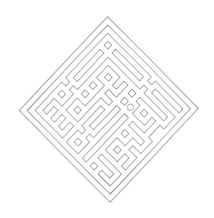

An Introduction
to the al-Sabah Collection

Marilyn Jenkins

In the spring of 1978, when I first met Sheikh Nasir, his passion for collecting Islamic art had only recently become all-consuming. At that time the al-Sabah Collection of Islamic art did not exist as such and the institution of Dar al-Athar al-Islamiyyah was not yet even an idea. The primary purpose of this essay is to trace the steps resulting in the formalization of the al-Sabah Collection and the birth of Dar al-Athar al-Islamiyyah, both of which occurred simultaneously during the fifteen-month period from December 1981 to February 1983. As a corollary, the history of these events can also serve as a blueprint to aid others in organizing public and private collections and in creating future museums.

At the center of this remarkable metamorphosis was the patron himself, Sheikh Nasir Sabah al-Ahmad al-Sabah, who was helped during his years of collecting by his wife, Sheikha Hussah Sabah al-Salem al-Sabah, now director of Dar al-Athar al-Islamiyyah. In less than a single decade his collection of Islamic art was transformed from a series of fine, isolated works of art, adorning his various private residences throughout the world and seen by only a few individuals, into a comprehensive, world-class collection worthy and capable of filling an entire museum. Through Sheikh Nasir's inspired vision, sustained enthusiasm, humility, and magnanimity, these objects, important to the history of Islamic art and culture, can now be studied and enjoyed by everyone.

Figure 1. Exterior of the Kuwait National Museum complex with Dar al-Athar al-Islamiyyah on the right.

The story begins approximately thirty years ago, in the late 1950s, when competition for the design of a museum complex was held by the Kuwaiti government and won by Michel Ecochard of France. The actual construction of the five-building complex on the Arabian Gulf took place during the late 1970s (fig. 1). In the spring of 1981 the Ministry of Information asked UNESCO to organize a team of specialists (of which I was a member) to be sent to Kuwait to study the newly built complex and propose a plan for implementing the museum as a whole. This inspection trip was made and a report submitted, but for unknown reasons the study team's recommendations were not acted on. In December 1981, soon after this initial attempt to establish a museum complex in Kuwait, Sheikh Nasir asked me to help him organize his collection of Islamic art and create a museum in one of the five buildings of the original complex.

The museum complex had been designed not only without specific collections in mind but also so that each building connected with each other. Therefore, the building allocated to Sheikh Nasir for the display of his collection had to be modified so that it would be self-contained, with an interior design that could accommodate a collection of Islamic objects. The specialized function of the building necessitated a major modification of the amount of light admitted through a series of windows of varying sizes and shapes. The interior space, in fact, had to be redesigned, a task for which an exhibition designer was chosen. Security and lighting systems were also required, and, consequently, a lighting designer and a firm specializing in museum security systems were engaged.

While the interior construction work was progressing and the necessary systems installed, the process of organizing the collection began. The first step was to locate and actually see the entire collection as yet scattered around the world. Since Sheikh Nasir had not begun acquiring Islamic art with a view toward establishing a museum and records were practically nonexistent, the size and scope of his holdings were unknown even to him. Until they were ascertained, however, neither the selection of objects for exhibition or publication in the commemorative volume nor the precise layout of the exhibition space could be attempted. Due to the vast quantity of material and number of places involved, this enormous task consumed much time while taking on the aura of wide-ranging "archaeological excavations."

As the objects were gathered in Kuwait from near and far, each was numbered, measured, and catalogued. At the same time each object was evaluated vis-à-vis its conservation needs. Those pieces requiring treatment were sent with specific instructions to conservators in Europe and America who were chosen for their skill in various areas of expertise. As this process was being accomplished, a photographer was selected to go to Kuwait and make a complete photographic record of each object. When new objects were acquired for the collection or when conservation was completed, additional photographic documentation was assembled.

On completion of this cataloguing process, an order had been imposed on approximately seventy-five hundred works of art. It was now possible to choose the objects to be displayed as well as published and begin to plan the exhibition. This selection process was aided by the decision to divide all the objects into four broad chronological periods: early Islamic (seventh–tenth century), early medieval (eleventh–mid-thirteenth century), late medieval (mid-thirteenth–fifteenth century), and late Islamic (sixteenth–nineteenth century), a division that I had found helpful in organizing three earlier publications and one that is now becoming standard for comprehensive Islamic exhibitions and publications. It was then necessary to determine the amount of exhibition space to be allocated to each dynastic period represented in the collection as well as the ratio between those objects to be displayed in cases and those to be hung on the wall. Once these determinations had been made, the challenging task of laying out all the objects chosen for exhibition began.

This complex and crucial step was executed in New York using two-by-two-inch photographs and scale drawings of all the objects and cases in which they were to be displayed. Each object was precisely located in its specified case with the size of each necessary support block noted for construction before installation was to begin. Objects to be hung on the wall were also carefully located. A scale drawing of each case with every object in its proper location was then made, and this record was bound into notebooks, case by case and gallery by gallery for use during the final installation. Since only two months had been allowed for completion of the latter step and there was no museum infrastructure in place, nothing could be left to chance in the installation of approximately one thousand objects, most requiring mounts—manufactured and fitted by museum preparators—which would allow the objects to be viewed at the proper angle and height. The ease with which the installation was accomplished proved that a method had been devised whereby a museum could be organized totally on paper in a city far from the site of the building itself and all the installation needs could be anticipated before the on-site process was begun. As in the pioneering Islamic galleries at the Metropolitan Museum of Art in New York, the layout was chronological and each case contained objects of various media. Such organization provided great potential for using the museum as an educational tool.

To help the visitor understand the various historical periods of Islamic art, the objects themselves, and the layout of the building, a comprehensive interpretive graphics program was designed. Since all text was to appear in Arabic and English, a translator familiar with art-historical terms was employed. Descriptive text panels and object labels were written, maps drawn, and large color photographs of major Islamic monuments commissioned.

As a commemorative volume on the collection was to be published in honor of the opening of the museum, a selection of objects to be illustrated needed to be made and the text and captions written forthwith. The book design, including the decorative motifs and colors for the covers and endpapers, was chosen as well as a publisher who could produce high-quality Arabic and English editions within the time constraints imposed.

It finally became imperative that a name be chosen at once both for the building and the collection housed in it. The name Mathaf al-Kuwait al-Watani (Kuwait National Museum) was selected for the five-building complex and Dar al-Athar al-Islamiyyah (House of Islamic Antiquities) was chosen by Sheikh Nasir for the building designated for his collection, which was hereafter to be known as the al-Sabah Collection. As soon as the names had been decided on, a logo, signage, publication titles, posters, and stationery among other things could be selected.

The moment had finally arrived for the debut of the al-Sabah Collection on Kuwait's National Day, 25 February 1983. For several years before this event the field of Islamic art and the art world in general had been abuzz with the news that Sheikh Nasir was buying Islamic art with the goal of establishing a museum to house it. Very few individuals, however, were aware of the extent of his collection and an even smaller

number knew of its quality. The approximately three hundred scholars, collectors, and dealers in the field of Islamic art invited to Kuwait for the opening of Dar al-Athar al-Islamiyyah did not know what to expect. It was gratifying to see the response of these knowledgeable guests to the collection and its presentation (fig. 2). Praise was instantaneous. Not only was the reaction of the foreign guests laudatory, the Kuwaitis themselves responded favorably to the al-Sabah Collection and Dar al-Athar al-Islamiyyah. They were proud and rightly so. Here was their own new museum of Islamic art, housing a collection more comprehensive than any other in the Muslim world and one which at its inauguration could boast that it ranked with the other great collections of Islamic art in Berlin, Leningrad, London, New York, and Paris. When the week of festivities celebrating the birth of Dar al-Athar al-Islamiyyah and debut of the al-Sabah Collection were over, the al-Sabah Collection had become *the* national collection.

In 1982 I concluded the Introduction to the commemorative volume in this way:

> The collection introduced here is a living collection, one which will be augmented in years to come—its gaps filled, its weak areas strengthened, new masterpieces added. Thus, in time it will be even greater and more comprehensive than it is today. In forming this collection, Sheikh Nasser has greatly enriched the field of Islamic art, and in his decision to place it under the aegis of the Kuwait National Museum he has made an important cultural contribution to the world at large, the Middle East in general, and Kuwait in particular.

In retrospect, how accurate are these statements? Following the opening of Dar al-Athar al-Islamiyyah, Sheikh Nasir continued to add to the collection in an attempt to fill gaps and strengthen weak areas. Notably, he improved the early Islamic holdings, particularly those of the Umayyad and early Abbasid periods, and filled important lacunae in the pottery collection, especially those of the Ilkhanid and Ottoman periods. Indian and Turkish arts of the book and Islamic glass in general were significantly strengthened as well. These acquisitions during 1983 and 1984 were so important and numerous that it was decided to augment the original exhibition to accommodate them. This second phase opened in 1984, one year to the day after the inauguration of the al-Sabah Collection.

Thus, the collection is, in fact, greater and more comprehensive now than it was when Dar al-Athar al-Islamiyyah first opened. It has also greatly enriched the field of Islamic art. Proof of this lies in the circulating of the present exhibition as well as in the fact that objects from Dar al-Athar al-Islamiyyah have been requested for every major exhibition of Islamic art mounted since the introduction of the collection.

Figure 2. Interior of
Dar al-Athar al-Islamiyyah.

Let us hope that the reputation for fine and painstakingly cared for works of art and beautiful and well-documented exhibitions acquired by the al-Sabah Collection at its formalization and Dar al-Athar al-Islamiyyah at its birth continue to be enjoyed for years to come.

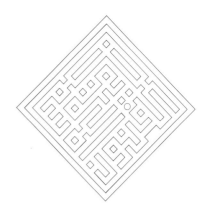

Patronage in Islamic Art

Oleg Grabar

Like most concepts and questions regulating the history and criticism of art, patronage has come to the fore of scholarly investigations and critical thinking because of its importance in the art of the Italian Renaissance and post-Renaissance western Europe. Patronage, it is suggested, transformed central Italian cities in the fourteenth century as ruling families, wealthy individuals, Christian orders, or civic organisms vied with each other in sponsoring buildings, monumental paintings and sculptures, and later, portable objects. A city like Florence is hardly understandable without a sense of who were the Medicis, Pazzis, and Strozzis and of the differences within the Signoria or between the Guelphs and Ghibellins, Franciscans and Dominicans. The best-known and most visible activity of patrons was then and is now to request, order, and finance the making of works of art. Scores of contemporary studies and thousands of archival documents, letters, and more or less literary accounts deal with this special relationship between sponsors and artists, the latter unable to survive without the former but the former requiring the talents of the latter for their glory, vanity, or commemoration. The immediate instrument of that relationship is the program, or, in architecture, the brief. Expressed orally or in written form, very detailed or barely sketched out, the program or the brief is a sort of agreement between a patron and a maker that the competence and perhaps the talent of the latter will be put to the service of the former for the execution of a specific task.

    While commissioning is no doubt the main aspect of the patron-artist relationship, it is not the only one and there are many forms of artistic patronage other than the making of works of art. There is collecting with various different ways of achieving one's ends. As has been well documented for the past one hundred years, there can be the support of artists whose works then enter a patron's living spaces or invested stock. There can be acquisitions through cash or exchange of works made or located elsewhere. There were, especially in Italy in the past and all over the world since the

Detail of **19**

27

early nineteenth century, legal or illegal excavations of ancient treasures. Although stricter controls have been established recently, outright theft, the bribery of venal, indifferent, or ignorant keepers of objects, and wanton looting have also been activities creating collections of art. Whatever the means, collecting and sponsoring works of art are the two principal efforts or purposes involved in patronage, and the first part of this essay will trace the ways in which Islamic history and culture encouraged, hindered, or otherwise affected the sponsoring and collecting of art.

The various studies on patronage in European art that have come to light in recent years have led to a number of additional and more profound questions about what seemed initially like a straightforward activity of sponsoring and collecting. Dealing no doubt with very different times and places than those in which Islamic art was nurtured, Francis Haskell indirectly questions what may well be asked of any culture with a major artistic tradition.[1] The question is of the effects of patronage on the arts. More specifically, is there a possible clash of wills between patrons and artists, which, within traditional structures of patronage, thwarts the creativity of the artist? Put in these terms, the question is hardly applicable to Islamic culture, which did not set the making of works of art at the same level of social, emotional, and even intellectual intensity as the Baroque Europe studied by Haskell. But in a perhaps more restricted sense than that of the creator's independent right to create whatever he or she wishes, the issue of the equilibrium between sponsor, maker, user, and object is an issue for all artistic traditions, and in the second part of the essay I will develop a few remarks on the art and the artist in Islamic art. Another issue derives from the subtitle of Haskell's book: the relation between art and society. The point is that patronage is the mechanism through which the making of art encounters the operation of society, and my third section will deal with art and society in Islamic art.

Such issues of broader import are not new in the study of Islamic art. In the past, however, they usually involved features of Islamic art like geometry or the attention given to writing, which were fairly peculiar, if not downright unique, to Islam and for which specifically Islamic explanations are legitimately sought.[2] Dealing with patronage is to ask of Islamic art questions that are not a priori peculiar to it but to which it may well have provided unique answers. In our time of ideological concern for whatever it is that makes an art or a culture independent and different, it is important to stress that the issue of patronage is universal and it is post-Renaissance Europe that argued that it was a significant factor in the forms taken by art rather than just a practical example of demand and supply of works of art.

Two preliminary difficulties remain. One is the absence of even tentative statements or hypotheses about patronage in the Islamic world. The Arabic root most appropriately used to mean "patronage" is *raaya*, whose verbal noun, *riaya*, was borrowed by classical Persian and Ottoman Turkish. The implication of the root is one of protection, as over one's flock, and such was, in part, the role of the patron in any culture, whether the protection affects artists through support for their life or works of art through hoarding and conserving. It would be useful to know whether other terms were used to indicate various aspects of patronage, as highly literate societies, like the traditional Muslim one, usually reflected in their language the subtleties of their thoughts and behavior. One example may suffice. In very recent years some attention has finally been given to the extensive *waqfiyya*s (legal endowment deeds) that regulated so much of the construction and maintenance of large buildings and of urban ensembles.[3] Some work is being done on the technical vocabulary of these documents, on the names given to architectural spaces and building methods. The economics implied by these deeds as well as the social hierarchies suggested by them have also received some attention. But these documents may well also contain the vocabulary of sponsorship of building and an expression of the social and ideological expectations aroused by buildings, in short, the very essence of patronage of the simplest kind. Such data, unfortunately not yet gathered, would no doubt sharpen our understanding of an unexplored process.

The second difficulty is that the nature of patronage and what we know about it has changed enormously over the centuries. It is dangerous, if not downright wrong, to push back into time the fairly bureaucratic and formalized ateliers of painters and calligraphers, the official sponsoring of certain techniques of ceramics or of weaving, and the existence of a corps of architects, which are ascertained in the great empires of the fifteenth and later centuries. These premodern centuries have left masses of written documents absent from earlier times, and, especially in the Ottoman and Mughal realms, they shared a number of characteristics and procedures with Europe, among others a more forceful and frequent identification of the person for whom or on whose order a building was built, a manuscript copied and illustrated, a carpet woven, or a candlestick made and decorated. For the first six centuries of Islamic history, as for the Middle Ages in Christian Europe, information is sparse and remarkably uneven. A Fatimid building like the Mosque of al-Hakim (1013) can be explained with the help of a large number of complementary sources, and several accounts with different contexts have been left of Fatimid treasures.[4] But it is difficult to know whether the information available for Cairo in the eleventh century is applicable elsewhere or whether it reflects unique circumstances.[5] In most instances it is from the remaining objects, works of art, or buildings and from tantalizingly pithy statements that we must today imagine the complex processes by which these works were created.

A single example of a written source illustrates the point. Several scholars have commented over a rather striking passage in Masudi's *Muruj al-Dhahab* (Golden meadows), a particularly legible and original chronicle from the tenth century. The great historian mentions, almost in passing, that the Abbasid caliph al-Mutawakkil (r. 847–61) introduced a new kind of textile (probably silk woven on cotton) for the manufacture of elaborate garments and a whole set of new architectural forms, whose exact interpretation is still under discussion.[6] We seem to be dealing with a significant change in taste, which is attributed by a particularly original and trustworthy chronicler of patronage by the caliph. One can easily imagine a critical reaction to the text arguing that, while caliphs may have been major arbiters of taste, they probably did not compel changes of taste nor invent the techniques on which taste exercises itself. Some other factors—social, regional, technical, economic—must have been involved, which then became sanctioned by the caliph. This may well be true, just as no one knows whether the Umayyad caliph Abd al-Malik (r. 685–705) decided at the end of the seventh century on his own to change the coinage or created a committee to advise him on such matters. But, in fact, we shall never really know what al-Mutawakkil's or Abd al-Malik's exact roles may have been in regard to artistic changes attributed to them. Early texts rarely satisfy the questions raised by today's historians or critics, and it is most often the study of and penetration into objects that provide answers to the questions of our own day. This is so, provided our questions are truly historical, that is, fully focused on explaining and understanding the past, not only on identifying the time, place, and possible attribution of the work of art in order to set the value of an artifact rather than illuminate its context.

An essay on patronage in general must navigate between two extremes. At one end lies the unique moment for the creation of an object. Unfortunately, too few of these moments have been investigated in a manner useful to the study of patronage, and the uniqueness of a given moment or work of art often diminishes the value of either for a general theory of any kind. At the other end lies an equally undemonstrated generality, that the very phenomenon of an Islamic culture created conditions for patronage that differentiated the Muslim from those, mostly European, cultures that first developed the notion of patronage. The following remarks are but first and very tentative steps toward finding an appropriate course between two unelucidated extremes. They are preliminary steps to be honed and modified by future research both on individual works and on theoretical approaches. They are far from forming a coherent system or valid explanation. They are an invitation for in-depth research on monuments, for difficult searches in all sorts of documents, and for the additional elaboration of a theory of patronage in Islamic art or in the arts in general.

The Arts within Islamic Culture

Nearly from the beginning of its history two strands affecting the arts operated within the Islamic world, and both are expressed, if not directly in the Quranic revelation, at least in the rich traditions on which rests so many of the Muslim's practices and beliefs. One strand, intimated by the Prophet Muhammad's preservation of an image inside the Kaaba (the major shrine for Muslim pilgrims in Makka) or by his approval of the textiles owned by his young wife, Aysha, is that the making and possession of beautiful things are not wrong in themselves, only in the uses made of these things, as in the most obvious case of idolatry. The other, ascetic, strand sees evil in almost anything that can distract the faithful from correct living according to the precepts of the faith. This strand dominated those traditions that threaten all painters with eternal damnation and have affected more than one moralist within Islamic thought who saw in expensive materials and beautifully ornamented surfaces means to destroy or weaken the follower of the straight path enjoined by the faith.[7] Both strands and their practical or ethical implications lead to the same logical conclusion. Some one person, institution, doctrine, or set of rules must exist to ensure that limitations or restrictions on visual creativity are properly observed. The existence of control mechanisms is necessitated by the absence within theoretical Islam of a separation between independent realms of life as exist in post seventeenth-century Europe and America; by the absence of theoretical doctrines as existed in Europe with the use and reuse of Vitruvius to establish a "classical" architecture and with post-Iconoclastic manuals within Byzantine Christian art, which formulated norms of representation; even by the absence of a continuous ethical or ideological discourse in art, as appeared around Impressionism and within the consistent reappearance of arguments and proclamations about the central issue of representation. I shall return later to the question of how artists and artisans may have been affected by such restrictions. At this stage the point is simply to wonder whether controls were controls of taste, as with controls issued from academies, or moral and ideological controls.

In theory, within Islam such authority should have been vested with the *sharia* (a legal system based on the Quran), and we know from much later sources that, at least for architecture and town planning, judges assumed some part in shaping the environment or at least in preventing developments that would harm the community or individual Muslims.[8] But most of the examples to have emerged so far from *hisba* manuals, court records, or legal texts and opinions relate to the fabric of the constructed environment not with major monuments or works of art.[9] Such classical texts do not deal with what are normally known as the arts, at best with the quality control of some techniques, quality being, of course, understood in a sense other than aesthetic. It is thus apparently not within or through the *sharia* that controls were channeled in the making or keeping of art.

A hypothesis on how the system worked can perhaps be derived from the extraordinary *Muqaddima* (Introduction [to history]) completed in 1377 by Ibn Khaldun (1332–1406), the most original interpreter of history to have emerged out of the classical Islamic world.[10] Ibn Khaldun did not write directly about the arts, a point of some significance as we shall see presently, but he refers to the arts and especially the crafts in many different sections of his book.[11] His concern is precisely ours, in trying to figure out how patronage operated, for he wants to understand and then explain the relationship between existing artifacts—a city, a large mosque, a small mosque, Makka, the Dome of the Rock, expensive textiles, rugs, handsomely written pages, and so on—and whomever or whatever made them possible. He assumes that an artist or artisan is competent but needs a motive, a sense of need, from elsewhere. An order is required, and it is interesting to note that the standard formula identifying the patron of an object or building is *amara bi-amal* or *bi-bina hadhi*, that is, "has given the order for making or the building of."

Who gives the orders? According to Ibn Khaldun (although he does not put it that clearly), there are three types of patronage. One is the caliphate, the institution that through many vagaries succeeded to the rule of the Prophet in Madinah in Saudi Arabia, the only institution shared in theory by all Muslims. The Shiite minority rejected the succession of the Prophet and established its own caliphate in Egypt and Tunisia in the tenth century and laid claim to the rule of all Muslims. After the defeat and execution of the last Abbasid caliph by the Mongols in 1258, the institution lost much of its practical authority but remained until the early twentieth century as a symbol of the possible unity of all Muslims.

Several functions of patronage are the privilege of the caliphate and its direct representatives, the governors of the major cities and provinces of the Islamic world. The most important caliphal privilege is protecting congregational mosques, as the caliph alone is, in Ibn Khaldun's view, responsible for maintaining a space where the whole community of Muslims can gather. Then there is minting coins, manufacturing fancy cloth, and assembling bound books and official documents. These activities are tied to the caliph because each contains expressions of power and signs of Islamic presence. The wording on coins has since the late seventh century been carefully chosen to proclaim the principles of the faith and its mission to all humankind. Clothes were the main gifts given by rulers to each other and to whomever was received at court; they were the charged souvenirs of the successors of the Prophet. Books and documents were means to transfer and communicate to others knowledge and beliefs but also to guarantee agreements and disseminate orders. All these activities required writing as the formal seal of quality. Thus, the extraordinary coincidence of the needs of a faith revealed and transmitted through words and of a state trying to hold together a huge empire with very diverse people speaking many languages found its most consistent expression in an Arabic script becoming identified with Islam wherever it occurred. More than half the items illustrated in this publication contain writing. In ways that still await their historian and philosopher, writing has become associated with Islam so that even imitation of writing has a cultural, if not a sacred, connotation.

A second form of patronage suggested by Ibn Khaldun is urban. He recognized, although at times almost regretfully, the permanence of the great cities of the Arab world. These were not only caliphal capitals like Baghdad or Cairo. They included all the Spanish cities almost entirely lost to the Reconquista by the time he was writing, the cities (Fez, Marrakesh, Meknes, Rabat) that will be the backbone of Morocco, the ruined Fatimid cities of Algeria, the old cities of Syria like Aleppo or Damascus. And our list could easily continue to include the cities of Iran, which by the late fourteenth century had been revived as centers for economic life and for the arts. In these urban settings with their checkered histories of successes and failures Ibn Khaldun recognized, it seems to me, two forms of patronage. One is a miniaturized version of the grand caliphal order gone by the time he wrote. The other is related to local artistry, and his comments on how Spanish writing styles were brought to North Africa and on the competence of makers of textiles and other objects show well his awareness of continuous local traditions controlled less by a prince than by a collective agreement on what is good or bad for the community, to paraphrase the traditional judicial formula of Islam.

This brings me to a third type of patronage, which was profoundly affected by the needs of the faith. For Ibn Khaldun, this patronage, which may be called communal, is most telling when he talks about the three holy cities of Jerusalem, Madinah, and Makka. The control effected by the community required that visually perceived forms, whether in buildings or objects, must be meaningful to all the faithful. Artists and architects presumably found a language recognizable by all, and it is this communal control that maintained for so many centuries the commonality of certain forms or at least approaches to forms within Islamic art. The existence of that commonality overwhelms whenever one comes to Islamic art from other traditions. It is important to add that commonality need not mean sameness. The aesthetic of a Mughal mosque is far removed from that of a Mamluk one, and the elegance of a page written in Iranian *nastaliq* (a type of cursive script) is hardly comparable to the assertiveness of one employing kufic (angular script), but neither can be confused with Chinese or Gothic art.

In a sense the communal patronage operated with the caliphal one as centripetal forces vying to unify among other ways by writing, geometry, or other types of ornament. Local urban patronage may well have been more centrifugal as it sought to emphasize the pride and achievement of an area or person as different from some other one. The tensions between the two are still present today within the Muslim world and they could be as creative now as they have been in the past.

These hypotheses derived from Ibn Khaldun's writing may help explain what type of patronage was made possible by the existence of a worldwide Islamic community. How it operated in practice requires analyses of individual monuments within categories such as those I have proposed. But then the reading of other Muslim thinkers, especially the *adab* (writers of belles lettres and good manners), who reflected and at times created the taste of various periods, may bring out alternate or complementary hypotheses on how the elaborate Muslim order operated to control the arts.

Islamic Art and the Artist

Traditional approaches to the study of patronage have always assumed that the involvement of the patron was the central motivation affecting the working process of the artist and, after the nineteenth-century revolution in the very concept of the artist, that strong patronage stymied a creative process understood by then as an independent form of its own.

The second of these ideas—artists thwarted by a conservative patronage in the accomplishment of their ambitions and expression of their feelings—is not at first glance appropriate to the traditional arts of the Muslim world, just as it is hardly appropriate to a discussion of most medieval or precontemporary arts anywhere. And yet everywhere among the eccentric painters and calligraphers of China and Japan or among European painters like Pietro Testa (1611–1650) in early Baroque Italy, there was a counterpoint to the norms established and accepted by official patronage.[12] Whether these alternate approaches would be understood in the ideological terms of twentieth-century art criticism is perhaps doubtful. Some artists were indeed eccentrics, and too much socio-political meaning should not be read in many of them. However one is to interpret them, such peculiar individuals and creations do exist within the classical Muslim tradition. There are rather wild designs on certain northeast Iranian ceramics and deformations in the representations of people and animals in Iraqi ceramics that have a fascinating surrealist quality hardly fitting with the "high" tradition of the time.[13] The wilder representations from the fifteenth century found in the İstanbul albums and eventually affecting high Iranian painting, as in Sultan Muhammad's wonderful monsters in the circa 1530 great *Shahnama* (Book of kings; written for Shah Tahmasp I [r. 1524–76]), are another example of approaches to images of people and animals that seem contrary to the norm.[14] There are similar developments in calligraphy, especially after the sixteenth century, where strange, unexplained, and at times even absurd shapes were created.[15]

Eccentricities also appear in stories told about artists and artisans. During the sixteenth century one Maulana Abd al-Karim was a great calligrapher but decided to call himself "emperor" (*padshah*) and signed his work with the bizarre statement "written by a giraffe."[16] He may have just been crazy, but the lives of many painters in sixteenth- and early seventeenth-century Iran suggest the existence of a counter-culture to which some artists belonged.[17]

A popular story about the architect who worked for Timur (r. 1370–1405) in Samarqand, Uzbekistan, would fit with the idea of artists as free agents threatened by the behavior of royal patrons. The architect, it is told, had been ordered to finish the mosque of Samarqand while the conqueror was off on some expedition. Timur's wife, Bibi Khanum (whose name is still carried by the mosque built ca. 1398–1405), was put in charge of the operation. During the work the architect fell in love with her and refused to complete the mosque until he had kissed her. Finally, as Timur was coming near, she agreed to his demand, but put a pillow on her cheek to soften his passion. His kiss was, however, so ardent that it went through the pillow and left a burn mark on the cheek of the queen. The architect finished the mosque. Timur came back, was pleased with the result, and then noticed the wound on his wife's face. After she told him what had happened the emperor sent guards to apprehend the architect, who had climbed on top of one of the beautiful minarets he had just completed. As the guards were about to catch him, he jumped. Because he was a good architect, angels picked him up and flew him to Mashhad in Iran, where he went on building.[18] Less directly related to supernatural intervention is the story of Farhad, the sculptor with whom the princess Shirin falls in illicit love. It is a tragic story, ultimately a story of death. In it the artist is depicted with several different sides. He is the creator of wonders, as many a painting shows him and Shirin in admiration in front of sculptures, always inspired by the rock carvings of Taq-i Bustan in western Iran. But he is also someone who willfully or not inspires evil. In some deeper sense, as portrayed by the poets Nizami (1141–1202/3) and Amir Khosrau Dihlavi (1253–1325), he may symbolize the contradictory and perhaps incompatible feelings of "high" Islam toward art, but for our purposes Farhad can be seen as a sort of rebel for art.[19]

Unless and until scholarly research demonstrates that belonging to mystical circles and participating in their activities was a political act in the sixteenth and seventeenth centuries, that angels help those who go against the wishes of kings, or that the representations of personages and animals as frightful but powerful monstrosities were made to glorify marginal existence and an alternate way of life to the high urban or courtly ones, the criticism found in literature of the behavior of a few artists should be construed as a judgment of taste and life-style and not an expression of ideological concerns. It is anachronistic to project our own contemporary attitudes about artists onto the traditional past, even if the contrast between different modes of representation as well as recorded incidents or popular legends seem relatable to nineteenth- and twentieth-century manifestos or to forms made to shock or annoy.

We are on much safer ground in asserting that the artist worked to meet the expectation of a patron. To stay with Timur, a major patron of the arts, one Umar Aqta presented the great conqueror with a copy of the Quran that could be fitted under the socket of a ring. Timur was not impressed by something so small. So the resourceful Umar wrote a Quran manuscript so big that it had to be tied to a wheelbarrow in order to be brought to the emperor, who came out to see it with his court and rewarded the writer with all sorts of favors.[20] While few stories are as obvious in establishing a patron's arbitrariness, nearly all assert or imply that works of art were made to please, glorify, or otherwise enhance rulers or their immediate surrogates, the viziers and other ministers. An architect imprisoned in Fustat (old Cairo) hears that Ibn Tulun (r. 868–84), the nearly independent and powerful governor of Egypt, wanted a fancy minaret for his new mosque. He then "invents" the spiral that will interest the ruler and guarantee his liberation. It was a Fatimid vizier who initiated a competition between painters that served to establish criteria for representations.[21] The story itself is dubious because it smacks of a type of rhetorical narrative used since antiquity, but the conclusion that princely patrons usually make a judicious choice is constant in stories about patronage.

Another notion derived from stories is that the artist had to be the master of the *ajib*. The term means "wonderful" or "amazing," but its implication for the arts is that an object or a building must possess a certain unexpected quality, something that would make one wonder. It could be the slightly simpleminded wonderment at the sight of one of the automata at work, as little balls fall every hour into bowls in a toylike reproduction of a celebrated clock in Damascus or as a mechanical scribe scribbles something on a tablet (see **49**). It could be the sheer power and brilliance of wealthy materials, as in Nizami's magnificent palaces built for the Iranian hero-king Bahram Gur (see **74**) or in many stories from *The Thousand and One Nights*.[22] And I suppose that it could also be, as in poetry or music, where they have been studied, exhilarating variations on known themes by which an enlightened patron sought to distinguish the work he or she sponsored from something ordered by someone else. Today we may not be able to detect these variations in the composition of letters on pages and pages of writing, in the arrangement of personages on manuscript illustrations, or in the floral and geometric orders painted on ceramics or chased on metalwork. Yet if there is some truth to the effects of patronage on the making of works of art, distinctions were in their time recognized and appreciated. There is no doubt, I believe, about an aesthetic requirement made of the artist or artisan by a patron, but we have not yet learned to penetrate into its ways.

Two examples studied in recent years show well the interaction between patron and artist that existed in sixteenth-century Iran. The first example is the *Shahnama* of Shah Tahmasp mentioned earlier. Martin Dickson and Stuart Cary Welch have proposed a complex series of attributions for its paintings and often related the artists' expression of competence to the fascinating, broody personality of the emperor himself. It is not important that every one of their judgments be correct; the nature of the process itself has been brilliantly demonstrated, whatever one may think of individual solutions. The second example is that of the other masterpiece of Shah Tahmasp's time, the beautiful *Haft Avrang* (Seven thrones) of Jami (1414–1492) made between 1556 and 1565 for Ibrahim Mirza (ca. 1540–1,577) and kept at the Freer Gallery of Art in Washington, D.C. The study of its colophons and codicological details led Marianna Shreve Simpson to the extraordinary conclusion of a sort of mail-order production that served to proclaim the glory of its patron.[23] Copyists, illuminators, and presumably painters worked all over Iran, apparently orchestrated by the patron, Ibrahim Mirza.

Both these examples are manuscripts with a considerable amount of internal written evidence and with references in external sources like chronicles. Internal written evidence, usually inscriptions, led to at least reasonable hypotheses about earlier works of art like the Dome of the Rock in Jerusalem (691/92),[24] the Great Mosque of Córdoba (784–86; 987), or many examples of twelfth- and thirteenth-century metalwork, to some of which I shall return from another point of view in the third part of this essay. In all these instances the artist is the intermediary between the patron's will or needs and a typology of available forms. To identify the uniqueness of one or the other is impossible without hundreds of as yet unwritten monographs. Nor is it likely that the patronage of Muslims by Muslims was theoretically or practically different from patronage elsewhere except on one point. It is that the rate of involvement of potential patrons in the sponsorship of artists and of art fluctuated enormously according to factors requiring further investigation. One factor was space, as a place like Cairo became a museum of architecture between 1260 and 1520, but the same is not true of, for instance, Baghdad. Another factor is time, as the period of, say, 1390 or 1450 saw extraordinary creativity almost everywhere and in all techniques. A third factor is individual whim, as Qaitbay (r. 1468–96), Süleyman the Magnificent (r. 1520–66), or Timur outdid many equally brilliant rulers.

The place of the maker of art is difficult to assess properly in the traditional cultures of Islamic lands. He was the follower of the patron's fancy, yet he could be independent. It is possible that he attracted a patron's attention by his skill, thus essentially marketing himself and compelling a patron to transform the creator's solutions into expressions of the patron's own taste. Such may well have been the case with Sinan (ca. 1490–1588) giving visual shape to Ottoman ideas of power and rule in his architecture. Something of the same phenomenon may have occurred with Behzad (ca. 1450s–ca. 1530s), whose novelties may have been accepted by the painter's patrons rather than requested by them. A curious example in this context is the celebrated brass basin known as the Baptistère de Saint Louis (see fig. 17), where the artist, Muhammad ibn al-Zayn, signs his name many times as though advertising his talents and successes for further commands.[25]

Art and Society

Patronage, I have argued earlier, is one of the mechanisms that trigger the success or perhaps the failure of the operation of a work of art in society. Since the Renaissance and especially since the eighteenth century, a battery of means, from continuous copy and imitation to critical judgment, exists to evaluate and ascertain the continuous appreciation and understanding of art over the centuries.

It is much more difficult to draw comparable pictures for the Muslim world. Written sources are very few, and it is, in fact, only for Iranian painting between 1300 and 1650 that we possess retrospective manuals, all too short for the most part, which carry judgments of quality and imply a relationship of impacts between patrons, artists, and works of art.[26] Although the examples themselves have never been put together in a systematic way, it is generally recognized that the evolutionary dialectic of Iranian painting from the early fourteenth century onward has been made possible by the recognition of aesthetic values in the art of previous generations by a patronage that sought through that recognition to establish its legitimacy. So it seems to have been with the Timurids and then with the Mughals, Safavids, and even Ottomans in relationship to the Timurids and this conclusion can be illustrated through specific paintings.[27]

We do, of course, have individual examples of a patron's decision affecting a given work of art by providing it with references presumably understood by society. Thus, the thirteenth-century Mamluk rulers Baybars (r. 1260–77) and Qalaun (r. 1280–90) both sought in early buildings, from Cairo in the case of Baybars and from Jerusalem in the case of Qalaun, models for their own constructions. They did so with very specific ideological, political, and emotional purposes in mind.[28] Something similar must have happened with the spread of a mosque type throughout the Ottoman Empire. Literary references argue for a filiation between the great imperial mausoleums, from Sanjar's in Merv in Turkestan to Timur's in Samarqand, but I am less certain that the filiation was understandable to anyone but the literati of the culture.

Fancy architecture lends itself to this type of explanation because the public and official character of most examples is talked and written about in all sorts of documents before, during, and after construction, because the investment in building requires a particularly complex range of technical competencies, and even more so because the expectations of architecture were always higher than those of other arts. This elevated position of buildings is made clear in the Muslim tradition by the moralizing criticism of architecture as a work of vanity. One can always hide a picture or another object; buildings as signs of vanity are destroyed by God or nature.

When we turn to art objects and books, which form the majority of the works at an exhibition or in private and public collections, the evidence is less clear or rather it is more difficult to demonstrate how patronage operated. We can only suggest a few ways. It is a commonplace of the discourse on Islamic art that during the period of nearly two hundred years, from the mid-twelfth century to the beginning of the fourteenth, large numbers of functionally common objects were made in bronze or brass inlaid with silver and often covered with all sorts of representations. It is further agreed that this type of manufacture began in Herat in western Afghanistan and from there spread westward to Egypt and Yemen. Since some of the earliest examples from Herat were made for, and in one case by, merchants (see fig. 12), the further conclusion is easily reached that this art of metalwork had been sponsored by the wealthy bourgeoisie of the large cities of the Islamic world. In reality, of course, this is not quite so, as many later objects were made for feudal lords or at least contain statements of allegiance to the princes of the time.[29] Feudal lords and rich merchants, the patrons of inlaid metalwork during these centuries were neither the caliphs and the central court nor the mass of the population. In ways that we are only beginning to understand, the decoration, figurative or not, of these objects met the need of a small and reasonably well-delineated segment of society. It is difficult to decide whether the objects of metal for these classes were ordered by them or were made by artisans hoping to please their patrons. For the central, so-called classical centuries I favor the latter explanation, but there are examples for the opposite position.

Among the techniques of Islamic art, metalwork has been unusually well studied, but I feel that a relatively similar equilibrium between maker and eventual user can be established for most decorated and carefully scripted manuscripts, which multiply after the tenth century. There, too, as we know from their own statements, the copyist was praised for his success in meeting the expectations of a buyer-patron. Although we are little used to dealing with beautiful writing, we have much more trouble in understanding how the appreciation of writing operated.[30]

Next to an imperial court, which "ordered" things to be made (and always bearing in mind considerable differences between periods and regions), there would then have been a high feudal or mercantile order, which acquired objects presumably made for them but not always nor necessarily at their direct request. For the rest of the population our direct information is almost absent. Yet it is likely, for instance, that the vast majority of the pottery shards and glass fragments found in excavations were used by the silent majority of the past. One could argue that all these fragments are part of a functional and practical ethnographic record to which the judgment of art historians is not pertinent. Yet complete objects of nearly all glazed types found in the Muslim world have become coveted treasures and some are among the masterpieces of Islamic art. Somewhere in the development of the many techniques of glass and ceramics a decision about meaning was introduced, which implies a patronage. It is, of course, unlikely that everyone went to a ceramicist and ordered an individual, personalized, piece. Such objects exist, but in most cases it seems more reasonable to assign them to the local urban order of feudal lords and merchants.[31] Most objects were made for a market and therefore reflect an artisan's guess or knowledge about the taste of social groups. Even though we hardly know how it worked nor how size, decoration, or technique related to each other and to the society that used the wares, we do know that the wares worked, as they were repeated, copied, or otherwise transformed.[32] It is possible that artisans created the taste of their patrons, but it is likely that they belonged to the same class or group as their patrons and therefore were satisfying their own needs while serving others. Patronage here becomes a bond between the many functions of objects and their transformation into works of beauty.

The great originality, I believe, of traditional Islamic art, at least until the fourteenth century, has been the presence of this third level of patronage at which user and maker are, so to speak, one, for they share the same social values. Ceramics is the medium in which this particular streak of the arts within the Muslim world is most clearly apparent, but it is probable that a study of textiles, including the carpets of later years, as part of the social contract between diverse members of society, would also emphasize a sense of symbiosis between a patron-user and maker. Clothes and carpets deserve more thorough studies than the purely descriptive and taxonomic ones that they have received so far.[33] But in a more general sense the patronage of ceramics and textiles is at the opposite end of the spectrum from the patronage of architecture. The latter tends to consist of a series of individuals or small groups putting together a building by sharing technical competencies, financial means, and social or other purposes. The former is a patronage of a society in action, meeting as attractively and as interestingly as possible its basic needs and functions.

These remarks and notes are but a few sketches toward an evaluation of patronage within Islamic culture. Too much remains to be studied, too many questions are still to be asked of objects, buildings, and written testimonies to allow for a true survey of how patronage of the arts developed within the Islamic world and especially of how it changed over the centuries to reach a stage comparable, at least in a few places, to what is known to have been attained in Fatimid Cairo, Ottoman İstanbul, and Mughal Delhi. Primarily in these capital cities and probably in a few others like Baghdad, Córdoba, Herat, Isfahan, and Samarqand, rulers collected and gathered objects from the past and from the present. Their individual motives varied, but the result was always the same. Thanks to the patronage of the arts, the past served to make the future through the care of the present.

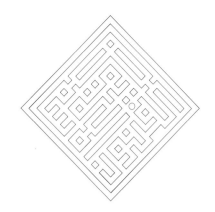

Early Islam
Emerging Patterns (622–1050)

Estelle Whelan

As the Muslim conquerors spread rapidly across western Asia, North Africa, and parts of southern Europe during the seventh and early eighth centuries, they came into direct contact with the imperial courts of late antiquity. In Iraq they fell heir to the state treasury and institutions of the defeated Sasanian dynasty (224–651), which had ruled its vast empire from Ctesiphon, a few miles south of the later site of Baghdad. Farther west they became familiar with the administration and ceremonials of the Byzantine emperors, both in the captured provinces of Egypt and Syria and through continued diplomatic contact with their court at Constantinople (later called İstanbul). It is only natural then that the Umayyads, who founded the first dynasty of caliphs in Islam, should have sought to rival and even surpass the grandeur of both Iranians and Greeks. Although the scale of their expenditure on luxury and display was thus usually "royal" in the full sense of the word, it was many centuries before a centrally organized structure of workshops under the patronage of the court came into existence.

Some production units were under state control even in the earliest period, but they tended to be decentralized and not subject to a single coherent pattern of administration. Perhaps the best known were the mints, which in most instances continued preconquest establishments and practices under local governors and officials, with only loose direction from the caliphal capital.[1] Although variations in the minting practices of different regions make it difficult to draw conclusions about development, it can be noted that imitations of Byzantine gold and Sasanian silver coins generally predominated for the first sixty years after the Muslim conquest.

A second state-controlled production apparatus consisted of specialized weaving establishments called *dar al-tiraz* (from the Persian word *tiraz,* meaning "embroidery"), which produced cloth and embroideries for the caliphs' own use, for presentation to officials, and for diplomatic gifts. State officials were appointed expressly to oversee the work and account for raw materials and output. Like the mints, these establishments appear to have been modeled on Byzantine and Sasanian predecessors, although it is not certain that actual pre-Islamic workshops were taken over and kept in operation.[2]

Patronage at Court

Despite these institutional roots, however, the products of the state workshops had a character distinct from those of their predecessors. For example, in 696/97 the fifth Umayyad caliph, Abd al-Malik, instituted a decisive reform at the mint of Damascus, which set the pattern for the official coinage of Islam thenceforth: the elimination of images in favor of purely epigraphic coins, on which Quranic phrases and the names and titles of the rulers were engraved in an angular, monumental script now known as "kufic" (fig. 3), though the identification is by no means certain. Although the early history and organization of the *tiraz* workshops are more obscure, they too seem to have specialized in epigraphic designs, usually embroidered in gold and colored threads and bearing the names and titles of caliphs and various officials. The earliest caliph who can definitely be said to have operated *tiraz* workshops is the Umayyad Hisham (r. 724–43); the earliest surviving example of such a textile is a fragmentary woven silk from the *tiraz* workshop in what is now Tunisia, with an embroidered inscription probably attributable on both paleographic and historical grounds to Marwan II (r. 744–50), the last Umayyad caliph (fig. 4).[3] Much has been made of a report by the fourteenth-century Tunisian historian Ibn Khaldun that "the houses within the palaces in which such garments were woven were called '*ṭirāz* houses.'"[4] Although it is not yet possible to identify the specific locations of other sites of *tiraz* units in the Umayyad period, the existence of the one in Tunisia, so far from the caliphal capital, nevertheless suggests that, like the mints, the textile workshops were decentralized and administered locally. Ibn Khaldun's report, based on knowledge of conditions closer to his own time, must thus be recognized as an anachronism when applied to the first centuries of Islam. In fact, much of the confusing and apparently contradictory information that has been reported about the early *tiraz* system probably reflects an inconsistent pattern of administration comparable to that observed in connection with the mints.

Figure 3. Gold dinar minted during the reign of Abd al-Malik in Damascus (?), obverse (top) and reverse (bottom), Syria, dated 696/97. New York, American Numismatic Society (1002.1.406).

It is clear that these state-controlled media had considerable political importance. The inclusion of a ruler's name on his coins and textile inscriptions was an acknowledgment of his sovereignty; equally, its omission signaled a change of rule or a challenge to his authority. They do not seem, however, to have given rise to a pervasive pattern of court workshops catering to the caliphs' requirements for luxury and public display.

Aside from textiles, the primary media of royal patronage in the early centuries seem to have been architecture and architectural decoration. The first great Islamic architectural monument was the Dome of the Rock in Jerusalem, constructed by Abd al-Malik as a kind of ideological statement made concrete, announcing through the grandeur of its form and its gleaming marble, bronze, and glass-mosaic decorations

Figure 4. Fragment of woven silk of Marwan II, Tunisia, second quarter eighth century. London, Victoria and Albert Museum (1314–1888 and T. 13–1960).

the triumph of the Muslim faith in the most holy Christian city.[5] Nothing is known about the circumstances of its construction. On the basis of slight but suggestive evidence about the building projects of Abd al-Malik's son and successor, al-Walid I (r. 705–15), however, it can be assumed that the work force consisted of a combination of hired and impressed labor rather than of court personnel. It was al-Walid who built the first great congregational mosques, in Madinah, Damascus, Fustat, and Jerusalem. Official documents on papyrus from Aphrodito and other sites in upper Egypt show that funds to pay for tools, materials, and wages for the mosques and other structures at Damascus and Jerusalem were requisitioned from this province— and probably, therefore, from other provinces of the empire as well. Occasionally, a district might be required to send workmen and provide for their support, but for the most part it seems that local workmen were hired and paid by means of assessments.[6]

The specialized artists and craftsmen employed to decorate these mosques as well as palaces and other important buildings with mosaics, inscriptions, carved stone and wood, wall paintings, ceramic revetments, and so on were probably also not part of a permanent court establishment. For example, the gold inscriptions in the mihrab (prayer niche) of the Great Mosque of Madinah (705–10) were designed by Khalid ibn Abi al-Hayyaj, a renowned calligrapher who also transcribed Quran manuscripts and wrote official documents for al-Walid. That he worked independently on commission is demonstrated by an incident in which a slightly later caliph, Umar ibn Abd al-Aziz (r. 717–20), asked him to prepare a copy of the Quran text but then objected to the price and refused to accept the finished book.[7] The artists who produced the mosaic panels for the mosques in both Madinah and Damascus may even have been Christians, although there is controversy over whether they came from the Byzantine capital or from Syria.

In the Umayyad period, then, the caliphs, although lavish in their patronage, especially of architectural decoration, commissioned artists or craftsmen to perform the work. There is no evidence of a centralized apparatus of workshops administered

Figure 5. Fragment of wall painting from the palace of Jawsaq al-Khaqani, Samarra, Iraq, ninth century (after Herzfeld, *Malereien von Samarra,* pl. VI).

as part of the court itself. On the other hand, the caliphs and their courtiers were naturally in a position to pay for special quality and initiate fashions.

Under the early Abbasids, who in 750 succeeded the Umayyads in the caliphate, court life reached new heights of luxury. For example, *tiraz* workshops seem to have been quite numerous and were especially concentrated in the Egyptian delta, an important area of textile production since before the Islamic conquest. For the first time, too, there is firm evidence that some of these workshops were actually income-producing units, manufacturing textiles for the marketplace as well as for courtly needs. Unlike their predecessors, the Abbasids constructed great cities, most notably the new capital at Baghdad, which was built by many thousands of workmen in less than three years, between 762 and 765; these workmen were brought together from all over the empire and worked under the direction of four engineers from Kufa, a city south of Baghdad.[8] Less than a century later, in 836, construction of a new city was begun farther up the Tigris at Samarra, also with workers from all over the empire;[9] it served as capital for only about fifty years before the caliphs returned to Baghdad. Although there are almost no surviving traces from Baghdad in this period, the extensive remains of the once splendid palaces and mosques at Samarra were excavated early in this century. They yielded fragments of glass mosaic, luster-painted ceramics, millefiori glass, and carved stuccowork. Despite the new and more grandiose scale of caliphal patronage under the Abbasids, its fundamental nature appears not to have changed. The founder of Samarra, al-Mutasim (r. 833–42), brought craftsmen from all over the Islamic world to work there, including glassblowers and mat weavers from Basra in southern Iraq, potters from both Basra and Kufa,[10] and marble workers from workshops at Latakia on the Syrian coast. Industries ''of all descriptions'' flourished in the city, and each craft was allotted a separate area in the bazaars. Wages for a number of craftsmen were included in the household budget of one of al-Mutasim's successors, al-Mutawakkil. Almost all were employed in connection with the wardrobe, the living quarters, the stables, and the armory, however, and there is no indication that this work force amounted to more than a large domestic establishment.[11]

Other evidence suggests, in fact, that the caliphs continued to commission independent workmen for the decoration and furnishing of their palaces. In this connection it is striking that the extensive wall paintings found in the private residential quarters of the first caliphal residence in the new city (fig. 5), the palace of Jawsaq al-Khaqani (ca. 836), are identical in style with the painted labels on wine bottles probably purchased from nearby Christian wineries (fig. 6). These similarities suggest that painters were accustomed to executing commissions of diverse kinds for patrons from different segments of society.

Already in the ninth century, however, the Abbasid caliphate was growing weaker, owing to a variety of causes, among which dynastic rivalries, political intrigue, and fiscal extravagance were prominent. Independent power centers had begun to emerge in other parts of the empire, although most rulers still nominally accepted the authority of the Abbasid caliphs. As provincial governors seized more and more power, they too adopted the accepted models of authority, adding their own names to inscriptions on coins and *tiraz* fabrics and building mosques and palaces to adorn their capitals. By the late tenth century the caliphs had become little more than figureheads, even in Baghdad, where the central government, including the *tiraz* factories, was controlled by the Buyids, a Shiite family that had initially come to power in southern Iran. At almost the same time a rival caliphate, the Fatimids, was established in Cairo. The rivalry was based on the fact that the Fatimids claimed descent from the Prophet's family and thus a right to the caliphate, in opposition to the Sunni rulers in Baghdad.

Despite the political weakness of the Abbasid caliphs, tastes in fashion and art prevalent in their capital during this period actually gained in prestige throughout the Islamic world and were emulated in many provincial centers. In 862/63, for example, the Aghlabid governor of Tunisia sent to Baghdad for marble panels and teakwood for the congregational mosque (836–75) that he was building in his capital, Kairouan. The wood was used for the minbar (pulpit), and the marble panels, carved in openwork designs, can still be seen in the mihrab. Set above the mihrab, on the frame of the niche and the wall, are 139 luster-painted tiles (plus several fragments) of the same period; some are known to have been made by a man from Baghdad, although it is not certain whether he was working there or had come to Kairouan.[12]

Ibn Tulun, who was governor of Egypt at about the same time, built a congregational mosque (879) with stucco ornamentation in the beveled style of carving associated with Samarra. This style, which is characterized by curvilinear motifs interlocked in such a way that the distinction between figure and ground tends to disappear (fig. 7), retained considerable prestige and was adopted for wood panels and doors

Figure 6. Fragment of painted ceramic wine bottle from the palace of Jawsaq al-Khaqani, Samarra, Iraq, ninth century (after Herzfeld, *Malereien von Samarra,* pl. LXVII).

in mosques constructed or renovated by the Fatimid caliph al-Hakim (r. 996–1021). At the opposite end of the empire, in the northeast Iranian province of Khorasan, the Samanid governor Nuh ibn Mansur (r. 976–97) ordered embroidered garments for himself and some of his officials from the Baghdad *tiraz* factory, causing the powerful Buyid amir Adud al-Dawla (r. 978–83) some dismay at his presumption.[13] A silk and cotton textile in the Musée du Louvre in Paris, bearing a woven inscription with the name of an official of one of Nuh's predecessors, Abd al-Malik I (r. 954–61), and sharing some technical and stylistic features with textiles from Iraq, may have originated in one of the Abbasid *tiraz* workshops.[14]

Perhaps the most striking evidence of the prestige of fashions from the Abbasid court survives from an area that was completely independent of the caliphate, Islamic Spain, where the descendants of the Umayyads still ruled, with residences at Córdoba and, especially in the second half of the tenth century, at the nearby courtly city of Madinat al-Zahra (see **23**), perhaps built in emulation of Samarra. Coins were struck in both cities, although the only *tiraz* factory definitely identified from this period was at Almería. At the Spanish Umayyad court there was a particular vogue for styles originating in Baghdad: in food, coiffures, music, luxurious furnishings, and objets d'art. For example, fragments of imported Iraqi luster-painted ceramics have been found at Madinat al-Zahra.[15] Furthermore, after the fall of the dynasty in 1031 and the breakup of the kingdom into a number of smaller principalities ruled by the Muluk al-Tawaif (Party kings), the prestige of the arts of the Abbasid realm continued high. Their influence can be seen in the local ceramic production of Almería in the eleventh century and in at least one Spanish silk textile of the same period with an inscription falsely claiming Baghdad as the city of manufacture.[16]

From the "courtly art" of the Spanish Umayyads themselves, however, the most intriguing survivals are a series of beautifully carved ivory boxes in various shapes inscribed to members of the royal house and high officials in the last half of the tenth and early eleventh centuries. Because of these inscriptions, some of which refer explicitly to Madinat al-Zahra, it has been assumed that the ivories were made in a court workshop there. On the other hand, John Beckwith suggested that some pieces in a coarser style (see **22**), many uninscribed or expressing only generalized "good wishes" to anonymous owners, were copied for the commercial market from works of the "palace school." Ernst Kühnel considered the style and iconography of this second group so different from those of the first as to indicate an entirely different production center, probably Córdoba.[17] It is possible that some of the ivory boxes were made in a workshop within the court, although such an arrangement would have been contrary to the overall pattern of loosely organized princely patronage in this period. Several factors suggest that they probably were not. First, as ivory carving did not have the official status of the mints and *tiraz* factories and as the level of demand could not have supported a wide range of state establishments, it is unlikely that the court would have sheltered more than one workshop for such production. Yet both Beckwith and Kühnel have provided convincing evidence that at least two ivory-carving workshops were active in this period. Had one of them been producing exclusively for the court, it is not clear how objects made there could have been accessible for study and imitation by commercial carvers. If both groups were working in close proximity or if their products were circulating in the market, then such cross-fertilization would have been relatively easy. Second, according to the inscriptions, boxes were ordered on behalf of highly placed recipients by a variety of officials and retainers. It seems probable that, had there been an organized workshop administered within the court, the intervention of such a range of agents would not have been necessary. This point is confirmed by the comparatively informal wording of the inscriptions themselves, which is generally parallel to that on commissioned objects and buildings throughout the Islamic world, in contrast to the protocols usually found on contemporary coins and textiles from the state workshops. Finally, in the eleventh century ivories were carved at the relatively minor town of Cuenca to the order of members of the ruling family of Toledo (ca. 1026–85) and their officials, probably continuing the pattern of the immediately preceding period. As at Madinat al-Zahra, craftsmen who signed some of these pieces also signed others entirely without inscriptions and thus probably not made to order.

These ivories exemplify yet another aspect of court patronage at the provincial level. Despite the appeal of fashions from Baghdad and Samarra, provincial rulers throughout the empire relied on local craftsmen for most of the luxury goods and decorations with which they surrounded themselves. In this way deeply rooted local artistic traditions, many of which had been evolving for generations, were nurtured and developed, often to levels of high art. This evolution is particularly clear in architectural decoration and ceramics. For example, the sensitive wood carving and elegant inlay work of Egypt seem to have owed much to Coptic traditions, and the elaborate brick-patterned architectural surfaces of northeastern Iran and Transoxiana (the region between the Oxus and Jaxartes rivers in central Asia) may also have sprung from local roots. Provincial courts may thus be said to have contributed in significant ways to the proliferation of regional artistic styles that is one of the most striking aspects of Islamic civilization from the ninth century onward.

It is clear that the caliphs surrounded themselves with every kind of refined object, whether commissioned, collected in tribute, or received as diplomatic gifts. Although their taste for luxury was highly developed, there was a political motivation as well:

to impress rivals and supporters alike with their wealth and power. The latter dimension is dramatically illustrated in the reports of preparations made by the Abbasid caliph al-Muqtadir (r. 908–32) to receive two ambassadors from the Byzantine emperor. After being kept waiting in Iraq for four months while these preparations were completed, the ambassadors were finally treated to an exhausting tour of several palaces, where rich textiles, jewels, exotic animals, and even gilt-silver trees with singing birds were arrayed for their benefit.[18]

The Fatimids may actually have surpassed their Abbasid rivals in the richness of their state collections. A contemporary account of what was looted from their treasury during a period of chaos between 1061 and 1069 fills several pages and includes vast quantities of carved rock crystals, amber figurines, jewels of all kinds, precious metal objects, and especially rich clothing and textiles.[19] Although most of these splendors do not survive, several rock crystal objects inscribed with the names of early Fatimid rulers and officials are known. Once again, the evidence suggests that in the early eleventh century the craftsmen worked in commercial workshops (see **21**). In about 1049 the celebrated scholar al-Biruni (973–ca. 1050) described the organization of the craft of rock crystal carving in Basra, and at almost the same time the Iranian traveler Nasir-i Khosrau (1003–ca. 1061) reported the existence of workshops in the markets of Cairo.[20] The rich treasures kept in the Abbasid and Fatimid palaces and perhaps on a smaller scale in some provincial courts do not, however, appear to have been genuine collections consciously formed by princely connoisseurs. Rather, they were dazzling accumulations of luxury objects for the enjoyment of the rulers and advertisement of their wealth.

One aspect of court patronage that deserves special mention is the role of women. Although rarely in a position to sponsor works of political significance, women from the caliphal families and the nobility were especially active in pious commissions. Some endowed fountains and other conveniences for the benefit of Muslim travelers making the annual pilgrimage to Makka. Amat al-Aziz, known as al-Zubayda, wife of the Abbasid caliph Harun al-Rashid (r. 786–809), was famous for her generosity in constructing such facilities.[21] Others provided ornaments and furnishings for mosques and other religious establishments. For example, a number of women associated with the Zirid governing family of Tunisia under the Fatimids donated Quran manuscripts to the Great Mosque at Kairouan.[22] In about 914 Naim (also called Shaghab), the powerful mother of the Abbasid caliph al-Muqtadir, sent richly carved wood doors to al-Aqsa Mosque (ca. 709–16) in Jerusalem. Although the patronage of these women differed little from that of their male contemporaries, there were also rare occasions when women can be said to have introduced genuine innovations in Islamic artistic and architectural practice. Perhaps the best-known example from this early period involved the "Byzantine" mother of the caliph al-Muntasir (r. 861–62), a woman called Habashiyya in the Arabic texts.[23] After her son's death she constructed an octagonal domed canopy, now known as Qubbat al-Sulaybiyya, on the west bank of the Tigris River across from Samarra and thus apparently became the first person to break the taboo on construction of mausoleums that had been in force since the time of the Prophet. In the ensuing centuries mausoleums of diverse types proliferated throughout the Islamic world, perhaps satisfying long-repressed local preferences.[24]

The impact of Habashiyya's innovation on subsequent architectural practice underscores the necessity of exploring the role of the harem as a conduit for new artistic ideas in Islam.

Widening Circles

Perhaps the most significant consequence of the reliance by princes and governors on independent artists and craftsmen was the rapid and thorough percolation of artistic ideas through many levels of society. As potential purchasers circulated through the bazaars they could see the craftsmen at work. The tastes of the court were thus to some extent accessible to imitation or adaptation, depending on the customer's pocketbook. Furthermore, new ideas could spread quickly by means of trade to other parts of the empire. The same types of luster-painted ceramics from Iraq that were so much admired in Tunisia, Egypt, and Spain have been found in the ruins of private houses at Nishapur in northeastern Iran, along with local imitations painted in colored slips instead of metallic oxides. At Cairo a great many luster-painted ceramics from the same period have been found (see **9**). Their overall quality is so high that it is difficult to determine whether individual pieces were imported from Iraq or made locally.[25] Jonathan M. Bloom has emphasized the importance of the pilgrimage to Makka, during which Muslims from every part of the empire had an opportunity each year to mingle and exchange ideas and goods.[26]

Beautiful writing was, however, the art form most admired in the Islamic world. From the earliest decades after the conquest scribes had sought to glorify the Word of God by writing it as beautifully as possible and also often by adding ornamentation in gold and colors. The appreciation engendered by the development of this art form was expressed in other spheres of life as well: in highly refined manuscripts of secular texts, monumental inscriptions, and decorated luxury objects. Most important, the arts of calligraphy and illumination seem to have been patronized by a broad spectrum of society, in which at least three distinct levels can be discerned.

In court circles the natural locus for development of Arabic script was the diwan, the chancery responsible for official correspondence. Although this department had existed as part of the imperial administration since the time of the Umayyad Abd al-Malik and perhaps earlier, it first emerged as an intellectual and artistic center in the time of the Abbasid al-Mamun (r. 813–33), and the secretaries continued to gain steadily in political and cultural influence throughout the ninth and tenth centuries, often rising to high positions in government. It is possible, in fact, that the diwan should be viewed as a kind of court workshop, comparable to the mints, although there is no evidence that the caliphs took any sustained interest in the artistic aspects of its work. Instead, the participation of many of the secretaries in the broader intellectual and particularly literary life of the period seems to have engendered an atmosphere conducive to high levels of connoisseurship in relation to their craft. Although few official documents survive from the early diwan, the secretaries' concern with clarity and elegance in the writing of Arabic is attested by several instructional manuals in which the principles of good writing were set forth, sometimes with examples.[27] It was, in fact, the secretaries of the Abbasid diwan who first codified

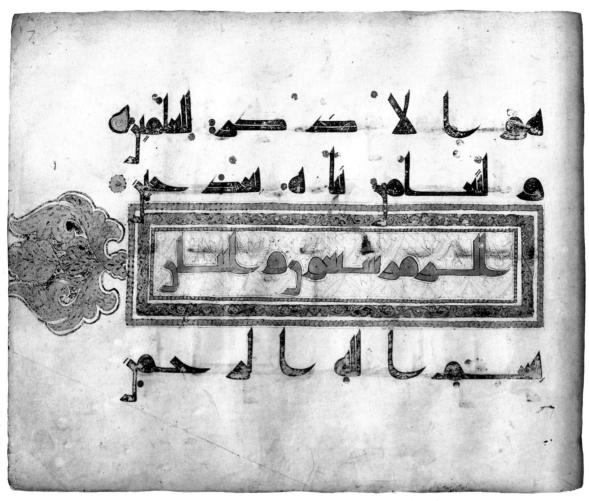

Figure 8. Illuminated folio with kufic script from a dispersed Quran manuscript, Iraq (?), ninth century. Oxford, Bodleian Library (MS Marsh 178, fol. 34a).

several basic varieties of Arabic script. One, Ibn Muqla (ca. 886–940), who eventually became vizier, is said to have invented "proportioned" cursive writing, in which the dimensions of each letter were determined in relation to the tall vertical stroke of the first letter of the alphabet, although, according to some sources, it is his brother who should be credited with this invention. Whatever the truth may be, it was Ibn al-Bawwab (d. ca. 1022), who served for some time as librarian to the Buyid Baha al-Dawla (r. 989–1012) and was active in official circles, who perfected this type of script. The primary achievement of the professional class of court administrators and secretaries during the ninth and tenth centuries was thus the rationalization of fine Arabic writing. Eventually, the standards that they formulated came to predominate in the copying of all kinds of secular and religious texts, including that of the Quran. In fact, the earliest dated Quran manuscript of this type known to have survived was copied in about 1000 by Ibn al-Bawwab himself.[28]

There was, however, already a long-established tradition of manuscript copying in the Islamic world, which continued to flourish and develop outside the court during the two centuries in which the secretaries were evolving their standards for fine writing. Among the most attractive manuscripts that survive from the first four centuries of Islam are copies (*masahif*) of the Quran text in a simple, undecorated, but monumental kufic script similar to that on early coins and in a few surviving

Umayyad inscriptions.[29] They are often adorned with bands of decoration in gold and colors separating the divisions of the text (fig. 8; see 2–3). According to the court secretary Ibn Durustuyah (871–957), these manuscripts were copied by members of the ulama, the class of learned men who functioned as leaders of the Muslim religious community.[30] This report is confirmed by an examination of the principles on which the Quranic script was constructed; they differ in many important aspects from those fostered by Ibn Durustuyah and his colleagues and successors. In addition, many of the finest kufic Quran manuscripts had obvious liturgical functions. They were divided into equal sections to be read publicly in specified periods of time (for example, one thirtieth on each day of the month). They were often provided with ornaments to indicate the fourteen points at which the congregation should stop for prostration and prayer. As a convenience for religious scholars, an array of colored markings helped distinguish the various systems of vocalizing the text for public readings.

Such manuscripts were frequently presented as waqfs (endowments) to mosques in Damascus, Cairo, and elsewhere, and they may even have been commissioned expressly for that purpose. Although some pious rulers endowed institutions in which they were interested, no surviving kufic Quran manuscript appears to have been commissioned by a member of the court. This lack may not be entirely coincidental, for in the early ninth century the Abbasid caliphs strongly supported the Mutazilite heresy, the leaders of which claimed, among other things, that the Quran was "created," that is, not eternal. They were thus seriously at odds with the religious teachers among whom the kufic Quran manuscripts were copied. The only prominent historical figure so far identified among donors of such manuscripts is Amajur, a Turkish governor of Damascus in the late ninth century. The other known waqf notices from this early period are in the names of private donors. The elegant kufic script that distinguishes these manuscripts was almost never adopted for other kinds of texts; nor does it seem to have evolved in significant ways. The style of the accompanying illuminations had a wider impact, however, which can be gauged by imitations produced among religious minorities in far-flung parts of the empire. For example, similar illuminations occur, on one hand, in a Karaite Jewish codex copied in 895 in Tiberias, Palestine, and, on the other, in Mozarabic Christian manuscripts of Spain, including the Biblia Hispalense of 960.[31]

A third group who specialized in calligraphy in the ninth and tenth centuries comprised the *warraq*s, professional scribes who were also booksellers or worked for booksellers—the distinction is not always clear—copying a variety of texts for whomever wished to buy them. Although their works also did not conform to the "rules" being developed by the secretaries, they differed in style from the kufic Quran manuscripts copied by members of the ulama. It seems to have been the *warraq*s who were responsible, at about the turn of the tenth century, for the gradual stylization of the clear, cursive Arabic "book scripts" into an elegant, angular type commonly known as "broken" or "eastern" kufic, although it is more appropriately designated "broken cursive" (fig. 9; see 4).[32] By the end of the century Quran manuscripts were also being written in this script; the earliest known example is dated 972.

It seems, then, that through the ninth and tenth centuries three distinct groups of calligraphers were active, at least two of them working primarily for patrons outside

يعقوبانِ وعنهما أخذه النّحو
وعليهما فواتِ كتاب سيبويه
وبركعتهما ممّن تحلّك علم
البصريّن بعلم الكوفيّين أبو بكر
بن شقير وأبو بكر بن المبارك:

تمّ الكتاب بحمد الله ومنه

قويم وصحّ وعوّض بعون الله

تعالى

بن شاذان الواذي في شهر جمادى
الأوّل سنه ستّ وسبعين وثلثمايه
الحمد لله كفاء فضاله وصلّى الله على محمّد وآله

the court. By the beginning of the eleventh century, however, Quran codexes transcribed in the old monumental kufic, a conservative style that had been given up even on coins, were beginning to disappear. They were apparently supplanted in the public taste by copies in more dynamic styles: the broken cursive that had developed in the marketplace and the proportioned cursive scripts used by the secretaries.

Cross-fertilization between the court and the private sector was manifest not only in wide geographical and social diffusion but also in the mutual enrichment of different media, fostered by the open atmosphere of the marketplace that has already been noted. Once again, calligraphy and illumination seem to have played a special role. The illuminations of the early kufic Quran manuscripts, which had provided the models for ornamentation of sacred books produced by minority religious groups, had an equally powerful influence on the design of objects in other media. For example, in many Quran manuscripts the lettering of the section titles was surrounded by white contours so that it would stand out from the patterning of the decorative band in which it was placed. In the same period major motifs on luster-painted ceramics were set off from the patterned metallic backgrounds by means of similar white contours reserved from the luster. Even more striking is the appearance of both kufic and broken cursive scripts in the calligraphic decoration of some ceramics excavated in northeastern Iran and Transoxiana, some in private houses at Nishapur.[33] These and similar pieces are decorated with inscriptions in black slips on white. The austerity and monumentality of their designs, nearly unique in the corpus of early Islamic ceramics, have often been noted. They seem to be matched only by the bold dark lettering on the clean parchment of early Quran manuscripts and may very well have been inspired by them, although the potters seem very quickly to have gone beyond the models, elaborating the script with ornamental interlaces and curves (see 10) and sometimes even filling in the background with dots or hatching in red.

Figure 9. Folio with broken cursive script from al-Sirafi's *Kitab Akhbar al-Nahwiyyin,* a text on Arabic grammar, Iraq (?), dated 986. İstanbul, Süleymaniye Library (Şehid Ali Paşa 1842, fol. 191a).

Private patronage of the arts also manifested itself in the form of collecting, although information about this activity is regrettably sparse for the first four centuries of Islam. The impulse to collect was particularly directed toward manuscripts, as might be expected from the central importance of calligraphy among the arts of early Islam. Bibliophiles were numerous and their activities are relatively well documented. It is only when they can be demonstrated to have focused on calligraphy rather than on the texts themselves, however, that they can be classified as art collectors. Other kinds of works also appealed to collectors, who seemed especially attracted to ceramics. In the early eleventh century al-Biruni, for example, described an extensive array of Chinese porcelains that he had seen in a merchant's home in Rayy in north central Iran; it included many kinds of vessels for the table as well as lamps, lamp stands, and other objects.[34] That Chinese ceramics were widely appreciated in the Islamic world is clear from the many fragments excavated at sites from Cairo to Nishapur.

From this brief survey it can be concluded that in the first four centuries after the conquest a courtly art, in the sense of an art with definable characteristics identified exclusively with the ruling elite, had not yet been established in the Islamic world. Owing to their prestige and wealth, the caliphs and other powerful figures were frequently in a position to set fashions and determine taste and standards of quality for the society as a whole, but they nevertheless relied on commercial craftsmen to satisfy their needs and whims. The common cultural stock was thus frequently replenished from above while at the same time being subject to continual redefinition and cross-fertilization in the marketplace. In these relatively open conditions it was possible for ideas to circulate rapidly from country to country, town to town, class to class, craftsman to craftsman, engendering intense creativity in the arts throughout the Islamic world.

In the 1020s a new force appeared on the scene, the Seljuk Turks and their followers, originating from central Asia. Over the next several decades they surged across western Asia as far as the Mediterranean, easily overcoming what little resistance they met. They displaced the Shiite Buyids as mentors of the Abbasid caliphs at Baghdad and took command of most centers of political power in the region, establishing a capital of their own at Isfahan in Iran. Their arrival altered irrevocably the political and religious balance within the Islamic world and opened the way for major changes in the nature of patronage in the subsequent period.

FOLIO FROM A QURAN MANUSCRIPT

1

Tunisia (?), 9th century
Height 14.5 cm (5 ¾ in.), width 21.0 cm (8 ¼ in.)
LNS 203 MS

Early manuscripts of the Quran are distinguished by their horizontal format, use of parchment, and monumental script, with a few lines written on each page in black ink. Some rare examples commissioned by rulers or wealthy patrons were also transcribed in gold.

This detached folio contains five lines from the chapter Nisaa, the Women (IV:170–71). The compact, angular letters are characteristic of the ninth-century kufic style associated with the city of Kairouan in Tunisia. The gold script is outlined in black and enlivened by diacritical marks rendered in red, green, and blue. Fine diagonal strokes form the points of the letters. Placed in the outer margin is a red roundel with the verse number, "one hundred and seventy," written in two lines and enclosed by a gold beaded frame.

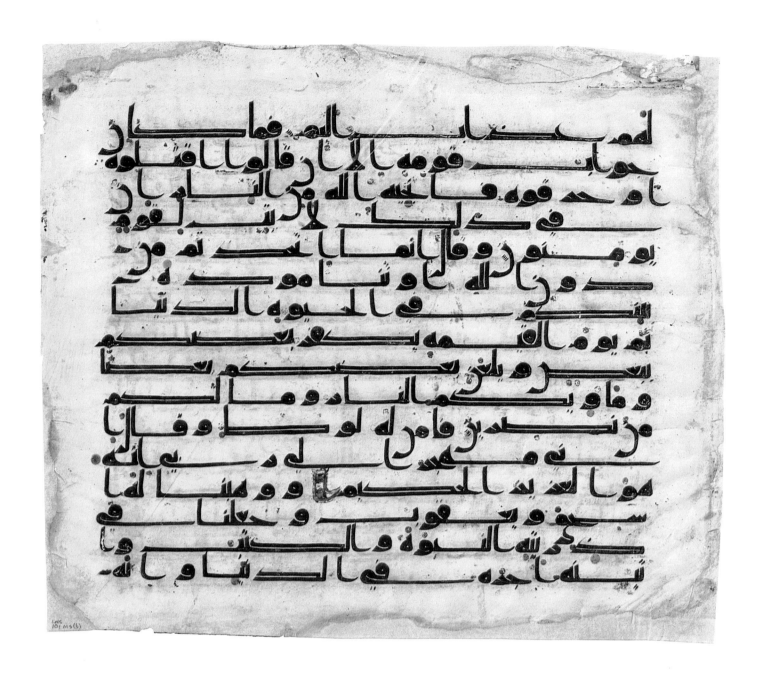

FOLIO FROM A QURAN MANUSCRIPT

2

10th century
Height 31.7 cm (12 ½ in.), width 37.0 cm (14 ½ in.)
LNS 101 MS (b)

It is difficult to identify the provenance of most early Quran manuscripts since many are fragmentary and contain no indication of where they were made. Most were written on parchment and transcribed in kufic with colored diacritical marks their only decorative feature.

In this detached folio, written in black ink on parchment, the diacritical marks are rendered in red and green with diagonal strokes used for the points of the letters. The verse stop (the division between the verses) is indicated by a series of small oblique strokes, and the mark for the fifth verse is the Arabic letter for *h*, which has the numerical value of five. The folio contains verses in sixteen lines from Ankabut, the Spider (XXIX:22–26).

56

FOLIO FROM A QURAN MANUSCRIPT

3

Tunisia (?), first half 10th century
Height 20.1 cm (7 ¹⁵⁄₁₆ in.), width 30.9 cm (12 ³⁄₁₆ in.)
LNS 2 CA (a)

The letters of the earliest kufic script are angular and the strokes do not extend below the text lines. At the turn of the tenth century a new version developed in Tunisia. Although derived from the parent script, it took a different direction by rounding the angular strokes and increasing the depth of the curves. The style spread from Tunisia to all of northwestern Africa and Spain after the tenth century.

This detached folio from a parchment Quran manuscript has three lines from Muminun, the Believers (XXIII:50), written in black or dark brown ink with red and green diacritics. The verse stop, a cluster of six roundels arranged in a triangle, and mark for the tenth verse are rendered in gold. The verse mark is a large concentric medallion, in the center of which is the Arabic word for "fifty," reserved in white and encircled with beaded bands and floral scrolls.

TWO FOLIOS FROM A QURAN MANUSCRIPT

4

Tunisia (?), late 10th century
Each: height 13.5 cm (5 ⁵⁄₁₆ in.), width 20.0 cm (7 ⅞ in.)
LNS 65 MS (a, g)

These parchment folios belong to a fragmentary Quran codex with ninety-three leaves, each with seven lines to a page. Representative of the Quran manuscripts produced in Kairouan, the text is written in broken cursive or curvilinear kufic with red and green diacritics. The verse stops are indicated by gold rosettes, and the mark for the fifth verse is the Arabic letter for *h*.

The folio illustrated above contains verses from Anam, the Cattle (VI:1–2), with the chapter title written in gold. A gold palmette with touches of white, blue, and green extends from the title into the margin.

The folio illustrated below is the left half of either a double frontispiece or finispiece and was conceived as an oblong with a palmette extension. The geometric design in the rectangle consists of interlacing circles and squares painted in gold and accentuated by green, blue, brown, and black. The floral elements in the border link the geometric composition and marginal extension.

CERAMIC BOWL WITH INSCRIPTION

5

Iraq, 9th century
Height 5.6 cm (2 ³/₁₆ in.), diameter 19.7 cm (7 ¾ in.)
LNS 128 C

A group of ninth-century wares made in Iraq is thought to have been inspired by Chinese ceramics imported to the Islamic world. Excavations in Egypt, Iran, and Syria indicate that this type of Islamic pottery was widely produced.

The Chinese influence is limited to the shape of these pieces, the majority of which are small bowls with low feet, flaring sides, and everted rims. A white opaque glaze—achieved either by an underfired alkaline glaze or by mixing tin oxide with a lead glaze—covers the earthenware body of these wares.

Islamic examples depart from Chinese pieces in their decorative repertoire, which incorporates inscriptions, floral motifs, or geometric designs, usually painted blue or green. With its understated elegance, the bowl is a typical example of this type of ware. It is decorated with a single word in Arabic, "blessing," rendered in blue kufic.

CERAMIC BOWL WITH SIX-PETALED BLOSSOM

6

Iraq, 9th century
Height 4.2 cm (1 ⅝ in.), diameter 16.1 cm (6 ⁵⁄₁₆ in.)
LNS 110 C

Similar to the previous example (**5**), this bowl with a low foot, flaring sides, and everted rim has a lead glaze opacified with tin. Decorating the interior is a six-petaled blossom with a hatched and stippled border painted blue. Green splashes appear inside the petals and extend beyond the lobes of the blossom into the rim.

Although the shape and opaque white glaze of the piece reveal the influence of imported Chinese wares, the decoration is indigenous. The use of blue, derived from cobalt, was an invention of the potters of Iraq and was known by the Chinese as "Muhammadan blue," in reference to its origin.

SPLASH-GLAZED CERAMIC BOWL

7

Iran, 10th century
Height 6.6 cm (2 ½ in.), diameter 24.1 cm (9 ½ in.)
LNS 278 C

A type of pottery called "splash ware" was produced throughout the Islamic world. Thought to have been inspired by the Chinese Tang dynasty (618–907) three-colored wares, it is characterized by underglazed designs incised through a white engobe (a fine semifluid clay used for coating) to reveal the red body underneath. Devised by the Muslim potters, the technique frequently incorporates splashes of green, purple, brown, and yellow.

This bowl with a low foot and flaring sides is a typical example of splash ware. Incised on the walls are six pairs of lobes with additional curvilinear and floral motifs placed in the interstices. In the center is a crosshatched medallion. The color scheme is predominantly green and yellow, except for the dark purple spots around the center, which is filled with haphazardly applied dots.

LUSTER-PAINTED CERAMIC PLATE WITH FLORALS

8

Iraq, 9th century
Height 2.0 cm (¾ in.), diameter 37.0 cm (14 ½ in.)
LNS 98 C

Luster painting is one of the major contributions and the unique invention of the Muslim potters. Although initially used on eighth-century glassware made in Egypt, it was first applied to pottery in Iraq. Iraqi luster-painted ceramics of the ninth and tenth centuries have earthenware bodies covered with an opaque white glaze, over which the metallic decoration was painted.

The earliest and most striking lusterware relied on a polychrome palette, but this type was short-lived due to the uncertainty regarding the proper adherence of the pigments. A more common type was painted in two colors, golden yellow and copper red or brownish red, as represented by this example.

The center of the plate is filled with stylized floral branches with checkered leaves, encircled by a frieze of ovals. The flattened rim contains the Arabic word for "sovereignty," written in kufic, repeated three times, and separated by panels with strokes, dots, and peacock eyes, that is, small circles with central dots.

LUSTER-PAINTED CERAMIC JAR

9

Egypt, 10th century
Height 22.5 cm (8 ¾ in.), diameter 18.4 cm (7 ¼ in.)
LNS 90 C

Lusterware with monochrome colors ranging from pale golden yellow to rich copper red was a further development of the dichromatic scheme (see **8**) and became commonly produced in Egypt and Iraq during the tenth century.

This earthenware jar has five applied handles on the shoulder, which is encircled by a raised band attached to the short neck with an everted lip. The surface is divided into horizontal panels filled with arches, connected heart-shaped motifs, or strokes and zigzags. The decorative layout of some panels echoes that of textiles. A turquoise blue droplet must have fallen onto the jar from another piece placed above it during firing.

SLIP-PAINTED CERAMIC BOWL WITH INSCRIPTION

10

Iran, 10th century
Height 6.5 cm (2 ½ in.), diameter 19.6 cm (7 ¾ in.)
LNS 119 C

A group of slip-painted pottery, known as "black-on-white wares," bears strikingly simple decorations consisting of bold or delicate inscriptions, stylized leaves, or birds. Found in Afrasiyab, a suburb of Samarqand in Uzbekistan, and Nishapur in northeastern Iran, these wares differ technically and aesthetically from contemporary products made in western Iran and Iraq. Covered with white engobe (sometimes brown or black), they are painted with slips under the glaze. The epigraphical group usually bears Arabic aphorisms, proverbs, or good wishes to the owner.

The earthenware body of this bowl is entirely covered with a creamy white engobe. Around the walls is a proverb written in kufic in brownish black slip: "He who talks much, errs much."

SLIP-PAINTED CERAMIC BOWL WITH SPOUT

11

Iran, 10th century
Height 7.4 cm (2 ¹⁵/₁₆ in.), diameter 21.8 cm (8 ½ in.)
LNS 160 C

Another group of tenth-century pottery is painted with polychrome slips on a white ground, employing black in combination with other colors, the most popular of which was red.

The earthenware body of this spouted bowl with a low foot and hemispherical shape is covered with a white engobe and underglaze painted with purplish black and red slips. The decoration consists of two motifs placed along the walls. The first is a large fanlike configuration combining various elements, such as half-palmettes, peacock eyes, and leaves. The second is a pair of half-palmettes flanking the spout. Details are rendered with delicate lines scratched through the slip as well as with strips left in reserve and filled with black dots. A chain of black dots, perhaps representing drops of water pouring toward the spout, connects the two main motifs.

GLASS GOBLET WITH APPLIED DECORATION

12

Iran or Iraq, 9th century
Height 11.0 cm (4 ¼ in.), diameter of rim 8.5 cm (3 ⁵⁄₁₆ in.)
LNS 85 G

The earliest glass vessels were produced by blowing into molds; later they were free-blown. The center of glassmaking in pre-Islamic times was Syria, which continued to be active after the coming of Islam and retained its reputation for producing fine wares with applied and trailed decoration. The same techniques were practiced in Iran and Iraq during the early Islamic period.

This free-blown goblet made of transparent blue-green glass is decorated with applied blue threads encircling the rim; thick blue-green threads applied to the body form a series of arches below a horizontal band. The cylindrical stem and splayed foot are devoid of ornamentation.

The shape and color of this example are characteristic of the period. Fragments of blue or blue-green glass dating from the eighth century were discovered in Kufa, an early Islamic city in Iraq, and contemporary vessels with similar decorations were excavated in Fustat (old Cairo).

MOSAIC-GLASS VESSEL

13

Iraq or Egypt, 9th century
Diameter 4.2 cm (1 ⅝ in.)
LNS 63 G

This diminutive hemispherical vessel was produced in the mosaic-glass technique, also known as millefiori, the Italian term for a "thousand flowers." In this technique different colored glass strips are fused together to create one rod, which is sliced transversely into sections. The sections are then placed in or around a mold and slowly heated until they fuse together to form the desired object, usually a small vessel, that is patterned with scrolls and circles of different colors.

The mosaic-glass technique, which dates to the second millennium B.C. in western Asia, was popular during the Hellenistic and Roman periods. It appears to have lost favor in the ensuing years, with only a few such pieces made in the Islamic world. This vessel is among the rare Islamic examples and employs red, green, yellow, dark blue, and white translucent mosaic glass.

MOLDED GLASS BOWL

14

Egypt or Syria, 9th–10th century
Height 4.3 cm (1 ¹¹/₁₆ in.), diameter 9.5 cm (3 ¾ in.)
LNS 127 G

The technique of mold blowing, established in the Roman period, continued into the early Islamic era and was fully exploited by the Muslim artisans, especially the Syrians, who were probably responsible for its revival. Decoration with ribbing, fluting, and faceting also dates to the Roman period.

   This small greenish blue glass bowl with seventeen ribs resembles, both in color and high-relief execution, Roman examples dating from the first century. The ribs encircling the walls start below the rim and curve under to form the base. The rounded rim has been ground and polished.

WHEEL-CUT GLASS BOWL OR LID

15

Iran, 10th century
Height 2.9 cm (1 ⅛ in.), diameter 14.0 cm (5 ½ in.)
LNS 88 G

This free-blown shallow bowl or lid with curving sides was made of blue-green glass decorated with elaborate wheel-cut designs. The outer surface is divided into concentric bands, in the center of which is a framed medallion surrounded by a hexagon enclosed by two bands. The inner points of the hexagon are accentuated by triple lines. A series of twelve teardrop motifs with double outlines embellishes the sides.

The design was formed by removing parts of the upper layers. This method, used in Egypt, Iran, and Iraq, probably originated with stone or stucco carving. The wheel-cut technique was generally applied to geometric designs, although stylized floral motifs or animal figures were also represented.

GOLD EARRING

16

Syria (?), 8th century
Length 5.3 cm (2 in.), width 2.9 cm (1 ⅛ in.)
LNS 55 J

This piece was fabricated from a thin sheet of gold, worked with punches against a bed of pitch, and reinforced around the edges with a beaded wire.

The main design consists of a realistic palm trunk that supports a stylized tree bearing half-palmettes and trefoils. In the center is a heart-shaped unit enclosing a pair of addorsed birds with half-palmette wings. The heart motif, beaded border, and half-palmettes are repeated at the sides of the tree.

The beaded wire and decorative motifs are associated with pre-Islamic traditions; but certain features, such as the overall composition and vigorous rendition, indicate that the piece belongs to the early Islamic era rather than to the late antique period. Thus the earring may be among the oldest extant examples of Islamic jewelry.

BRASS (?) EWER WITH FLUTED BODY

17

Iran, 8th century
Height 34.5 cm (13 9/16 in.), diameter 13.0 cm (5 1/16 in.)
LNS 85 M

Ewers of varying shapes and sizes produced during the formative years of Islamic art are often devoid of decoration. They are characterized by a certain boldness and strength attained through their simple and well-proportioned shapes. Their aesthetic appeal relies mainly on the relationship between the components or on faceting or fluting, as in this brass (or bronze) example, which was cast as a single piece and engraved.

Among the features of early Islamic ewers represented in this example are the elongated pear-shaped and fluted body, bipartite neck, and handle that functions as a unifying element. The curved handle joins the flattened rim with a pair of half-palmettes; embellished in the center with three beads, it is surmounted by a thumb rest shaped as a pomegranate.

BRASS (?) EWER WITH ENGRAVED DECORATION

18

Iran, 9th century
Height 29.2 cm (11 ½ in.), diameter 16.0 cm (6 ¼ in.)
LNS 132 M

This cast brass (or bronze) ewer is representative of a group of early Islamic examples related to that found in Egypt near the tomb of the last Umayyad caliph, Marwan II. It displays a similar spherical body, curved handle, and splayed foot as well as comparable proportions. These features, together with the slightly flaring neck with a ring at the base and pomegranate-shaped thumb rest, were employed in Iran through the twelfth century.

The dense, overall design covering the entire surface incorporates such pre-Islamic decorative elements as winged palmettes, bunches of grapes, and calyxes, which are adapted and reinterpreted. Early Islamic ewers with overall surface decoration appear to be exceptional and not commonly produced.

BRASS ASTROLABE

19

Made by Nastulus (or Bastulus)
Iraq, dated 927/28
Height 22.5 cm (8 ¹³⁄₁₆ in.), diameter 17.5 cm (6 ⅞ in.)
LNS 36 M

The astrolabe, an astronomical instrument used for observing planetary movements, was indispensable for navigation. It was used also to determine the location of the Kaaba in Makka, in which direction all Muslims face during prayer.

Planispheric, or flat, astrolabes, such as this example, were more common than the linear and spherical types. In planispheric astrolabes the celestial sphere was drawn on a flat surface and represented on one plate.

This astrolabe, made of cast brass, is the earliest known dated example and bears the name of its maker. The inscription at the back of the *kursi,* or throne, is written in kufic and states that the astrolabe was made by Nastulus (or Bastulus) and gives the date, which corresponds to 927/28. The date is rendered in Arabic letters, whose numerical values total 315, signifying the year in the Islamic calendar in which the astrolabe was made.

ROCK CRYSTAL BOTTLE WITH GILT-SILVER MOUNT

20

Egypt, 9th–10th century
Overall height 17.8 cm (7 in.), diameter 4.4 cm (1 ¼ in.)
Bottle height 7.0 cm (2 ¾ in.), diameter 3.7 cm (1 ⁷⁄₁₆ in.)
LNS 43 HS

Eleventh-century sources state that the city of Basra in Iraq imported raw rock crystal to be cut and fashioned into vessels, while Cairo produced objects of the highest quality.

The two examples illustrated here (see also **21**) were made in Egypt from the ninth to the early eleventh century, indicating that Cairo was an active center for rock crystal production at a date earlier than that suggested by the ancient sources. This small bottle with a sixteenth-century Spanish gilt-silver mount was wheel cut and drilled. It contains an intricate Arabic inscription written in kufic and rendered in relief, bestowing "blessing and felicity" to the owner.

A number of early Islamic rock crystal vessels were preserved in European churches and royal treasuries. This piece formerly belonged to the Hever Castle Collection in Kent, England.

ROCK CRYSTAL BOTTLE

21

Egypt, early 11th century
Height 10.5 cm (4 ⅛ in.), diameter 8.3 cm (3 ¼ in.)
LNS 3 HS

According to Arabic literary and historical texts, rock crystal objects—including ewers, plates, jars, bowls, bottles, and other similar items—were cherished in Egypt and preserved in large quantities in treasuries.

This bottle, probably a perfume container, represents the style of the period with its relief carving and floral decoration of half-palmettes flanking an axial tree, a theme that is repeated on both flattened sides. The bevel cutting defining the elements is characteristic of the age. Similar to the previous example (**20**), this piece was also in a European collection, that of a countess of Béhague in Paris.

CARVED IVORY BOX

22

Spain, early 11th century
Height 9.9 cm (3 ⅞ in.), diameter 7.5 cm (3 in.)
LNS 19 I

This cylindrical box, known as a pyxis, was produced from a single piece of ivory. The exterior is intricately carved in deep relief with green paint applied to the background.

Like most Spanish ivories, it is covered with profuse foliage inhabited by animals and birds. The creatures are placed within interlocking medallions and arched cartouches encircling the base. These units are outlined with beaded bands. Inside the medallions are pairs of animals alternating with pairs of birds. The docile animals have intertwining ears or necks, while the ferocious birds attack one another. The arched cartouches are decorated with palmettes and half-palmettes.

A series of triangular panels adorns the edge of the lid, each representing a human face flanked by a pair of deer. The flat top of the lid contains an undeciphered inscription, in the center of which is a four-petaled rosette.

The function of such boxes is explained in an Arabic inscription found on a similar example in the museum of the Hispanic Society of America, New York, a part of which reads: "I am a receptacle for musk, camphor, and ambergris."

CARVED MARBLE CAPITAL

23

Made for Caliph al-Hakam II by Falih
Spain, dated 972/73
Height 38.2 cm (15 in.), width 41.0 cm (16 ⅛ in.)
LNS 2 S

This marble capital belongs to a series of hundreds of columns made for the royal palace at Madinat al-Zahra near Córdoba begun in 936 by Caliph Abd al-Rahman III (r. 912–61) and continued by his son al-Hakam II (r. 961–76).

The surface of the capital is divided into horizontal registers and is entirely covered with deeply carved floral motifs. The lower registers are decorated with alternating rows of projecting acanthus leaves, while the head of the capital has four large volutes protruding from the corners. Above is a narrow panel with inscriptions, interrupted by four projecting triangles.

The Arabic inscriptions, rendered in kufic, include the names of al-Hakam and the supervisor of the project, Taled, and end with the date 362 A.H. (972/73). The name of the maker, written on one of the triangular projections, is given as Falih. Other capitals from the same structure are in the Metropolitan Museum of Art in New York, Musée du Louvre in Paris, Museo Arqueológico in Madrid, and in situ on the original site.

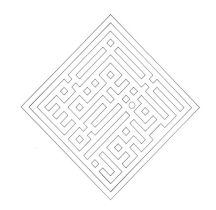

The Classical Period (1050–1250)

JONATHAN M. BLOOM

The patterns of patronage in Islamic art become more clearly defined from the mid-eleventh to the mid-thirteenth century due to the increased amount of information provided by the objects themselves, which include some of the most splendid examples of classical Islamic art. In this period magnificent buildings were decorated with dazzling glazed tiles; illustrated manuscripts began to proliferate; two of the most important techniques, inlaid metalwork and luster-painted ceramics, reached their apogee; and figural ornament was used to an unprecedented degree. The comparatively large number of surviving objects in varied media is complemented by the increased role of decorative inscriptions, which often identify the patron or class of patron involved. Historical and literary texts and legal documents provide supplementary information.

The period is most often defined by events in the history of the Abbasid caliphate with its capital at Baghdad: in 1055 an army of Seljuk Turks led by Tughrul Beg (r. 1038–63) entered the city and put the caliph into tutelage; Tughrul assumed the title of sultan, and he and his successors ruled most of the eastern Islamic world.[1] Afghanistan and northern India, however, remained under the control of the Ghaznavids and Ghurids, while the rich agricultural region in the lower Oxus River Valley was ruled by the semi-independent dynasty of the Khwarazmshahs. In 1258, two centuries after the Seljuk conquest, an army of Mongols led by Hulagu (r. 1256–65), a grandson of Genghis Khan (r. 1206–27), sacked Baghdad and effectively ended the caliphate there.

Detail of 29

These dates also mark significant moments elsewhere in the Islamic world. Anatolia, which had previously been a province of the Byzantine Empire, was first opened to Muslim settlement in the late eleventh century, after the definitive defeat of the Byzantines by the Seljuks in 1071 at the battle of Malazgirt (Manzikert) and a host of petty Islamic dynasties was established there. The most important were the Seljuks of Rum (Anatolia), who ruled until the beginning of the fourteenth century. In northern Syria, eastern Anatolia, and upper Iraq, several dynasties arose in the Seljuk wake, including the Artuqids in Diyarbakır and the Zangids in Aleppo and Mosul. In Egypt the political, economic, and social crisis of the mid-eleventh century was resolved in 1073, when the Shiite Fatimid caliph summoned Badr al-Jamali (d. 1094), erstwhile governor of Damascus, to restore order. As viziers, he and his successors assumed power from a line of increasingly and deliberately ineffectual caliphs. The Fatimid caliphate in Egypt was abolished a century later in 1171, and an Ayyubid sultanate recognizing the spiritual authority of the Abbasid caliphs of Baghdad was established there and in Syria. But the Mongol invasions also had an effect in Egypt and Syria, where the Mamluks, former slaves to the Ayyubids, seized control in 1250 and ten years later defeated the Mongols at Ayn Jalut in Syria.

These two dates of 1050 and 1250 are significant even in the western Islamic lands. In Spain the Umayyad caliphate had dissolved by 1031 to be replaced first by some twenty-three local dynasties, collectively called the Muluk al-Tawaif, and then by the Almohads and Almoravids, reforming dynasties of North African origin, which successively but briefly united the Maghrib (North Africa) with Spain until their defeat by the resurgent Christian forces. By the mid-thirteenth century the Muslim presence in Spain was reduced to the Nasrid sultanate of Granada and the Maghrib was ruled by regional powers.

The Patrons

In a period in which power was increasingly fragmented, rulers with regional or local authority replaced the caliphs, who had—or pretended to have—universal power and built and spent accordingly. Those caliphs who continued to reign in this period were forced to limit themselves to more modest projects, such as the madrasa (theological college) founded in 1233 in Baghdad by the Abbasid caliph al-Mustansir (r. 1226–

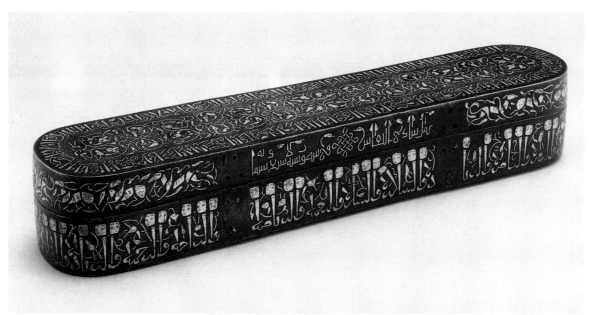

Figure 10. Brass pen box inlaid with silver and copper made for Majd al-Mulk al-Muzaffar by Shazi, Afghanistan, dated 1210/11. Washington, D.C., Freer Gallery of Art (36.7).

Figure 11. Luster-painted ceramic plate made for an unnamed official by Sayyid Shams al-Din al-Hasani, Iran, dated 1210. Washington, D.C., Freer Gallery of Art (41.11).

42) or the domed pavilion and arcades that the Fatimid caliph al-Hafiz (r. 1131–49) added to the court facade of the great al-Azhar Mosque (begun 970) in Cairo.[2] Most acts of patronage formerly in the caliphs' domain passed into the hands of the sultans and viziers, who actually controlled the power and money. The Seljuk sultan Malik Shah (r. 1072–92) restored the dome of the Great Mosque of Damascus in 1082–83, and the Fatimid vizier Badr al-Jamali ordered Cairo refortified with stone walls and gates in 1087–92.[3] Accompanying commemorative inscriptions briefly mention the ruling caliph but enumerate at great length the titles of the actual patrons.[4] Often inscriptions on major works ignore the caliph entirely: the inscription around the interior of the south dome of the Great Mosque of Isfahan (1086–88) mentions only the sultan Malik Shah, his vizier, and the treasurer.[5]

Sultans and viziers undoubtedly ordered objects as well, but comparatively fewer of them have survived. Among the exceptions are the brass pen box inlaid with silver and copper made in 1210/11 for Majd al-Mulk al-Muzaffar (d. 1221), the grand vizier of the last Khwarazmshahs (fig. 10), or the inlaid brasses made for thirteenth-century rulers in northern Iraq and Syria, such as Badr al-Din Lulu (r. 1232–59) or Najm al-Din (r. 1240–49), the Ayyubid sultan of Egypt and Syria.[6]

Military officials, occupying such ranks as amir, atabeg, *isfahsalar*, and rais, were some of the most prolific patrons, commissioning a wide range of artistic projects, from buildings to ceramics. The Chehel Dukhtaran Minaret in Isfahan was ordered in 1108 by the *isfahsalar* Abu'l-Fath ibn Muhammad ibn Abd al-Wahid al-Hujid.[7] A century later, a man occupying the ranks of amir and *isfahsalar* ordered the splendid luster-painted plate in the Freer Gallery of Art (fig. 11).[8]

Figure 12. Bronze (?) bucket inlaid with silver and copper made for Rashid al-Din Azizi ibn Abu'l-Husayn al-Zanjani, Afghanistan, dated 1163. Leningrad, State Hermitage Museum (IR-2268).

Religious officials were also patrons of the arts. The *qadi* (judge) Abu'l-Hasan Muhammad al-Khashshab ordered a minaret for the Great Mosque of Aleppo in 1090.[9] In the following year work at the Great Mosque of Diyarbakır was ordered by the sultan, directed by the vizier, and carried out by a judge.[10] Work at the Great Mosque of Tlemcen in western Algeria was ordered in 1136 by a jurisconsult (faqih) and judge, Abu'l-Hasan Ali ibn Abd al-Rahman.[11]

Members of the urban merchant class are occasionally known as patrons. The most famous example is the bath pail known as the Bobrinski bucket, made in 1163 for a merchant most likely in Herat (fig. 12).[12] In 1116 Muhammad ibn Umayr (?) ibn Yamur built three shops in Almería, constituting their revenues as a waqf for a neighboring cemetery and mosque.[13] Other patrons, known only by name, are often thought to have been prosperous and pious merchants: Abu Ismail Muhammad ibn al-Husayn ibn Ali ibn Zarkarya built a minaret at Sin near Isfahan in 1132, Abu Bakr ibn Muhammad ibn Ahmad Kilay ordered a minbar in Yazd in central Iran in 1151, and Abu Tahir al-Husayn ibn Ghali ibn Ahmad ordered a dome chamber and iwan (a barrel-vaulted hall open at one end) for the mosque of Ardistan also in central Iran in 1158–60.[14] Extremely important and powerful individuals occasionally presented themselves without their usual titles, especially in pious foundations; thus the Seljuk vizier Nizam al-Mulk (1018–1092) is identified only by his personal names and genealogy, al-Hasan ibn Ali ibn Ishaq, on the inscription around the south dome chamber at the Great Mosque of Isfahan.[15]

During this period women are rarely recorded as patrons. An inscription at the Zahiriya Madrasa in Damascus records that in 1110–11 the mother of Duqaq, the Seljuk ruler of Syria from 1095 to 1104 and son of Taj al-Dawla Tutush (r. 1078–95), founded this *mashhad* (martyrium) and mausoleum. Ruzayn bint Abd Allah, wife of the Abbasid caliph al-Mustazhir (r. 1094–1118), established an endowment in favor of female mystics in Makka.[16] Al-Darika (?), mother of Amir Ali, son of the amir and chamberlain Faris al-Dawla, built a mosque at Muarriba in Syria around 1136.[17] They are all identified by their male relatives, from whom one may imagine their power and wealth derived. Only in the areas controlled by Turks did women begin to become important patrons in their own right, but their patronage would become particularly strong only after the Mongol conquests.

The Patronage of Architecture

In this period far more is known about the contemporary patronage of architecture than about all the other arts combined. The new class of regional rulers had neither the need nor the resources to found new cities as the caliphs had done at Samarra or Madinat al-Zahra or to expand older cities with enormous new districts as the Fatimids had done in Cairo. It is only in western Islamic lands, always somewhat of an exception, that a new city, Marrakesh, was founded around 1060 as a military base. Its excellent location, controlling the routes south across the High Atlas Mountains, allowed it to replace Sijilmasa as an entrepôt for the Saharan trade and ensured its continued survival.[18] Instead, during this period cities were fortified and repaired. The caliphate had nominally guaranteed security within the lands of Islam, and only the border regions, particularly the frontier with Byzantium, had regularly been subject to raids. The breakup of the caliphate allowed regional chiefs to see any neighbor as a tempting conquest, so that strong city walls and gates became defensive necessities. Cairo, for example, was threatened not only by the Seljuk Turks but later by the Crusaders. It was repeatedly fortified, first by the Fatimid vizier Badr al-Jamali and then, beginning in 1171, by the Ayyubid sultan Salah al-Din (r. 1169–93).[19] The latter moved the seat of government from its traditional locus in the palace set within the city to a citadel set astride the city walls. Aleppo, Damascus, and Diyarbakır all had their walls and citadels built or rebuilt at this time.[20]

Religious architecture had always been an important focus of patronage, and this period was no exception, although once again the scale of patronage was necessarily smaller than in earlier centuries. In the cities of Anatolia that had newly come under Muslim control, new congregational mosques were built under the patronage of the Seljuk sultans of Rum. At Konya, the new Seljuk capital, the Ala al-Din Mosque was begun around 1155. The Great Mosque of Sivas was built in 1197; at Malatya, which had passed for centuries between Muslim and Christian hands, the congregational mosque dates from 1224.[21] Elsewhere, in regions that had long been within the lands of Islam, cities already had congregational mosques, and only in exceptional cases were new ones founded (for example, the Zangid sultan Nur al-Din [r. 1146–74] constructed a new mosque for the lower town of Hama in Syria in 1163).[22] Otherwise, potential patrons repaired or enlarged existing mosques or commissioned other types of buildings. In 1082–83 the Seljuk sultan Malik Shah rebuilt the great wood dome of the Great Mosque of Damascus, which had been destroyed in 1069 by fire. In 1086–88 his vizier, Nizam al-Mulk, had a great freestanding brick dome chamber, covering many of the bays in front of and around the mihrab, inserted into the hypostyle mosque of Isfahan, and a few decades later the dome chamber was connected to the court with a massive iwan.[23] Smaller dome chambers and iwans were added to other hypostyle mosques in Iran, such as the one ordered for Ardistan in 1158–60.[24] The Qarawiyyin Mosque of Fez was enlarged and extensively restored by the Almoravid sultan Ali ibn Yusuf (r. 1106–42). The prayer hall was deepened by three bays along the qibla (Makka-oriented) wall and a series of magnificent *muqarnas* (stalactite) vaults was added to the aisle leading from the court to the mihrab. In addition, two portals of the mosque were remodeled. Although contemporary inscriptions ascribe the reconstruction to the sultan, later accounts claim that it was the work of two local judges who paid for it out of the mosque's endowments to ensure the purity of the money.[25] There were more modest ways to improve an old building since these massive projects must have been expensive. The Fatimid caliph added an arcade all around the court of the splendid al-Azhar Mosque in Cairo. Not only did it increase the covered area of the mosque, but it also gave an elegant new aspect to the building's court facades without changing its basic structure.

Far more popular was the addition of a minaret to a preexisting mosque. The minaret was unknown in the earliest centuries of Islam, and only gradually did it become generally accepted as a desirable, although not essential, feature of mosque architecture. Its widespread popularity during this period was ensured by the contemporary view of it as a symbol of Sunni Islam, as championed by the Seljuk sultans. Dozens of stone and baked-brick minarets survive in Afghanistan, Soviet Central Asia, Iran, Iraq, Syria, and Turkey, sometimes independent of any adjacent building. Their inscriptions reflect a wide range of patronage, indicating that to all classes a minaret gave good value for the money.[26] For example, the Ghaznavid sultans Masud III (r. 1098–1115) and Bahram Shah (r. 1117–49) erected magnificent brick minarets at Ghazna, their capital in Afghanistan.[27] Abu Harb Bakhtiyar, the governor of a region in northern Iran for the Ziyarids, built minarets for the mosques of Damghan (Tarik-Khana; probably 1028) and Simnan (1031–35).[28] Judges added minarets to the mosques of Kashan in central Iran (1073–74) and Aleppo (1090). For all classes of patrons, minarets were gratifyingly visible and not as expensive as a new mosque or other building.

The madrasa was an important new building type introduced during this period. The madrasas were established by regional and local figures who sought to strengthen Sunni Islam through the teaching of its tenets and to perpetuate their names through the pious endowments that supported these institutions. These buildings normally provided space for teaching (often an iwan) and residential chambers for the students and teachers. Nizam al-Mulk, vizier to three Seljuk sultans, founded madrasas at Baghdad, Balkh in Afghanistan, Basra, Herat, Isfahan, Nishapur, and Tus in Iran. Nur al-Din, the Zangid sultan of Syria, built them at Aleppo, Baalbek, Damascus, Hama, Homs, Manbij, al-Rahaba, "and all the towns of his kingdom." Other figures, such as amirs, freed slaves, or otherwise-unidentified individuals, established madrasas as well.[29]

The founders of madrasas frequently placed tombs within or adjacent to the complex to ensure that their memory might be perpetuated after their death. Although the orthodox frowned at the erection of sumptuous tombs, a pious foundation such as a madrasa or hospital might deflect some disapproval, and tombs—both freestanding and attached to other buildings—continued to proliferate during this period. Tombs had formerly been identified primarily with the Shiite veneration of descendants of the Prophet or with princes and were most common in Fatimid Egypt and the Caspian provinces of Iran, but increasingly they began to be erected over the graves of Sunni religious and secular figures throughout the Islamic world. At Kharraqan in northwestern Iran two subprincely Turks or Iranians erected freestanding mausoleums for themselves in 1067 and 1093.[30] The last of the Seljuk sultans, Sanjar (r. 1118–57), erected at Merv an enormous mausoleum for himself within a large complex that also included a mosque and a palace.[31]

Caravansaries were another focus of patronage. Royal patrons supported and encouraged commerce by building facilities for travelers and merchants along the major trade routes. The approximately one hundred stone caravansaries located at intervals of one day's stage (about thirty-two kilometers) along the key commercial routes radiating from Konya are among the most spectacular monuments of the period from Turkey. At least eight were erected between 1200 and 1270 by Seljuk sultans and several others were founded by members of the royal family, but the great majority were built by members of the ruling military-bureaucratic elite to open Anatolia to international commerce and enhance the prosperity of the Seljuk state.[32]

The palaces of the rich and powerful were certainly centers of lavish patronage of the arts, but few have survived in such condition to make precise statements about them. They were generally built of less-durable materials and were usually abandoned rather than repaired and restored. Excavations in Afghanistan have brought to light palaces of the Ghaznavid sultans; the one at Ghazni (1105) is decorated with Persian verses and the one at Lashkari Bazar (twelfth century) with wall paintings.[33] In 1154 Sultan Sanjar's wife refurbished the caravansary Ribat Sharaf in Iran as a palace, which preserves splendid brick and stucco decoration.[34] In Turkey some of the tiled and stucco decoration of the summer palaces of Ala al-Din Kayqubad (r. 1219–37) near Kayseri, known as Kayqubadiye (1224–26), and on Lake Beyşehir, known as Qubadabad (1236), have been preserved.[35]

The Patronage of Art

Increasing amounts of information are available about the production and patronage of manuscripts during this period, probably because books became more common. This was undoubtedly due to the increased availability and use of paper for all kinds of manuscripts, including Quran texts. Paper had been introduced to the Islamic world in the eighth century but apparently was not used initially for Quran manuscripts, as the earliest surviving dated paper Quran codex is from the year 1000. Paper soon replaced parchment for all Quran manuscripts, except in western Islamic lands. Simultaneously, the cursive script that had been used for ordinary writing was regularized and began to be used for transcribing the Quran, although the old angular scripts were still retained for headings and decorative uses. Rich individuals might order sumptuously decorated and bound Quran manuscripts for their own use or as gifts to mosques and shrines. Their patronage is normally recorded in colophons, library marks, or endowment records. The illuminated double frontispiece of the eleventh-century Quran manuscript (**24**) written in an angular script indicates that it was the seventh of a thirty-volume set, notable for the elegant script and extremely fine gold illumination and marginal decoration. The leaf with four lines of angular script decorated with an undulating vine scroll (**25**) is from another dispersed thirty-volume Quran manuscript. Facing pages of this set were decorated with matching vegetal decoration in the same colors. In neither case can the patronage be determined, but the stylized nature of the script, quality of the work, and lavish use of gold on the former Quran volume would suggest that it was no ordinary production.

Among the few examples of a manuscript known to have been commissioned by a sultan is Abu Bakr Muhammad's *Kitab Khalq al-Nabi wa Khulqih*, a work on the physical and moral characteristics of the Prophet, which was ordered for the library of the Ghaznavid sultan Abd al-Rashid (r. 1050–53), son and third successor to Mahmud of Ghazni (r. 998–1030).[36] Written on paper in a cursive hand, the layout and lavishly illuminated headings in gold and colors with marginal rosettes are related to contemporary luxury Quran manuscripts (fig. 13).

Figure 13. Right half of a double title page from Abu Bakr Muhammad's *Kitab Khalq al-Nabi wa Khulqih* ordered for the library of Sultan Abd al-Rashid, Afghanistan, circa 1050. Leiden, University Library (MS 437, fol. 1b).

The atabeg Badr al-Din Lulu is known to have been a great patron of the arts of the book. A manuscript by an author known as Pseudo-Galen, now in the National-bibliothek in Vienna, is thought to have been produced in Mosul during his reign,

بِسْمِ اللهِ الرَّحْمَنِ الرَّحِيمِ

قَالَ أَبُو بَكْرٍ مُحَمَّدُ بْنُ عَبْدِ اللهِ بْنِ عَبْدِ الْعَزِيزِ

رَضِيَ اللهُ عَنْهُ وَعَنْ وَالِدَيْهِ

الْحَمْدُ لِلّٰهِ عَلَى نِعَمِهِ الظَّاهِرَةِ الْبَاطِنَةِ وَلَهُ

الشُّكْرُ عَلَى آلَائِهِ السَّالِفَةِ وَالرَّاهِنَةِ أَحْمَدُهُ

and he may be portrayed on its frontispiece.[37] He is clearly identifiable in frontispieces to the surviving volumes of a twenty-volume set of the *Kitab al-Aghani* (Book of songs) by the tenth-century poet al-Isfahani (fig. 14).[38] The five dedicatory paintings show the sovereign engaged in typical royal activities: seated on a throne, giving audience, riding in ceremony, hunting with falcons, and celebrating with concubines and musicians.

Physicians, scientists, and engineers continued to need illustrated scientific and technical works. Surviving examples indicate that the tradition of practical book illustration known from Hellenistic times continued in the Islamic world. The illustrated collection of treatises on astrolabes (26) is one example of a genre that included the Arabic translation of Dioscorides's *De Materia Medica* (several thirteenth-century copies are known) and al-Jazari's *Kitab fi Marifat al-Hiyal al-Handasiyya* (Book of knowledge of mechanical devices), in which automata based on the mechanical discoveries of Greek scholars were represented.[39] In the latter many of the devices—such as hand-washing and bloodletting machines—seem to have been designed for a prince's pleasure (see 49 for a later copy).

Most significant during this period is the appearance of the first surviving illustrated literary texts. While illustrated books had been produced earlier, the illustration of texts such as al-Hariri's *Maqamat* (Assemblies) and Ibn al-Muqaffa's translation of *Kalila and Dimna* appear to be a distinctly new phenomenon of the last decades of this period.[40] The quality of the script and illustrations for the circa 1200–1220 *Kalila and Dimna* and the 1237 *Maqamat* suggests that these books were not produced for a princely clientele but rather for a reasonably well-educated bourgeois audience that appreciated the morals of the fables as well as the verbal pyrotechnics of al-Hariri's Arabic text.[41] The *Maqamat* illustrations, in contrast to the royal imagery of the *Kitab al-Aghani* frontispieces, reflect the world of the bourgeoisie and traveling merchants and depict villages, caravans, ships, and mosque interiors (fig. 15).

Many of the finest Islamic ceramics are dated to the two centuries before the Mongol conquest, but in only a few cases can patronage be specified on the basis of inscriptions. Pious individuals are known to have commissioned sets of luster-painted tiles to decorate the walls of Iranian mosques and shrines, such as the large mihrab commissioned in 1226 from al-Hasan ibn Arabshah for the Maydan Mosque of Kashan, but the patrons' names are rarely given.[42] One exception is the set of tiles for the cenotaph of Fatima (daughter of the Prophet) at Qum in central Iran, which was commissioned in 1206 by the great-grandson of Sultan Sanjar's vizier.[43] One of the most famous ceramics from the period is a flat luster-painted plate made at Kashan in 1210 by Sayyid Shams al-Din al-Hasani (see fig. 11). The fragmentary inscription offers good wishes to an individual whose titles are included but whose personal names are missing. The unusual iconography, which depicts a sleeping groom, has been shown to have royal and mystical overtones.[44] The plate was pressed in a mold with twenty-nine scallops, which was also used to produce at least four other pieces. Three are decorated with luster, a particularly expensive process, but a fourth is simply painted in black under a turquoise glaze, one of the more common techniques of Islamic ceramics (see, for example, 28). This suggests that the workshop that owned the mold made pieces for various levels of society.

Figure 14. Frontispiece of volume 17 from al-Isfahani's *Kitab al-Aghani* made for Badr al-Din Lulu, Iraq, circa 1218–19. İstanbul, Millet Library (Feyzullah Efendi, 1566, fol.1a).

Figure 15. Discussion near a Village, illustration from al-Hariri's *Maqamat* by Yahya ibn Mahmud al-Wasiti, Iraq, dated 1237. Paris, Bibliothèque Nationale (MS Arabe 5847, fol. 138a).

Many *minai* (overglaze-painted) wares produced in Iran during the twelfth and early thirteenth centuries are painted with scenes of royal pastimes, such as enthronements, feasting, riding, and hunting. The iconography and expense of the technique suggests that they were destined for the rich, but their inscriptions rarely assign them to royal or princely patronage (fig. 16). Painted ceramic tiles were used to decorate royal palaces, such as the Seljuk one at Qubadabad.[45] Some ceramics, such as the white bowl with carved and pierced decoration (**27**), must have been made for a clientele whose taste had been formed by exposure to Chinese wares of the Song dynasty, which were imported at great expense into the Islamic world. Other pieces, such as the luster-painted bowl (**33**), are of a type that seems to have been made in several Syrian cities for the flourishing bourgeoisie.

An unusually wide range of patrons encouraged the florescence of Islamic metalwork during this period. Different copper alloys were cast, spun, and hammered to make

Figure 16. Overglaze-painted bowl made for Abu Nasir Kermanshah, Iran, late twelfth–early thirteenth century. Washington, D.C., Freer Gallery of Art (27.3).

107

a variety of utilitarian objects, such as ewers, basins, and candlesticks, which were lavishly decorated in repoussé as well as with raising, engraving, chasing, and inlay with epigraphic, vegetal, and figural motifs (38–41). Many of the finest pieces are inscribed with the names of patrons and artisans, indicating not only a wide range of patronage but also the importance of the craft. The Persian inscription on the Bobrinski bucket (see fig. 12), for example, states that Abd al-Rahman ibn Abd Allah al-Rashidi ordered it, Muhammad ibn Abd al-Wahid cast it, and Hajib Masud ibn Ahmad the engraver worked it and that it was made for Rashid al-Din Azizi ibn Abu'l-Husayn al-Zanjani, a merchant.[46] The inscription on an aquamanile, or water vessel, in the shape of a zebu, now in the State Hermitage Museum in Leningrad, states that it was made in 1206 for an Iranian lord, and that on the pen box in the Freer Gallery of Art (see fig. 10) indicates that it was made for a vizier to the Khwarazmshahs.[47] Many other pieces, such as the brass candlestick (39) or bronze mirror (41), are inscribed with a series of good wishes for an anonymous owner, suggesting that artisans made them without specific patrons in mind. Nevertheless, the quality of some anonymous pieces is equal to those made for specific patrons.

Comparatively few pieces in precious metals have survived from this period, primarily because gold and silver vessels and jewelry were considered to be currency reserves, which could be melted down and struck into coin during financial emergencies. A gilt-silver bowl in the Kier Collection in Richmond, England, is inscribed with the name and titles of Badr al-Din Qaragöz, a local ruler in western Iran between 1198 and 1219. It was broken roughly and purposefully into large pieces, probably at the time of the Mongol invasions, in order to mint coins.[48] In pre-Islamic and Islamic Iran, small silver bowls and ewers were essential tableware for the wine-drinking (bazm) ceremony, an elaborate feast with music, poetry, and merry-making. When silver was unavailable, white, or high-tin, bronze (see 38) seems to have been substituted.

Other media also illustrate the wide range of patronage in the two centuries before the Mongol conquest. Textiles woven with bands containing the name of the ruling Fatimid caliph continued to be produced in Egyptian court workshops to the mid-twelfth century. They were intended as seasonal gifts for the members of the court, who would have had them made into garments. Silk textiles decorated with repeat patterns of medallions containing animals and inscriptions were popular with the rich in the eastern Islamic world.[49]

Ivory was by its expense a material reserved for the richest clientele; the hunting horn (45) was probably made in Sicily or southern Italy by artisans familiar with Islamic decorative motifs, but there is little evidence that such ivories were produced for Muslim patrons. Elaborately carved wood was used for a variety of rich architectural fittings and mosque furniture, such as minbars, Quran stands, and cenotaphs (see, for example, 46). The Zangid sultan Nur al-Din, for example, ordered exquisite wood minbars for his new mosque in Hama and for al-Aqsa Mosque in Jerusalem.[50]

The two most important features common to all forms of Islamic art of this period—the increased role of Arabic inscriptions and the extraordinary development of figural ornament—can be understood in terms of changes in patronage. The prevalence of Arabic inscriptions points to the deep Islamization of the world conquered by Muslim armies several centuries earlier. Large segments of the population under Islamic rule had remained Christian, Jewish, or Zoroastrian until the tenth century, but conversion to Islam necessitated the adoption of Arabic as the language of religion and consequently of literature and the arts.[51] Thus the objects produced during this period are not just for Muslim patrons but are the products of an Islamic society.

The remarkable development of figural ornament seen in this period is less clearly understood, but surely it marks a momentous change in taste, which did not survive into the fourteenth century. While individual scenes (such as enthronements or the royal hunt) or cycles of images (such as the labors of the months or the signs of the zodiac) have been identified, little work has yet been done to explain why such scenes were suddenly appropriate decoration on all kinds of objects produced for all types of patrons. The most intriguing hypothesis, proposed several years ago by Oleg Grabar, suggested that the change in taste was due to the dispersal of the Fatimid treasuries in the mid-eleventh century.[52] Figural representations had been characteristic of earlier princely objects but relatively unknown to the bourgeoisie, but the looting and public sale of the incredible wealth accumulated by the Fatimid caliphs would have made a type of decoration suddenly available to the general populace. Some nonroyal objects decorated with figural imagery seem to predate the dispersal of the treasuries and events in Egypt do not necessarily explain a phenomenon characteristic of a much larger region, but this hypothesis remains the best attempt so far to interpret this significant episode in the arts of the classical period.

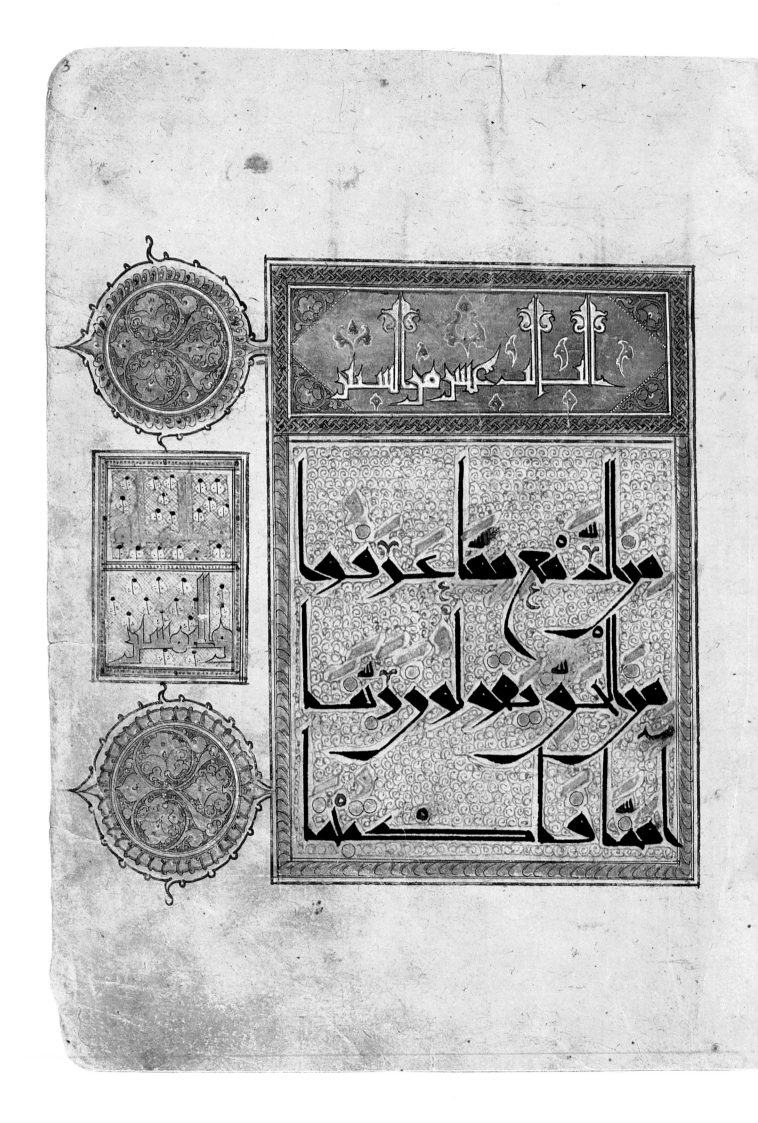

110

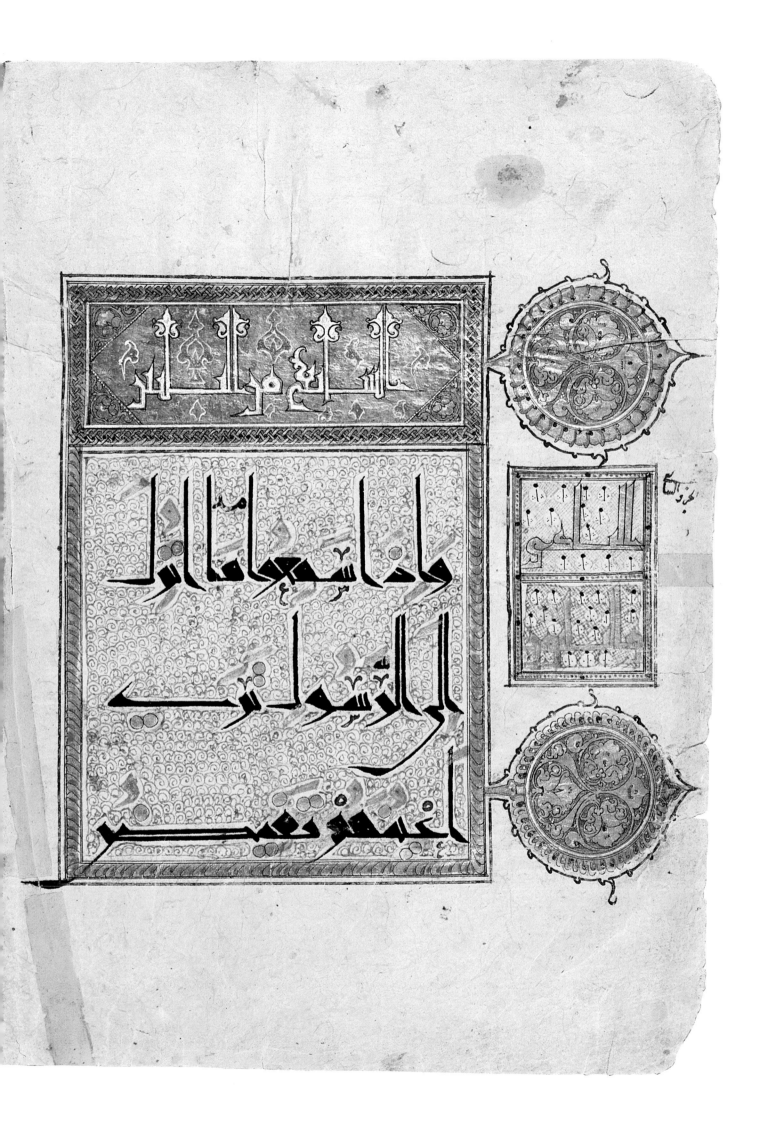

DOUBLE FOLIOS FROM A QURAN MANUSCRIPT

24

Iran, 11th century
Each folio: height 27.0 cm (10 %16 in.), width 20.5 cm (8 in.)
LNS 6 MS (fols. 2b–3a)

This manuscript was originally part of a thirty-volume set, each volume containing one *juz,* or section of the Quran read on each day of the Muslim month, which has thirty days, following the lunar calendar. This part has twenty-two folios and includes verses from Maida, the Table Spread (V:83–120). The work opens with an illuminated double frontispiece decorated with gold foliated designs on a red ground. The next pair of folios contains the text, illustrated here, and is decorated in mirror image. In the central square are three lines of black kufic placed against a tightly wound brown scroll. The diacritics, rendered in red, gold, and blue, alleviate the boldness of the script. Projecting into the margins are square panels inscribed with the *juz* number, "thirty-two," flanked by two medallions bearing floral scrolls enclosing blossoms.

The text is written in the so-called eastern kufic script developed in the tenth century. It remained in use in Iran until the thirteenth century and was later employed in chapter headings. This style of angular writing is more delicate than the parent kufic, with its long verticals and swooping extenders.

The emergence of this type of kufic coincided with two significant developments in the manuscripts: the vertical format was favored over the horizontal and paper replaced parchment.

Illustrated on the preceding pages

FOLIO FROM A QURAN MANUSCRIPT

25

Iran, 11th century
Height 34.0 cm (13 ³⁄16 in.), width 24.0 cm (9 ½ in.)
LNS 63 MS (b)

This folio, together with three other examples in the collection, belongs to a widely dispersed Quran manuscript thought to have been produced in Mashhad in eastern Iran. Written in ink on paper with four lines to the page, the text was transcribed in an elegant script erroneously known as "Qarmatian," a variant of the tenth-century kufic. In this style the horizontal letters are more compact and the verticals are considerably taller than the earlier kufic, giving the script a majestic appearance. The vertical format of the page is most suitable to accommodate the tall letters of the script. The use of red and blue diacritics rendered as short vowels instead of colored dots facilitates the reading of the script.

The bold rendition of the text, from Nisaa (IV:173–75), contrasts the finely drawn pale ground with floral scrolls enclosing blossoms (see also **24**). Similar designs appear on contemporary ceramics and metalwork.

113

وضع على اى موضع واستحسنتا[ن] لمواضع القطعة الى الاطواف محركا مساكبالبدوبداربه

الكوكبون وتكون ثلا[ث]كمن الاصبعان مضبطه ثم نعل مظهر عضان اما محرفة او

قايمة بلتفتيرمعقودبربا اواوساطهما وقطبا ونساوحلقة ونضع كل وادرى موضعه

وقدم لنا الاصطرلاب الثمالى الاعمال التى لابدمنها وسلبنى ودكرى الاصطرلاب

الجنورعلى الزيادات التى يلى بالاصطرلاب ونوع ما يهتم اليه اعمالها وهذه صور الكوكبون

الثمالى وساير الالات التى بها ينبع الاصطرلاب

عمل الاصطرلاب الجنوبى   واما الاصطرلاب الجنوبى فنقله

عالم ما ذكرناه لاطلعته وقطب بعضه طبيعى فانه يصير بناحمة اليمن وهو نفظة

هـ فى مدار الجوراعنى النقطة المقابلة بالنقاطر التى ذات فى استعمال وطب التسطيح

ثم يختلف وضاعه كلها اما المدارات اولاغانها ثلثا ل سوى مدار الحمل والميزان

مصيرمدار الجر والدنى ميله الى الجنوب الى مقدار واحداعنى ان يصير مدار السرطان هو مدار

الجدى

CONSTRUCTION OF A DISC

26

Illustration from a collection of treatises on astrolabes
Turkey, dated 1230/31 and 1237/38
Height 25.0 cm (9 ⅞ in.), width 16.5 cm (6 ⅞₆ in.)
LNS 67 MS (fol. 68b)

This manuscript with 195 folios was produced in two cities in Turkey. Incorporating four treatises on the theory, construction, and use of the astrolabe, it was written in Arabic by al-Biruni, Kamal al-Din ibn Yunus, al-Saghani, and al-Shirazi. The first two treatises were copied by a calligrapher named al-Mushi in 628 A.H. (1230/31) in Sivas, the third treatise was transcribed in 635 A.H. (1237/38) in Kayseri, and the last is undated. The second, third, and fourth treatises contain diagrams and tables drawn in red and brown.

The folio illustrated here belongs to al-Biruni's section and describes the part of an astrolabe representing the southern hemisphere. Al-Biruni was a celebrated eleventh-century scholar and his work on the astrolabe became the standard text for this instrument.

CERAMIC BOWL WITH PIERCED DECORATION

27

Iran, 12th century
Height 7.0 cm (2 ¾ in.), diameter 15.8 cm (6 ¼ in.)
LNS 279 C

An extremely fine group of twelfth-century wares displays a hard white body, frequently decorated with carved and pierced designs in an attempt to simulate the translucency of Chinese Song dynasty (960–1280) porcelains. The decoration was at times enhanced by splashes of color, as in this example.

The shape of the bowl with a low foot, flaring sides, and straight rim was also inspired by Chinese wares. The decorative repertoire, especially the scrolls bearing leaves and blossoms, however, is purely Islamic. Bowls of similar shape and decoration were also monochrome glazed in turquoise and purple, another characteristic feature of this type of Islamic pottery.

CERAMIC JAR WITH CARVED DECORATION

28

Iran, 12th–13th century
Height 29.0 cm (11 ½ in.), diameter 15.0 cm (6 in.)
LNS 207 C

A group of ceramics made in the twelfth and thirteenth centuries has a hard white paste covered with a black engobe, which was carved out to expose the white body underneath. The designs were left in relief and the details were incised. The pieces were then coated with a transparent turquoise or off-white glaze, which tinted only the sunken white areas. A similar "silhouette" effect was also achieved by painting the white body with a black slip and then glazing the piece.

This jar with a low foot, cylindrical body, sloping shoulders, short neck, and everted rim represents the carved and turquoise-glazed type. The lower portion of the body is divided into wide and narrow vertical stripes, above which is a panel with a foliated kufic inscription set against a floral ground. The Arabic inscription repeats the words "prosperity" and "progress." Vertical stripes, a popular decorative device used on these wares, appear on the shoulder. A meander motif encircles the neck.

MONOCHROME-GLAZED CERAMIC JAR

29

Egypt, 12th–13th century
Height 42.8 cm (16 ⅞ in.), diameter 29.5 cm (11 ½ in.)
LNS 350 C

Monochrome-glazed wares were popularly produced in the Islamic world during the twelfth and thirteenth centuries, although examples made in Egypt are rare. Frequently decorated with incised and carved designs, they were covered with various shades of blue, green, and purple.

The white body of this exceptional Egyptian jar is decorated with incised and carved designs and covered with a transparent green glaze that stops above the splayed foot. The Arabic inscription placed around the body and set against foliated scrolls reads "glory and prosperity and . . . peace and . . . long life to its owner." Encircling bands bear floral scrolls, while the neck contains a series of interlocking circles enclosing blossoms.

LUSTER-PAINTED CERAMIC BOWL WITH LION

30

Egypt, 12th century
Height 7.1 cm (2 ¾ in.), diameter 26.5 cm (10 ⁷/₁₆ in.)
LNS 167 C

In contrast to the earlier lusterwares made in Iraq and Egypt, which were painted within white contours, twelfth-century Egyptian wares reserved the main themes in white against the luster ground with the details painted in luster. This stylistic feature provided the potters with greater freedom to represent complicated scenes as well as movement and volume.

Typical of a group of Fatimid wares decorated with single animals, this bowl has an earthenware body covered with opaque white glaze and is painted in copper red luster. The flaring sides contain a kufic inscription set against spiraling scrolls. In the center is a stalking lion surrounded by a leaping hare and several sprays of leaves.

LUSTER-PAINTED CERAMIC BOWL WITH FIGURE

31

Iran, late 12th–early 13th century
Height 5.7 cm (2 ¼ in.), diameter 14.9 cm (5 ⅞ in.)
LNS 295 C

Iranian lusterwares produced in the twelfth and thirteenth centuries epitomize the technical achievements of the Muslim potters. The pieces represent diverse figural compositions, ranging from enthroned princes and mystical gatherings to astrological themes. The finest wares were made in Kashan, which was renowned for its exquisite vessels and tiles.

This unusual bowl with three feet and straight sides characterizes the lusterwares identified with Kashan. In the center is an enthroned figure wearing a robe decorated with spirals. The figure displays the physiognomy of an idealized Seljuk prince—round face, almond-shaped eyes, straight nose, and small mouth—and wears a headdress identifiable with the Turkish ruling class. Reserved on a luster ground, the solitary figure projects a hierarchic image, his head encircled by a white halo.

LUSTER-PAINTED CERAMIC BOWL WITH BIRDS

32

Iran, dated January 1218
Height 8.1 cm (3 ³/₁₆ in.), diameter 23.7 cm (9 ⁵/₁₆ in.)
LNS 210 C

The shape of this bowl with four flanges on its rim follows a metalwork prototype. The decorative scheme represents a variation of Kashan artistry and is devoid of human figures but includes floral and bird motifs as well as inscriptions.

Forming a scroll with four large volutes in the center of the bowl is a medallion with half-palmettes and plump flying birds, characteristic features of this style. In the background are a series of spirals scratched through the luster. Around the central medallion is a band with Persian inscriptions written in *naskhi,* or cursive script, and reserved on luster. Painted in luster on the inner walls is another *naskhi* inscription rendered in Arabic. Arabic is also used on the exterior walls in the kufic band, which is partly deciphered as ''glory and good fortune.''

Touches of blue define the branches of the scroll in the central medallion, edges of the four flanges, and exterior kufic band.

LUSTER-PAINTED CERAMIC BOWL WITH FLORALS

33

Syria, late 12th–early 13th century
Height 12.0 cm (4 ¾ in.), diameter 24.0 cm (9 ⁷/₁₆ in.)
LNS 24 C

The production of lusterwares flourished in Syria during the late twelfth and early thirteenth centuries, as attested by finds in Damascus, Hama, and Raqqa. This bowl represents the wares often attributed to Raqqa, which are characterized by a greenish tinged glaze; the decoration is overglaze painted in copper red luster as well as underglaze painted in turquoise or blue. In this example the underglaze painting appears in the roundels on the interior walls.

The reserved decoration on the luster-painted ground consists of half-palmettes and Arabic inscriptions. The half-palmettes fill the central medallion and decorate two of the four compartments on the interior walls. The remaining compartments are inscribed with the words "comprehensive" and "happiness." Wide concentric circles painted in luster appear on the exterior walls.

OVERGLAZE-PAINTED CERAMIC BOWL WITH RIDER

34

Iran, late 12th–early 13th century
Height 8.7 cm (3 ½ in.), diameter 20.6 cm (8 ⅛ in.)
LNS 306 C

Overglaze-painted Seljuk wares, known as *minai,* generally depict figural compositions. When inscriptions were used, kufic normally appears on the inside and *naskhi* on the outside.

The interior of this bowl with a high foot and flaring sides is divided into concentric bands. The central medallion represents a rider framed by a turquoise band and enclosed by a panel with six seated figures interspersed with stylized trees, their palmettelike branches extending over the heads of the personages. The panel is bordered by a repetitive series of letters rendered in kufic and placed over scrolls. A Persian inscription written in *naskhi* appears on the exterior walls. The motifs are both underglaze and overglaze painted in blue, black, brown, pale purple, and turquoise.

GLASS JUG WITH STAMPED INSCRIPTION

35

Egypt, 11th–12th century
Height 16.7 cm (6 %6 in.), diameter 10.9 cm (4 ¼ in.)
LNS 124 G

This jug was free-blown in colorless transparent glass; the handle was made separately and applied to the body. Confined to the slightly flaring neck, the decoration consists of stamped Arabic inscriptions separated by pincered lines. Written vertically, the inscriptions repeat five times the words "enjoyable drinking."

The technique of free-blowing was the most important innovation in the glass industry. Attributed to Syrian glassmakers, it was developed in the first century B.C. and resulted in the production of a large quantity of vessels all over the Roman Empire. Less time-consuming than the earlier method of mold blowing, this technique permitted the products to be cheaply made and thus more widely accessible. It also introduced a larger variety of shapes, sizes, and decorative themes and motifs.

MOLDED GLASS BOTTLE

36

Iran, 11th–12th century
Height 20.8 cm (8 ³⁄₁₆ in.), diameter 10.5 cm (4 ⅛ in.)
LNS 8 G

This bottle of transparent blue glass combines two techniques: the body was blown in a two-part mold while the neck was free-blown. Molds used for glass vessels were made of wood or clay and usually consisted of two or more parts. A seam generally appears at the joint but is often camouflaged by the design. The decoration of this bottle, consisting of four pairs of addorsed palmettes with lozenges in the centers and roundels at the points of intersection, does not cover the seam.

Glass bottles of a similar shape were produced in Iran between the ninth and twelfth centuries. The same shape also appeared in metalwork.

Illustrated on the following page

SMALL MOLDED GLASS BOTTLE

37

Iran, 12th century
Height 9.2 cm (3 ¹¹/₁₆ in.), diameter 7.8 cm (3 ⅛ in.)
LNS 113 G

Molds have been used for relief designs in western Asia since the first century B.C. They were employed in Iran during the pre-Islamic era and reached a high level of perfection during the Seljuk period.

The decoration on this transparent yellowish green bottle was achieved by mold blowing, the same technique used in the example discussed previously (36). Popular in Iran during the eleventh and twelfth centuries, the design consists of repeated palmette and calyx motifs, bordered at the bottom by a series of triangles. The use of the palmette, an ancient motif, spread throughout the Islamic world and was applied to diverse materials.

The trailed purple thread applied to the rim of the flaring neck adds color to the piece and contrasts with the overall relief decoration of the body.

HIGH-TIN BRONZE BOWL

38

Afghanistan, 11th–12th century
Height 12.0 cm (4 ¾ in.), diameter 26.9 cm (10 ½ in.)
LNS 3 M

The hemispherical bowl, hammered from a sheet of metal, is decorated with engraved and punched designs. The surface reveals three patterns placed in six vertical panels radiating from the roundel at the base. They include hatched lozenges, small circles, and double circles with seven-dot rosettes characteristic of the decorative repertoire of Afghanistan and eastern Iran.

The metallurgical composition of the piece consists of approximately 90 percent copper and 10 percent tin, known either as high-tin, or white, bronze, due to the lighter color resulting from the addition of tin. High-tin bronze wares were produced by the Chinese, Romans, and Sasanians. According to early Arabic sources, the material (called *asfithruy*) was used as a substitute for gold and silver. It became popular during the eleventh and twelfth centuries.

Detail

INLAID BRASS CANDLESTICK WITH ANIMALS

39

Afghanistan, late 12th century
Height 31.0 cm (12 ³/₁₆ in.), diameter 35.2 cm (13 ⅞ in.)
LNS 81 M

This eight-sided candlestick belongs to a small group of faceted examples. It was hammered from a sheet of brass, chased, and inlaid with silver and copper. Such inlaying, rarely seen on earlier pieces, became common during the twelfth and thirteenth centuries, together with the decorative techniques of engraving, piercing, and chasing.

The candlestick is decorated with horizontal panels of varying widths. Arabic inscriptions repeating such good wishes and invocations as ''glory, happiness, contentment, bounty, mercy, health, power, perpetuity, and blessing'' appear in the panels on the socket, shoulder, and body, written in both kufic and *naskhi*. At the top, base, and wide central panels of the body are figural compositions executed in repoussé. The upper and lower registers depict seated lions and birds, while the central zone represents pairs of animals in combat, symbolizing imperial power.

INLAID BRASS PEN BOX

40

Syria or Turkey, first half 13th century
Height 3.5 cm (1 ⁵⁄₁₆ in.), length 21.5 cm (8 ½ in.), width 4.8 cm (1 ⅞ in.)
LNS 17 M

Metal pen boxes with separate compartments for pens, ink, and sand were used throughout the Islamic world. They were produced in various shapes, the most popular being rectangular with rounded corners, similar to this example.

This pen box was raised from a sheet of brass, engraved, and inlaid with silver and gold. It is decorated with Arabic inscriptions and scrolls interspersed with roundels bearing geometric designs. Two medallions filled with scrolling split-palmettes flank a poem inscribed on the lid: "Do not write with your hand except that which will delight you to see on Judgment Day." The other inscriptions encircling the sides are invocational and end with the phrase wishing the owner life "as long as a pigeon coos." This phrase also appears on a fifteenth-century helmet (see **68**) attributed to eastern Turkey.

BRONZE MIRROR

41

Turkey, early 13th century
Diameter 11.4 cm (4 ½ in.)
LNS 102 M

This cast-bronze mirror has a pierced central boss with a pair of addorsed sphinxes enclosed by a band of benedictory inscriptions written in foliated kufic. The curving wings of the creatures were joined together to form a symmetrical tree, with additional floral sprays placed in the background. The Arabic inscription incorporates blessings to the owner: "Glory and perpetuity and presidency and high rank and appreciation and joy and eminence and rulership, growth and power and bounty to its owner forever."

Circular cast-bronze mirrors were found in eastern Iran as well as in Iraq, Syria, and Turkey, suggesting that they were made throughout the Islamic world. The same type was produced as early as 1200 B.C. in China and central Asia, from where it must have spread westward. Mirrors of this type, with a central boss for suspending it from a cord, appear to have been used for divination.

INLAID SILVER SPOON AND FORK

42

Iran, 12th century
Length 14.8 cm (5 ⅞ in.), width 3.3 cm (1 ¼ in.)
LNS 104 M

This remarkable piece combining a fork and spoon attests to the creativity and practicality of the Muslim artists. The folding spoon and fork was cast in silver, engraved, and inlaid with niello (a black enamellike alloy). Its decorative scheme incorporates animals as well as Arabic inscriptions written in kufic. Placed around the bowl of the spoon are the phrases: "Power is God's, sovereignty is God's, thanks is God's, greatness is God's, glory is God's, reverence is God's."

A bird occupies the central medallion of the spoon and a winged lion appears in the roundel between the spoon and fork. The contrasting background, filled with niello, highlights the figures.

PAIR OF GOLD BRACELETS

Syria (?), 11th century
Each: diameter 7.1 and 6.9 cm (2 ⅞ and 2 ¾ in.), width of clasp 3.2 cm (1 ¼ in.)
LNS 7 J (a–b)

These hollow bracelets, fabricated from a thin sheet of gold, are filled with a hard yellow substance, probably a sulphur compound. Hinged at midpoint with a ball-and-socket joint, the cylindrical shanks of the bracelets are decorated in low relief with bands containing affronted birds or kufic inscriptions.

The wide triangular areas flanking the clasp are decorated with granulation. Tiny grains are lined up between pairs of twisted wires bent to form scrolling branches.

Many comparable bracelets are known. Some have triangular shank terminals, as here; others are crescentic with an opening for the wrist, have heart-shaped ends, or are without clasps or hinges.

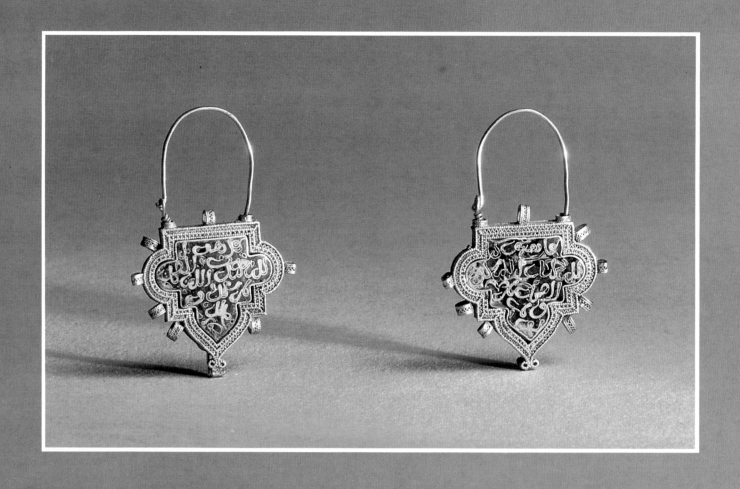

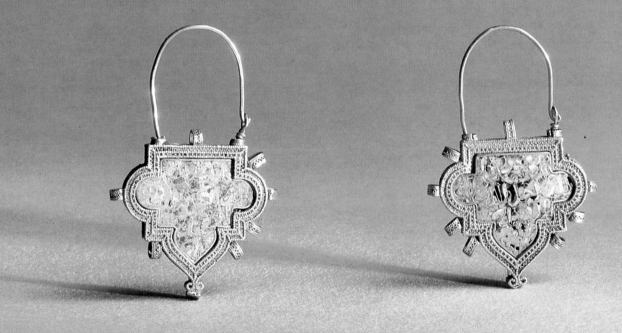

PAIR OF ENAMELED GOLD EARRINGS

44

Spain or Morocco, 12th century
Each: length with ear wires 4.8 cm (1 ⅞ in.), width 3.1 cm (1 ¼ in.)
LNS 30 J (a–b)

Into both faces of each earring is set an enameled unit, in which the first part of the Quranic chapter Ikhlas, the Unity (CXII), is executed in cloisonné. In this type of enameling the vitreous compounds are applied to compartments created by metal wires soldered to the back.

Although the cloisonné technique and boxlike frame constructed of filigree and granulation link this unique pair to eleventh-century Fatimid pieces made in Egypt and Syria, the character of the Arabic inscriptions, together with analogies to local architectural forms, indicates that the earrings were produced in Morocco or Spain. Filigree work is found on a considerable amount of Spanish jewelry from the tenth to twelfth centuries. This technique as well as granulation and cloisonné enameling continued in Spain in the fourteenth and fifteenth centuries.

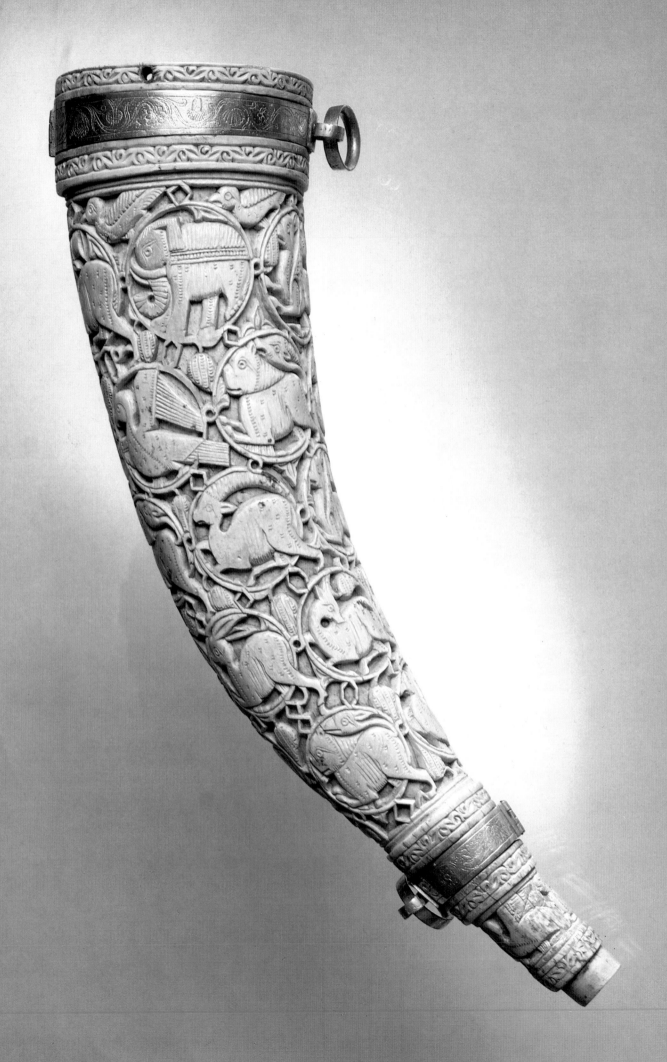

CARVED IVORY HUNTING HORN

45

Sicily, late 11th–early 12th century
Length 34.5 cm (13 9/16 in.), diameter 9.5 cm (3 3/4 in.)
LNS 12 I

Carved in relief from a single piece of elephant tusk, this horn is attributed to Sicily, one of the principal ivory-carving centers in the Mediterranean. The raised areas have flat profiles, in contrast to the three-dimensional or rounded surfaces of contemporary Spanish pieces.

The body is divided into five staggered rows of interlacing roundels composed of scrolling branches bearing pinecones or bunches of grapes. Inside the roundels are various animals and birds that extend their legs or heads over the frames. The tails of some creatures, such as the lion, terminate in dragon heads. Two narrow bands with foliated scrolls flank the incised brass fittings around the rim and base. At the very bottom is a panel with an elephant, deer, and bird.

CARVED WOOD PANEL

46

Egypt, 11th century
Height 32.9 cm (13 in.), width 152.7 cm (60 in.)
LNS 55 W

This panel epitomizes the high level of artistic expression achieved under the Fatimids. With traces of gesso indicating that it might have been painted, the piece is carved in relief, in departure from the earlier style of bevel cutting practiced in Egypt. A pleasing contrast is created by the energetic depiction of the two addorsed gazelles flanking the central palmette, their prancing movement counteracting the static effect of the symmetrical composition and abstracted motifs. This lively and naturalistic representation is characteristic of Fatimid art.

The panel is one of several discovered in Cairo during repairwork carried out in 1911 at the thirteenth-century hospital of Sultan Qalaun. It is thought to come from the Fatimid palace that occupied the site, which was renovated in 1058. Other pieces are in the Museum of Islamic Art in Cairo.

The Postclassical Period (1250–1500)

SHEILA S. BLAIR

Detail of **68**

In 1258 Mongol forces took Baghdad and put an end to the Abbasid caliphate. This date is a convenient watershed to mark the beginning of the postclassical period, which continued until the foundation of the major empires by the Ottomans, Safavids, and Mughals in the early sixteenth century. By the time of the Mongol invasions international Islamic society had been established and many features from the previous period continued: the rule by military amirs, the organization of mystical orders, the patterns of Islamic expansion. But the Mongol conquests also introduced new elements into the historical situation, particularly new contact with distant cultures and new standards of art and patronage.[1]

In general, there is more evidence about patronage than in previous periods. More objects have survived. A recent survey lists 257 standing buildings erected in Iran and central Asia between 1360 and 1510, and another 140 are known from texts.[2] The Mamluk dynasty was responsible for another 250 in Cairo.[3] Textual evidence is more abundant and more varied. Some accounts are panegyrics composed in honor of a specific patron. One of the most florid authors was the fourteenth-century Persian chronicler Shihab al-Din Abd Allah ibn Fadl Allah al-Shirazi, whose epithet, Wassaf, means "Panegyrist" and whose style is so effusive that it had to be "translated" into prose for the modern reader.[4] Other accounts are told from different vantage points. For the Timurid period in Iran and central Asia, for example, the accounts by such court panegyrists as Hafiz-i Abru (d. 1430) and Sharaf al-Din Yazdi (d. 1435) can be set against those of virulent anti-Timurid writers such as Ibn Arabshah (1392–1450). External accounts of the dynasty include the Spanish traveler Ruy Gonzáles de Clavijo (d. 1412), ambassador from the court of Henry III of Castile to Timur.[5]

The Patrons

The kinds of patrons who had been active in the classical age were again active in the postclassical period. Sultans were usually the wealthiest; they controlled larger areas than had earlier rulers and had more money at their disposal. Among the most renowned were the Ilkhanids Ghazan (r. 1295–1304) and Oljaytu (r. 1304–17); the Timurids Timur and Shah Rukh (r. 1405–47); the Mamluks Nasir al-Din Muhammad (r. 1293–1341 with interruptions) and Qaitbay; the Marinid Abu'l-Inan Faris (r. 1348–59); and the Nasrid Muhammad V (r. 1354–91 with interruption). In North Africa sultans were almost the exclusive patrons because of the Maliki system of law that prevailed. According to other schools of law, the administration of a pious endowment could be reserved to its founder during his lifetime and to his successors to the end of the line, but this was prohibited in Maliki law, so private individuals had little incentive to set up pious foundations.[6]

Other members of princely families controlled vast resources that enabled them to be lavish patrons. In part, their power resulted from the arrangement of installing one's relatives as rulers of provincial cities. In the fifteenth century the Timurid princes Iskandar Sultan (1384–1415) and Ibrahim Sultan (1394–1435) maintained lavish courts at Shiraz in southern Iran, which included ateliers for the production of books. Shah Rukh's son Baysunghur (1399–1434), himself a famous calligrapher, maintained the foremost painting studio at Herat during his father's reign.[7]

Members of court also accumulated vast private fortunes and were substantial patrons of the arts. A good example is Rashid al-Din (d. 1318), vizier to the Ilkhanid sultans Ghazan, Oljaytu, and Abu Said (r. 1317–35). His funerary complex outside

Figure 17. Brass basin inlaid with silver and gold made by Muhammad ibn al-Zayn, Egypt, circa 1290–1310. Paris, Musée du Louvre (LP 16).

Tabriz in northwestern Iran was equal to those built by the sultans. It employed more than three hundred workers and had an endowment of nearly fifty thousand dinars (the annual revenues of the Ilkhanid state amounted to twenty-one million dinars).[8] Mir Ali Shir Navai (1440–1501), boon companion of the Timurid sultan Husayn Bayqara (also known as Husayn Mirza; r. 1470–1506), was credited with more than 120 structures, although much of the work may have only been repairs.[9]

The power of such men of the pen was balanced by that of the men of the sword, the amirs who surrounded the sultan and often upheld his throne. In 1304 the Ilkhanid amir Zayn al-Din Mastari (d. 1312) endowed a large shrine complex at Natanz in central Iran that included a hospice for mystics, or Sufis, a tomb, a congregational mosque, and a minaret.[10] The Mamluk amir Salar (d. 1310) probably commissioned the most exquisite piece of metalwork produced during the period, the so-called Baptistère de Saint Louis (fig. 17).[11] Other inlaid brasses (such as the basin and box, **66–67**) are inscribed with the titles of Mamluk officers, and some pieces of metalwork and ceramics (such as **60**) can be attributed to amiral patronage because of the blazons or insignia of rank inscribed on them.[12]

Few members of the ulama were patrons of large-scale buildings, but they did commission objects and furnishings. The inscriptions on the box for a Quran manuscript (**71**), for example, tell us that it was endowed by Izz al-Din Malik, who is identified as a *sadr*, a religious figure often involved in the administration of endowments, and that it was made by al-Hasan ibn Qutlubak for the tomb of his grandfather, Fakhr al-Din (d. 1344). In Egypt and Syria members of the Arabic-speaking educated class, which included the offspring of Mamluks and wealthy Arabs, were the main patrons for illustrated books. A tax inspector from Damascus, for example, signed a copy of the *Maqamat* that he bought in 1375, and a similar class of people were probably the intended owners of such manuscripts as the *Automata* of al-Jazari (1260–1338) copied in 1315 (**49**) and the *Sulwan al-Muta* (Comfort of rulers) of Ibn Zafar (1104–1170) made in Egypt or Syria during the second quarter of the fourteenth century (**50**).[13] The ulama also commissioned ceramics, since a fourteenth-century incised bowl found at Tod in lower Egypt is inscribed with the name of a judge, and a luster jar from Syria (fig. 18) is inscribed with the name of a patron whose lack of titles suggests a nonprincely origin.[14]

Women were the most significant new class of patrons during the postclassical period. They played an important role in traditional steppe societies, as in most nomadic cultures, which could not afford to preclude such a large segment of the population from the labor market. During the classical period a few Turkic women had already commissioned buildings, and with the assumption of power by non-Arab groups the role of women increased, although their sovereignty was never totally accepted. Shagarat al-Durr (d. 1257), widow of the last Ayyubid sultan, Najm al-Din Ayyub, is a good example. She concealed his death until her son Turanshah (r. 1250) could be installed, but the youth was so hated that he was assassinated after a two-month reign. Perhaps inspired by her authority, the Mamluks elected Shagarat al-Durr queen, but her claim to sovereignty was shaky and based on her regency for a dead infant. To boost her legitimacy, she married the commander-in-chief of the Mamluks, Izz al-Din Aybak (r. 1250–57), who was named sultan. After she had him

Figure 18. Luster-painted jar made for Asad al-Iskandarani by Yusuf, Damascus, Syria, second half thirteenth century. Kuwait, Dar al-Athar al-Islamiyyah (LNS 188 C).

murdered in the bath, the Mamluks rose up, put her in prison, and then handed her over to Aybak's former wife, who had her successor beaten to death with bath clogs.[15]

Women were particularly important in Mongol society. The earliest illustrations to Rashid al-Din's history of the Mongols, cut out from their original manuscripts and pasted in albums now in the Staatsbibliothek in West Berlin show women enthroned as equals with their husbands.[16] Women are frequently depicted in the Demotte *Shahnama* (ca. 1335/36; dispersed), the most important illustrated manuscript made under the Ilkhanids.[17] They are the main subject of several unusual paintings such as the representation of Ardavan's daughter seeking to poison her husband, Ardashir,[18] and even when not mentioned in the text, they are depicted popping out of windows and overlooking the scene. Scheming women are so common in the manuscript that they constitute one of its five themes, one that might be modeled on Baghdad Khatun, wife of Sultan Abu Said, who was accused of poisoning her husband.

Female patronage became most important under the Timurids, perhaps because of Timur's claim to legitimacy as "son-in-law" (*gurgan*) of Genghis Khan. Many tombs in the Shah-i Zinda, the extraordinary necropolis outside medieval Samarqand, were built for Timurid princesses, and women of the royal household founded madrasas and *khanaqa*s (hospices for Sufis) in the city itself.[19] The most outstanding was Gawhar Shad (d. 1457), daughter of a Chaghatay Turk notable and wife of the Timurid sultan Shah Rukh. Her architectural patronage outshone even that of her husband. She added a congregational mosque in 1416–18 to the Shrine of Imam Rida at Mashhad and engaged the same architect, Qawam al-Din Shirazi (d. 1438), to design an enormous mosque-madrasa complex in 1417–38 in the capital, Herat. She remained a busybody into her seventies, when she was executed by Sultan Abu Said (r. 1451–69) for plotting against him in league with her grandson Ala al-Dawla (1417–60).[20]

The Patronage of Architecture

These new and powerful patrons had the resources to order different kinds of art. Like the caliphs of the early period, they could create new cities. The Ilkhanids founded a new capital, Sultaniyya, in northwestern Iran in the middle of the plain, 120 kilometers northwest of Qazvin on the road to Tabriz. The outer city measured thirty thousand paces in circumference. The inner citadel, 250 meters wide, had walls broad enough for four horsemen to ride abreast and was protected by sixteen towers, a machicolated parapet, iron gate, and moat.[21] To expand and beautify his new capital of Samarqand, Timur recruited artisans from all the cities he had conquered in Iran and Syria. The Tughluqid sultans of India ordered a set of royal cities outside Delhi—Firuzabad, Jahanpanah, and Tughluqabad.[22]

Few palace complexes have survived in the Iranian world. The Mongols often used tent palaces such as the enormous ones erected by Timur in Samarqand, which Clavijo described as lined with fur and embroidered in silver and gold. Others have been destroyed by succeeding rulers or abandoned to the vicissitudes of time. All that is left of Timur's monumental White Palace (Aq Saray) in Shahr-i Sabz near his birthplace south of the Zarafshan Mountains in Soviet Central Asia are the pylons of its elephantine twenty-two-meter-wide portal.[23] The mainly fifteenth-century palace of the local dynasty of Shirvanshahs in Baku in Azerbayjan is better preserved, but its stone architecture is more closely related to the tradition of eastern Anatolia than to that of the Iranian world.[24]

The most evocative palace complex from the postclassical period is the Alhambra, a fortress-city built between the eleventh and fourteenth centuries, twenty-two hundred meters in perimeter with twenty-two towers, superbly situated on a spur of the Sierra Nevada overlooking Granada. Inside are two complete palaces organized around open courtyards, one around the Court of the Myrtles begun by Yusuf I (r. 1333–54) and the other around the Court of the Lions built by Muhammad V. Both have large throne rooms, the Hall of the Ambassadors with an extraordinary wood ceiling and the Hall of the Two Sisters with an elaborate *muqarnas* vault symbolizing the Dome of Heaven.[25]

Dynastic or imperial tomb complexes were other favorite architectural commissions. All that remains at Sultaniyya is the octagonal tomb (1305–15) of Sultan Oljaytu, but its enormous size (measuring some thirty-eight meters in diameter with a fifty-meter dome ringed by eight minarets) shows how much labor was involved in the original pious foundation that included places for prayer, instruction, Quran reading, residence, and medication.[26] Similarly, Gawhar Shad's dynastic tomb (1432) is one of the few elements remaining from her complex in Herat, and its melon-shaped dome and superb interior rib vaulting bespeak the high level of patronage and sophistication of the architects she was able to command.[27] The early Mamluk sultans continued the tradition of ordering tombs on the main street of medieval Cairo and had to shoehorn their mausoleums within space available. The tomb of Sultan Qalaun (1284/85), for example, occupies a trapezoidal plot on the site of the old Fatimid palaces. Later Mamluk sultans such as Qaitbay built in the cemeteries and were free to incorporate the various elements of fountain, primary school, and tomb in a more regular plan.[28]

Under the Ottomans these royal tomb complexes became known as *külliye*s. The one for Bayezid I (r. 1391–95) in Bursa in northwestern Turkey includes a madrasa, mosque, tomb, fountain, and kitchen loosely grouped on the top of a hill fronting a square, but in later tomb complexes built in İstanbul the individual elements are carefully aligned.[29]

Tomb complexes were not limited to the royal family. Rashid al-Din's suburb outside Tabriz was centered around the tomb built in 1300–1309 for him and his family, and local notables of Yazd—Rukn al-Din (d. 1334) and Shams al-Din (d. 1365)—copied his example there.[30] Mamluk amirs also built their own tombs in Cairo. The one for Salar and Sanjar al-Jawli (1303/4) is a picturesque grouping on the northwestern spur of an outcropping of the Muqattam Hills. Strung along a corridor are two mausoleums with ribbed domes, a combination school-hospice with two iwans, and a minaret with three differently shaped stories, the first of a kind that was to become standard in Cairo.[31]

Shrine complexes were also built around the graves of Sufi saints. The Marinid sultan Abu'l-Hasan Ali (r. 1331–48) turned the grave of the Andalusian mystic Abu Madyan Shuayb (d. 1197) into one of the important centers of instruction in the Maghrib (the scholar Ibn Khaldun, for example, worked there). Perched on a hill overlooking the city of Tlemcen, the complex (1338–46) includes a mosque, madrasa, ablution facilities, and residence in addition to the tomb. The madrasa had thirty-two cells for students, and the endowment deed inscribed on a marble plaque suggests that Sufis and pilgrims were meant to outnumber the students two to one. The sultan spent a great deal of money for the rich decoration—which includes tiled dadoes, carved plaster vaults, inlaid wood ceilings, bronze doors, and onyx columns and capitals—and endowed gardens, orchards, houses, windmills, baths, and land to maintain the shrine.[32] In 1397 Timur ordered a large shrine complex in honor of Sheikh Ahmad Yasavi (d. 1166) in the oasis of Yasi (now Turkestan City, Kazakh Republic, USSR) on the Jaxartes along the caravan route north of Tashkent. The spectacular *muqarnas* vaults over the assembly hall and tomb and innovative transverse vaulting in some of the smaller rooms attest to the high level of talent Timur was able to gather, even in this remote spot.[33] A quarter of a century later, the grave of Khwaja Abd Allah Ansari (d. 1089) at Gazur Gah, a village near Herat in northwestern Afghanistan, was turned into a major shrine complex, whose superb vaulting and elaborate tile patterns suggest an equally high level of patronage.[34]

Important patrons during this period also wanted to appear as pious Muslims and continued to endow traditional types of Muslim institutions. Sultans, amirs, and viziers ordered congregational mosques, most of which followed traditional plans. Those in Egypt and North Africa were usually hypostyle (like the ones ordered by the Mamluk sultan Muayyad Sheikh in 1415–21 in Cairo and by the Marinids at Mansuriyya outside Tlemcen in 1303–6), while those in Iran usually had four iwans around a courtyard and a domed sanctuary (like the one ordered by an Ilkhanid vizier from a local family at Varamin south of Tehran, constructed in 1322–26).[35] In Turkey congregational mosques built by the early Ottoman sultans introduced the domed profile that became the hallmark of later Ottoman mosques. The one built in Bursa by Bayezid I has twenty domes supported on twelve piers, while the Üç Şerefeli (Three-balconied) Mosque (1438–47) built by Murad II (r. 1421–51 with interruption) in Edirne, northwest of İstanbul, has a large central dome (twenty-four meters in diameter) demarcated by four tall minarets.[36]

Madrasas were the favorite type of pious construction by sultans in North Africa, due to the conservative Maliki system of law. The city of Fez is dotted with such splendid Marinid examples as the Attarin and Saffarin madrasas. The largest is the Bu Inaniyya (1350–55), built by Abu'l-Inan Faris, which also functioned as a congregational mosque.[37] Such schools were also popular in fifteenth-century Iran and central Asia. Timur's grandson Ulugh Beg (1394–1449) was a noted scientist and scholar, and in 1417, while ruler of Samarqand for his father, Shah Rukh, he ordered a large madrasa built there. Planned with four iwans and four domed halls in the corners, it had room for one hundred students in two levels of cells.[38] Ulugh Beg's scientific interests are also evident in the large observatory that he ordered in Samarqand.[39]

The Patronage of Art

Such architectural commissions often included furnishings inscribed with the name of the patron. Oljaytu ordered monumental Quran manuscripts for his tomb at Sultaniyya. The frontispieces to a thirty-volume set are decorated with patterns similar to those in stucco on the galleries of the tomb (figs. 19–20).[40] The similarity suggests a central design source, one which would have been the forerunner of the *naqqash-khana,* or central design studio, which flourished under the Ottomans.[41] A number of luxury Quran manuscripts (**47–48**) might also have been made for institutions founded by a sultan or his amirs.

Mamluk foundations were lit with enameled and gilded glass lamps, some bearing the patron's name or blazon. Sultan Hasan (r. 1347–61 with interruption) commissioned hundreds for his tomb in Cairo, of which at least fifty survive (fig. 21).[42] The vase produced in the same technique, with an inscription invoking glory to the sultan

Figure 19. Right half of a double frontispiece from part 23 of a thirty-volume Quran made for Sultan Oljaytu, transcribed and illuminated by Abd Allah ibn Muhammad ibn Mahmud al-Hamadhani, Iran, dated 1313. Cairo, National Library (72, fol. 1b).

Figure 20. Carved and painted stucco vault of the tomb of Sultan Oljaytu, Sultaniyya, Iran, built 1305–15.

(64), would also have been made for a royal patron, and the circular tile with the epigraphic blazon of Sultan Qaitbay (61) was obviously made for one of his foundations.

Lusterware was one of the most expensive types of Iranian ceramics, and luster-painted tiles (such as the star-shaped examples, 54) were often assembled in large dadoes and friezes for the most expensive monuments of the day (fig. 22). Examples have been discovered in situ in the Ilkhanid palace at Takht-i Sulayman in northwestern Iran and in numerous shrine complexes such as the one at Natanz.[43]

Other objects were made for royal or amiral households. The carved ivory box inscribed with the phrase "there is no victor but God" (70) probably belonged to the Nasrid court at Granada since the phrase was frequently used on objects commissioned by the founder of the dynasty, Muhammad I (r. 1230–72), and is inscribed all over the Alhambra walls. A series of inlaid brass bowls (such as 65) is inscribed with titles associated with the province of Fars in southern Iran,[44] but the generalized invocation of blessing and glory suggests that the bowls were not individual commissions but created for amiral households. Iranian ceramics decorated with figures in Mongol dress (55–56) might have been made for courtiers, but their generalized iconography suggests that they were not special commissions but were made for the market. Most portable objects of this period, however, are anonymous, and the specific patrons for which they were intended cannot be determined (see, for instance, 57–59 and 62–63).

Many of these types of portable objects in ceramic, glass, and metal are known from earlier periods; what is new in the postclassical period is the proliferation of illustrated books in Iran. Illustrated manuscripts had been produced in the classical Arab world, but only one Persian manuscript, a copy of Ayyuqi's *Warqa and Gulshah,* probably done at Konya around 1250, can be attributed to the classical period.[45] The reasons for the blossoming of the tradition of Persian book illustration in the fourteenth century are not entirely clear. It was part of the general cultural revival sponsored by the Ilkhanids and drew on the tradition of the illustrated scroll that they had known in China. It was also part of an increased interest in history.

The Islamic world had a long tradition of historical writing, but during the Mongol period three important things occurred: it became particularly prolific, was written in Persian rather than Arabic, and covered a far broader scope. In the classical Arab world illustrated books had included scientific manuals, animal stories, and popular literary works. These continued to be illustrated in the postclassical Arab (for example, 49–50) and Iranian (51) worlds, but a new type was added: historical works. For nearly a half century, from the enthronement of Hulagu until Ghazan's conversion in 1295, the Mongol rulers were non-Muslims, and much of the historical writing was meant to justify their rule. Events of the past were seen as analogous to those of the present, and important illustrated manuscripts were commissioned with ideological programs in mind.

The Mongol interest in history can best be seen in Rashid al-Din's *Jami al-Tavarikh* (Universal history; 1315). Ilkhanid rulers ordered the vizier to compose the first world history, one that would include the history of China, Europe, and India. The surviving fragmentary copies of his work are large-format manuscripts with striplike illustrations revealing a reliance on Chinese scrolls.[46] Many illustrated scenes were specifically chosen to justify the Mongols' right to rule. The section about the Ghaznavids in the fragment at the University Library in Edinburgh, for example, contains thirty folios with twenty-seven illustrations of the life of Mahmud, for the Mongols undoubtedly saw themselves in the same light as the great eleventh-century Turkish conqueror.

Historical manuscripts continued to be commissioned for ideological purposes during the fifteenth century. On the eve of his conquest of Khorasan, Sultan Husayn Bayqara commissioned a new copy of the *Zafarnama* (Book of conquest; 1467/68), Sharaf al-Din Yazdi's eulogistic account of the life of Timur.[47] The six double-page paintings added to the manuscript a decade or so later illustrate heroic episodes in the life of Timur and his son Umar Sheikh (1354–94): Timur's audience on his accession; victories in Urgench, on the Jaxartes, in Georgia, and in İzmir; and the construction

Figure 21. Enameled and gilded glass mosque lamp made for Sultan Hasan, Egypt, circa 1360. Cairo, Museum of Islamic Art (288).

Figure 22. Panel with star- and cross-shaped tiles from the shrine of Imamzada Yahya, Varamin, Iran, built 1262. London, Victoria and Albert Museum (1837-1876).

of the Great Mosque of Samarqand (fig. 23). They were chosen to underscore Husayn Bayqara's connection to the Timurid line and to justify his assumption of power.

This rhetorical use of illustrated manuscripts was not limited to historical texts; epics were also seen as history. The most popular was the *Shahnama*. The magnificent copy made at the end of the Ilkhanid period, known ignominiously as the "Demotte" after the dealer who cut it up in the early twentieth century, comprised two volumes amounting to three hundred folios (each about 40 x 29 cm) and nearly two hundred illustrations.[48] The paintings are clustered around specific events and stories, and unusual scenes such as the enthronements of Zav (fig. 24) and Garshasp were deliberately chosen as exemplars of dynastic legitimacy to prop up the moribund dynasty.[49] The patron has been identified as Ghiyath al-Din Muhammad (d. 1336), son of Rashid al-Din and himself a vizier who was charged with finding a suitable Ilkhanid heir following the death of Abu Said.

Later copies of the *Shahnama* were also made for polemic purposes. The one ordered by Prince Baysunghur in 1430 contains only twenty-one paintings, including a double-page frontispiece.[50] They do not illustrate scenes common in *Shahnama* manuscripts, such as Bahram Gur and Azada or Kay Khosrau in a snowstorm, but concentrate on events related to the life of the patron. The frontispiece, for example, does not depict a king enthroned but a prince hunting with musicians; and other scenes, such as Prince Luhrasp hearing of his father's disappearance and the young Bahram Gur consigned to the tutor Munzir, are unique to this manuscript.

These metropolitan manuscripts were produced in court-sponsored ateliers. The best example of a fourteenth-century scriptorium was founded by Rashid al-Din in the Rab-i Rashidi, his quarter outside Tabriz. Its endowment deed provided for the annual copying of Quran codices and religious manuscripts, and an addendum provided for annual copies of the vizier's collected works in Arabic and Persian. Some of the 220 slaves attached to the complex were assigned the tasks of calligraphy, painting, and gilding, and all manuscripts were to be prepared on high-quality Baghdadi paper in a neat hand, collated with the originals in the library, and bound in fine leather. Not all copies of Rashid al-Din's *Jami al-Tavarikh* were illustrated there, however, for the contemporary Baghdadi biographer Ibn al-Fuwati (1244–1318) mentioned meeting a famous master who was engaged in painting one of Rashid al-Din's works in the sultan's mobile camp in Arran in Transcaucasia.[51] Upon Rashid al-Din's death in 1318, the quarter was plundered, but the scriptorium must have survived since it is where the Demotte *Shahnama* was probably produced.

Timur's grandson Baysunghur established the most famous fifteenth-century atelier in Herat. A petition (*arzadasht*) preserved in an album in the Topkapı Palace Museum in İstanbul has been identified as a progress report sent about 1429 to the prince from Jafar Tabrizi (active 1412–31), the head of the atelier. It mentions twenty-two projects that are underway—manuscript designs, architectural works, tents, and other objects—and includes the names of twenty-three artists—painters, illuminators, calligraphers, binders, rulers, and chest makers—who worked individually or in teams.[52]

At the end of the fifteenth century the production of illustrated manuscripts flourished as part of the general cultural revival under the Timurid sultan Husayn Bayqara. The sultan patronized poets and scholars such as the mystic Jami and commissioned some of the most splendid Persian manuscripts, such as a *Bustan* (Orchard) of the poet Sadi (1184–ca.1291), dated 1488, copied by the celebrated calligrapher Sultan Ali Mashhadi (d. ca. 1520) and signed by the famous painter Behzad.[53] Paradoxically, this was a time of increased political fragmentation, and the expansion of cultural patronage may have been due to the growth of the *soyurghal*, a land grant with immunity from taxation and government interference, and other types of immunities and tax privileges connected with landholding.[54]

Illustrated manuscripts were also made under the patronage of other, smaller courts such as those of the Muzaffarids, Jalayirids, Qara Qoyunlus, and Aq Qoyunlus. A group of manuscripts with paintings rendered in vibrant colors (particularly bright reds and oranges), using such motifs as pointed hills and showing a naive, even slapdash style, has been identified with the Inju court in Fars on the basis of a dispersed *Shahnama* dated 1341 and dedicated to the vizier Qiwam al-Dawla.[55] A

Figure 23. Construction of the Great Mosque of Samarqand, illustration from Sharaf al-Din Yazdi's *Zafarnama* made for Sultan Husayn Bayqara, Afghanistan, dated 1467/68. Baltimore, Johns Hopkins University, Milton S. Eisenhower Library, John Work Garrett Collection (fol. 359b).

two-volume copy of the *Shahnama* (1493/94), known as the "Big-Head," was produced for Sultan Ali Mirza (r. 1478–1504), a local ruler of Mazandaran, a region on the southern coast of the Caspian Sea.[56] The specific role of these patrons and the organization of their ateliers remain, however, unclear.

Once the tradition of illustrated manuscripts had been established in Iran, it moved from a royal to a commercial level. Three early manuscripts of the *Shahnama* can be grouped together because of their small size, format, and style of illustration, including the lavish use of gold paint and the clear, precise outlines filled with a wide range of colors (see **52**). Their similarities suggest a common school, although its place and date are still a matter of lively discussion.[57] In the fifteenth century Shiraz was the center of a commercial school under Turkmen patronage (see **53**), and in the sixteenth century many manuscripts were churned out on a large scale.[58] This standardized production implies that any well-to-do citizen could acquire an illustrated copy of the *Shahnama* and equate himself with heroes from Iran's glorious past.

These, then, are the major features of patronage in the postclassical period. The Mongols are traditionally known as destroyers who ravaged much of the cultivated, settled land, carried out systematic mass exterminations in a series of towns, and irreparably upset the caliphate and unity of the Islamic world. Yet the postclassical period was hardly one of stagnation and decadence but rather one in which patronage continued to flourish, perhaps on an even more lavish scale than before.

Figure 24. Enthronement of Zav, illustration from Firdausi's *Shahnama*, Iran, circa 1335/36. Washington, D.C., Arthur M. Sackler Gallery (S86.0107).

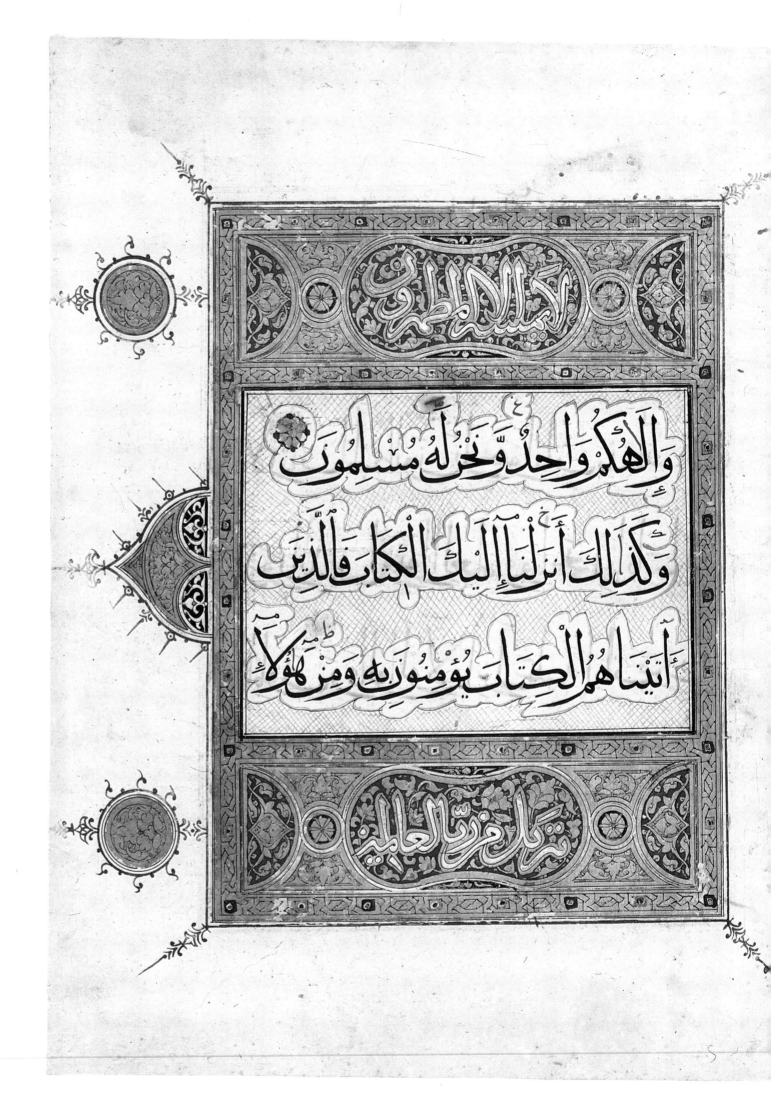

166

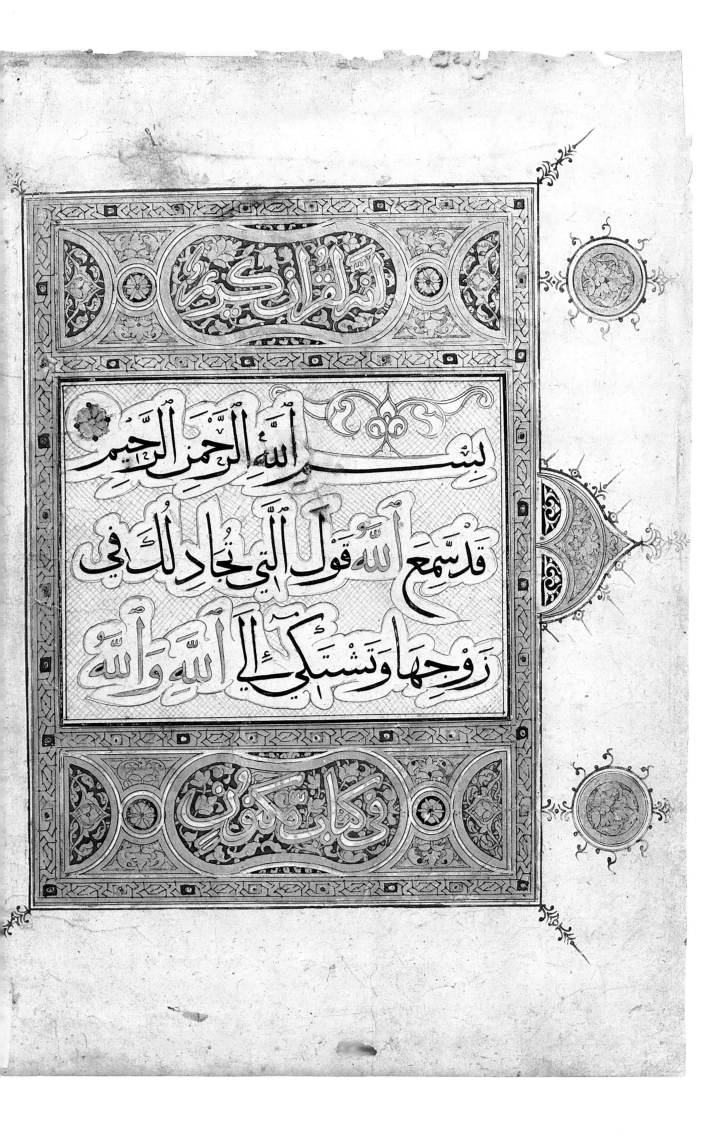

168

TWO FOLIOS FROM A QURAN MANUSCRIPT

47

Egypt, 14th century
Each: height 37.0 cm (14 ½ in.), width 27.0 cm (10 ⅝ in.)
LNS 74 MS (a–b)

The tradition of producing thirty-volume Quran manuscripts, each with one *juz*, was widely practiced in Egypt, Iran, and Syria during the fourteenth century. All the volumes in one set were written in the same script and used the same decorative layout and binding. These two detached folios are from a set attributed to Egypt.

The tripartite division of the folios is commonly employed in Mamluk frontispieces and finispieces. Gold braided bands frame the panels, which extend into the margins with circular and triangular formations.

The text in the wide central panel of the right folio contains the beginning of *juz* twenty-eight from Mujadila, the Woman Who Pleads (LVIII:1), written in *muhaqqaq* (a type of cursive script) on a crosshatched ground. The facing folio is the left half of the double opening pages of *juz* twenty-one and contains verses from Ankabut (XXIX:46–47).

The upper and lower narrower panels of both folios have oval cartouches with verses from Waqia, the Event (LVI:77–80), rendered in white *thuluth* (a type of cursive script) on a blue and gold floral ground. These verses, traditionally placed in the frontispieces of Mamluk Quran manuscripts, state: "Certainly this is a honored Quran, in a book well protected, which none shall touch it except the purified, it is a revelation from the Lord of the Worlds."

Illustrated on pages 166–67

DOUBLE FOLIOS FROM A QURAN MANUSCRIPT

48

Iran, 14th century
Each: height 21.0 cm (8 ¼ in.), width 17.4 cm (6 ⅞ in.)
LNS 44 MS (fols. 2b–3a)

After converting to Islam at the end of the thirteenth century the Ilkhanid rulers of Iran and Iraq encouraged the arts of the book and commissioned magnificent Quran codices. The decoration of Ilkhanid Quran manuscripts is similar to that of Mamluk volumes produced in Egypt and Syria.

Illustrated here is the left half of a double folio from *juz* sixteen of a thirty-volume Quran manuscript. The double folios contain wide central panels with the beginning of the *juz* from Kahf, the Cave (XVIII: 75–76), written in *thuluth* on a floral scroll reserved on a blue ground. The upper and lower narrower panels bear floral scrolls painted in gold with touches of blue. An interlacing band with the same color scheme frames both folios. A portion of the last word of the text extends into the left margin.

THE BEAKER WATER CLOCK

49

Illustration from the *Automata* of al-Jazari
Syria, dated December 1315
Height 31.5 cm (12 ⅜ in.), width 27.0 cm (8 ⁹⁄₁₆ in.)
LNS 17 MS (m)

A treatise on engineering entitled *The Book of Knowledge of Ingenious Mechanical Devices,* commonly known as the *Automata,* is devoted to the construction of fifty devices grouped under six categories. Written in Arabic by al-Jazari, it was dedicated to Nasir al-Din (r. 1201–22), the Artuqid sultan of Diyarbakır.

This volume, transcribed in *naskhi* by Farrukh ibn Abd al-Latif al-Yaquti al-Maulawi in Ramadan 715 A.H. (December 1315), is one of the earliest Mamluk copies. The manuscript, with 149 folios containing twenty-eight paintings and numerous drawings, is in the al-Sabah Collection, except for several illustrations that are dispersed among public and private collections.

This illustration, from the first category, which is devoted to clocks, shows how a scribe, seated on the flat cover of a beaker, marks time. The flow of the water in the beaker activates the pulleys that move the figure, enabling his pen to rest on the proper hour.

BEAR AND MONKEY

50

Illustration from the *Sulwan al-Muta* of Ibn Zafar
Egypt or Syria, second quarter 14th century
Height 25.0 cm (9 $^{13}/_{16}$ in.), width 17.6 cm (6 $^{13}/_{16}$ in.)
LNS 104 MS

The painting is from an Arabic book of fables written in 1159 by Ibn Zafar, known as al-Siqilli, the Sicilian. The intent of the stories was to teach rulers wise and ethical behavior by using animals as the protagonists.

The episode represented here is from the tale of the cruel bear and the monkey, illustrating that hypocrisy fails even against a modest intellect. The bear, pretending to be asleep, catches the monkey trying to escape, pulls him from the tree to the ground, and kills him.

The charming and naturalistic portrayal of the creatures is characteristic of illustrated Mamluk books on animals, which flourished during the mid-fourteenth century in Egypt and Syria.

قيل ولما انخرط في غاية المثل الذي ضرب به لهرام امسك عن القول

فقال له كهرام ما ابهجني بقربك واقر عيني ما تعيد ني من حكمك

وتضرب لي من امثال الكـ وتجلوه علي من ملكك ولئن بقيت الى ان

تدول لي دولتك لاجعلنك اول داخل علي واخر خارج عني

وسأروض نفسي بأدبك هذه مستعينا بالله فسجد حبس ودعا

PAIR OF ONAGERS

51

Illustration from the *Manafi al-Hayawan* of Ibn Bakhtishu
Iran, early 14th century
Height 26.5 cm (10 ⅜ in.), width 21.0 cm (8 ¼ in.)
LNS 59 MS

The *Manafi al-Hayawan* (Usefulness of animals) is a treatise on zoology written in 941 in Baghdad by Ibn Bakhtishu, the private physician of Caliph al-Muttaqi (r. 940–44). The Arabic text was translated into Persian in 1291 at the request of the Ilkhanid ruler Ghazan.

This folio from a dispersed copy illustrates two onagers, or wild asses, running in a landscape. Rendered in a calligraphic manner, the illustration resembles a tinted drawing. The painter displays an interest in depicting naturalistic movement as well as the texture of the animals' skin. The oversize lotus blossom and sparse foliage of the landscape reflect central or east Asian themes, which frequently appear in Islamic painting after the Mongol invasion of the mid-thirteenth century.

بعو فروشی ماکنبرا واب کاچوا کسے زاد مندک ادبستن بول کند نک شرد وجزن درتقترمانند

ماروعن کل معنید برود و اکر درجرب مالند نیک شود بید خرگور ماروغن کام سبید گداخته کردانند و طلی کند نه

بردوی کلف را برد شش خرگو خسک گونند با کندا و عسل یا ماهیز ند و کورند عم القفس را

دصیا ماروبر بزدا زابل کزدا رد مض گوهر یا میز ند یا بور ق وخولخان و یا جمار نبس طاب گزش

دلشت ازرزم نخا رکر مبه | زبوری دانش هنگار کرزند | جراس شه ره شاه جنگی سترو | بیاسود سره بهرام گرو | که اورزه افغاست وماه | کی ودادمونک بذد سنتگاه

بنداخت براهن بل زورد | جوحمند زدنو بای ووا کرد | گذار براب اورک کشت فرب | ساخت اموی بک ازس شب | زنجیر بازی جماجوی شد | بک روزبک شب باموی شد

بذرمنسربرم همی جست | سنان همی امرزع جست | عنای کار نادم رزند | همه لشکر شاه زرزند | حماجوی کشت شاه رماموغ | زمانه شاه زاک جون برجوغ

برازادکان جهان مستر | کی شاه دارا بلند اختر | سی براز خوز جا وخاکسار | همان برازخورد و رفت جوار | زبوری سجر کزاران | ترکان همرا کمشکن بذدش رو

کازدرنک خافان که کارشد

زعهد جهاندار سرزرت شد

بدسنت کردارن راشدن اکان

جولشکست نماز شدن بذنها

توخوز سره کاهاز سربز

ندخوب ابذازنابداران

کزنا می باش خواهی رواست

سنگ کناهاز مرزن جراست

همه دورز مندکان توم

بزرم اندازنکدن کران توم

دل شاه هولم ازازنشان خسی

بدست خدره وحشش بدو خت

بذرفتن هربال بازی کران | برشاه شد هنگ مهدران | دل مرا داشفه آهستد شد | جوم جهاندار سیته بن | برادشدشد شد شاه بندارنج | نخز بجتن سنت رکان بست

زجهیم ین زانزا برخو خواند | براسوزیک جهف ن لشکرساند | برازنک خسارو خندان دو | جوبرکشت واما زمن ترکان نما | برازباز دست دزترکان نما | ازا کارجز جوکام واشدزا

حقند مهن وباک وری رای ک | لشکرو اندرشاه سام | همان سنز عنج سابخ براه | لاشذکذجز دزبغان شاه | کنسترانراین ترک زرکنچ | براورد میلی سک زرکنچ

قامجواست امشکرجسی مرم | پفجود نازداودشد زبسی | دل شاه ازانزدشد مرشاحه | جوشدکار کرزوران مرزسنا | سدورا هنزوران زبین شا وکر | سرجنت اوافضیصا کند

خلاوندا رام ادر جرخ شزند | خداوندکرو دنج جرخ بلند | ازبنه بی برکردار جهان | سنامه بذد ازون مرز مان | زبیا کارترکان وکا رسا | نه هی کانامه یوشت شاه

نوشتم بنا مه ازمرزین | مرددرانس بابوازمن | همه یوذی برفرازاع ست | سرزکی خدی زبماز اوست

سرحت سدداد کرشدنکون | زرکز سد جندلا کفتی سباه | ازنج جنگ جویان ساندشید | هرانک گاه ازرزم خافان منبز

زان حرب ودرابزارخون کم | کنزن بسته اودرسی جبز | بندوج هرکه ده هیزارزد | بزم انزورن کزنگارشده

رفشندجوزر نعد غزار هی | کنزن زابن برمز آرا سباه | براه آمد دانکر نه ده اوژ | بذرفت باز ازانک نخواه بود

نهازدر هرکس آواز کوش | هرانک عرمودبرزاز بارشم | زشای بل ال شا بردمید | جرنامه بزرکدن سری سید

بزد زدامه کیهان خدبر | اندشته کزرفزان دیو | نبوری بزرگان هند شدند | دابی ماداران نشور شاه

همه بورش ما باید نهفت | جراح سوذنامه برخوشر | هان رای دانا ومسرد حرن | شکسنب این کرگان ماکرد | خافابه نفت ازرزکان درآس

نروزاکردازرود جون پش | سوزنامه راودباج تو | هان وی ازن شاه روزحکم | کزن رست رسی ازو جکم | سخت ازبزرکان ناکردنهاشاه

نه شاه ش بذبذ ته خست | نه ازبشنی بزدن ته شاه | موهندی ازراامدران ساه | کرفشد خاکان جبرز بنه | هاازن ببوم وذبرد ولنج

خاز ندار او کشتار وی داکشت | رفشاو اوبرکشتار انها | هرازها برکشتار شاه جهان | بیامذ بزرک شاه گشد جم | برازرفتن شاه اوبرنمهبر

176

BAHRAM GUR WITH THE TURANIANS

52

Illustration from the *Shahnama* of Firdausi
Iran, 14th century
Height 32.1 cm (12 ⁹/₁₆ in.), width 22.0 cm (8 ⁹/₁₆ in.)
LNS 33 MS

Illustrated copies of the *Shahnama,* the epic history of Iran and Turan (the area north of the Oxus River), written around 1010 in Persian by the epic poet Firdausi (940–ca. 1020), were among the earliest Ilkhanid manuscripts. The work recounts heroic exploits of kings and heroes from the beginning of history to the end of the Sasanian dynasty. Combining fact with fiction, the themes provided a rich source for pictorial representation.

This illustration, together with three others in the collection, belongs to a group known as the "Small" *Shahnama*s due to the size of their paintings.

As in this example, the characteristic features of this group include gold backgrounds, carefully painted details, vivid colors, expressive figures, and minimal settings. Such elements as banners, lances, and parasols frequently transgress the picture frame and extend into the margin.

SULTAN SANJAR AND THE OLD WOMAN

53

Illustration from the *Khamsa* of Nizami
Iran, dated 1487/88
Height 29.5 cm (11 ⁹/₁₆ in.), width 17.5 cm (6 ⅞ in.)
LNS 28 MS (f)

The painting belongs to the *Khamsa* (Quintet) of Nizami, a renowned lyrical and mystical Persian work composed in the twelfth century and popularly copied and illustrated after the fourteenth century.

This volume with 350 folios and sixteen paintings was transcribed in 1487/88. The stylistic features of the paintings indicate that the manuscript was produced in Shiraz, a major artistic center under the Aq Qoyunlu, or White Sheep, Turkmens, who ruled eastern Turkey and western Iran during the fourteenth and fifteenth centuries.

The first painting in the volume illustrates the dispensing of justice, the primary duty of the sultan. It shows a poor, old woman who confronts Sultan Sanjar during a hunting expedition and presents to him her grievances and complaints. The sultan listens with compassion and, fulfilling his obligations as a ruler, orders remuneration.

LUSTER-PAINTED STAR-SHAPED TILES

54

Iran, late 13th–early 14th century
Each: diameter 21.0 cm (8 ¼ in.)
LNS 55 C, 56 C, 58 C

The workshops of Kashan, a major center for luster-painted tiles during the Seljuk period, continued to produce the same type of wares after the Mongol invasion of the mid-thirteenth century and made star- and cross-shaped tiles to decorate the newly built Ilkhanid mosques and shrines. Those commissioned for the Shrine of Imamzade Jafar in Damghan, built in 1267, were among the most celebrated.

This group of three tiles is representative of the technique and decoration employed during the late thirteenth and early fourteenth centuries. The tiles are painted underglaze blue and turquoise with overglaze luster. The centers are reserved for floral or geometric designs, while inscriptions with passages from the Quran encircle the borders. The example on the top (LNS 55 C) contains verses from Kahf (XVIII:11–14); those on the left (LNS 56 C) and right (LNS 58 C) bear verses from Anam (VI:11–14 and 1–4, respectively).

STAR-SHAPED TILE WITH SEATED FIGURE

55

Iran, 14th century
Diameter 20.7 cm (8 ³⁄₁₆ in.)
LNS 363 C

Probably made for a secular building, this tile represents a type in which the border decoration is reserved in white on a blue ground. Here the letters are outlined in luster. Most such tiles are decorated with floral designs, but figural representations were also used.

A male figure, reserved on a luster-painted ground filled with flowering branches, sits under a lobed arch resting on two slender columns. The fine lines decorating the garment and two spandrels are painted in luster. The figure wears a Mongol-type headdress and garment typical of the period (see also **56**).

CERAMIC BOWL WITH STANDING FIGURE

56

Iran, 14th century
Height 10.8 cm (4 ¼ in.), diameter 20.8 cm (8 ³⁄₁₆ in.)
LNS 316 C

During the Ilkhanid period potters produced new types of underglaze-painted ceramics known as "Sultanabad" wares after the city in western Iran. They are generally characterized by dense compositions and somber coloring.

This bowl represents one of the Sultanabad types, with a low foot, angular sides, and flat, overhanging rim. A brownish gray engobe covers the white body, and the decoration is underglaze painted with a thick white slip that stands in relief; black is used for the outlines, details, and hatched background. A figure wearing a Mongol robe and hat stands in the center amid a densely foliated ground. A pearl band adorns the rim. An inscription encircles the upper walls of the interior, and radiating petals appear on the exterior.

CERAMIC BOWL WITH RADIAL PANELS

57

Iran, 14th century
Height 9.0 cm (3 ½ in.), diameter 22.0 cm (8 ⁹⁄₁₆ in.)
LNS 173 C

This bowl represents another type of Sultanabad ware. Compared to the previous example (**56**), it has thinner walls and a finer paste. The white engobe covering the body is partially exposed to contrast with the underglaze-painted blue, black, and turquoise pigments.

The rounded shape is enhanced by the panels radiating from the center. Filled with three alternating designs, the twelve panels are separated by blue and turquoise strips. The alternating designs consist of clusters of four small dots topped with an inscription band, interlacing motifs, and paired half-palmettes reserved on a hatched ground, also topped with inscribed bands. On the exterior are a series of petals, divided by chainlike vertical lines sprinkled with dots.

LUSTER-PAINTED CERAMIC JAR

58

Syria, 14th century
Height 28.2 cm (11 ⅛ in.), diameter 15.8 cm (6 ³⁄₁₆ in.)
LNS 218 C

Such jars with slightly concave sides and sloping shoulders, known as albarelli, were mostly used for transporting oils or dry goods from the Islamic world to Europe. A number of such pieces were found in Sicily, an active trading center.

This jar is covered with a deep blue glaze and overglaze painted with greenish gold luster. The body is decorated with four birds, a popular motif used on Syrian vessels (see also **59**). The animals are placed against floral scrolls that cover the entire surface. The shoulder bears a decorative inscription.

Luster painting flourished in Syria during the Seljuk and Ayyubid periods, especially in Raqqa. The technique continued in Damascus under the Mamluks. Damascus lusterwares generally employ greenish gold tones on deep blue grounds, differing from the designs favored by Raqqa potters, which incorporate copper reds with touches of blue or turquoise (see **33**).

CERAMIC JAR WITH STROLLING GEESE

59

Syria, 14th century
Height 29.8 cm (11 ¾ in.), diameter 16.9 cm (6 ⁹⁄₁₆ in.)
LNS 187 C

Blue and black underglaze-painted wares constitute the largest group of pottery produced during the Mamluk period. The most common shapes are bowls, jugs, and jars. The jars were generally used to contain spices and oils as well as to store herbs and medicines used by apothecaries. The concave sides of the jars facilitated their handling on crowded shelves.

The decoration on the jars is either confined within horizontal or vertical panels or executed freely, as in this example. The vessel is covered with four large geese—painted in reserve with bold greenish black outlines—strolling amid a loosely drawn landscape.

CERAMIC BOWL WITH CENTRAL BLAZON

60

Egypt, 14th century
Height 11.3 cm (4 ½ in.), diameter 22.6 cm (9 in.)
LNS 7 C

Roughly potted wares with red bodies covered by colored slips and incised designs are typical of the Mamluk ceramics produced in Egypt. Shaped mostly as large bowls, this type of ware apparently was made for the kitchens of the upper classes and many examples display blazons and inscriptions, characteristic features of the decorative repertoire of Mamluk art.

   The low-footed hemispherical bowl has an earthenware body covered with a yellowish slip through which the design was incised. The central four-petaled rosette (or blazon) and zigzag band along the exterior rim are underglaze painted. An Arabic inscription placed on the inner walls reads: "Made by order of the sheikh, the reverent, the respected, the masterful, the most generous."

TILE WITH EPIGRAPHIC BLAZON OF SULTAN QAITBAY

61

Egypt, late 15th century
Diameter 30.0 cm (11 ¹³⁄₁₆ in.)
LNS 190 C

The blazon on this circular tile—with the text placed in three horizontal fields reserved in white against a blue ground and bordered in black—belonged to the Mamluk sultan Qaitbay. The Arabic inscription follows the arrangement of the period and is read in the sequence of central field, upper panel, and lower panel. It states: "Glory to our master, the Sultan al-Malik al-Ashraf Abu'l-Nasir Qaitbay, may his victory be glorious."

Unique to the Mamluks, the epigraphic blazon was initiated by Sultan Nasir al-Din Muhammad around 1320 and became the emblem of all subsequent rulers. Offices held by the Mamluks were also identified by blazons, symbols of their rank. They were displayed on the owners' garments, arms, and armor and on the art and architecture commissioned by them.

GLASS PERFUME SPRINKLER

62

Egypt or Syria, 13th century
Height 11.1 cm (4 ⁵⁄₁₆ in.), diameter 6.9 cm (2 ¾ in.)
LNS 34 G

Free-blown of purple glass, the sprinkler has a flattened, oval body and thin, tapering neck with two trailed handles. The delicate neck and narrow mouth are functional, controlling the flow of the perfume when sprinkled.

The decoration consists of applied opaque white threads that were combed and marvered (rolled on a flat surface to smooth out the vessel walls), following a technique known to Egyptian glassmakers since the second millennium B.C. Continued by the Syrians during the Roman period, it regained popularity in the Islamic age and became commonly used between the eleventh and thirteenth centuries, especially in Egypt and Syria.

ENAMELED AND GILDED GLASS PERFUME SPRINKLER

63

Syria, 13th century
Height 11.8 cm (4 ⁹⁄₁₆ in.), diameter 8.7 cm (3 ½ in.)
LNS 48 G

Syrian glassmakers excelled in the production of a variety of enameled and gilded vessels, ranging from large mosque lamps, bottles, and vases to small personal items. This tiny perfume sprinkler bears floral scrolls on the shoulders and sides and two medallions on either side of the flattened body. Each medallion represents a courtly figure seated on a cushion and holding a beaker. The association of such princely activities as feasting and drinking enhances the luxurious implication of the item.

Figural representations, favored on glassware produced in Syria during the Ayyubid period, continued under the Mamluks but were gradually replaced by bold inscriptions and floral designs, which came to characterize the stylistic features of the fourteenth century (see **64**).

ENAMELED AND GILDED GLASS VASE

64

Egypt or Syria, first half 14th century
Height 29.0 cm (11 ⁷/₁₆ in.), diameter 17.0 cm (6 ¹¹/₁₆ in.)
LNS 69 G

This free-blown glass vase with applied handles represents a rare type of enameled and gilded Mamluk vessel. The trailed handles were attached after the piece was blown and its lip and foot were turned under.

The surface is divided into horizontal panels filled with Arabic inscriptions, floral scrolls, and birds. The widest panel on the body contains an inscription placed against spiraling scrolls bearing buds and leaves. The inscriptions read: "Glory to our lord, the sultan, the learned king." The narrow panel on the neck is occupied by a phoenix, an auspicious creature of central and east Asian origin. Interrupting the floral scroll on the upper neck are ovals bearing three-petaled blossoms, a characteristic motif of the period.

INLAID BRASS BOWL

65

Iran, early 14th century
Height 12.5 cm (4 ¹⁵⁄₁₆ in.), diameter 28.5 cm (11 ¼ in.)
LNS 116 M

Belonging to a group of fourteenth-century bowls produced in the region of Fars in southern Iran, this fine brass example was raised from a sheet of metal, engraved, and inlaid with silver and gold. The exterior is divided into horizontal panels combining images of princely activities with benedictory inscriptions written in Arabic and identified with the decorative repertoire of the region.

The narrow panel under the rim has three units with animals chasing each other, alternating with three inscribed sections that state: "Glory and prosperity and good fortune and worldly advancement and grandeur and abundance and generosity and knowledge and forbearance."

The widest zone on the body contains six inscribed oval cartouches alternating with six medallions, each bearing a rider with a hawk, arrow, or lance. Inscriptions placed against the scrolling branches read: "Glory to our master, the greatest king, the august sultan, the lord of the necks of the nations, master of the sultans of the Arabs and non-Arabs, the learned, the just, the triumphant, the supported [by God], the honored, the defender [of the faith], the warrior [of the frontiers], the supported [by God]."

The lower part of the bowl is covered with intersecting circles with floral motifs terminating with radiating lancet leaves. On the inside is a fantastic marine world with fish, eels, and other sea creatures revolving around a twelve-pointed star.

INLAID BRASS BASIN

66

Made for an officer of Sultan al-Malik al-Nasir
Egypt or Syria, first half 14th century
Height 22.2 cm (8 ¾ in.), diameter of rim 48.3 cm (19 in.)
LNS 110 M

Raised from a sheet of brass, engraved, and inlaid with silver, this striking basin not only represents the shape but also the bold epigraphic style characteristic of Mamluk metalwork. The Arabic inscriptions on the exterior, rendered in *thuluth* and interrupted by six medallions enclosing flying ducks, read: "His sublime excellency, the master, the great prince, the learned, the efficient, the war champion, the defender [of the faith], the warrior [of the frontier]."

A similar composition and text appear inside the rim, terminating with the words "[the officer] of al-Malik al-Nasir." A third inscription, repeating some of the same phrases but rendered in a circular formation, is placed inside the base. Incised at the bottom in casual *naskhi* is the statement, "made for my master Abd Allah ibn Ahmad," an individual who has not been identified.

Top of lid

INLAID BRASS BOX

67

Made for an officer of Sultan al-Malik al-Nasir
Egypt or Syria, first half 14th century
Height 11.6 cm (4 ½ in.), diameter 10.6 cm (4 ⅛ in.)
LNS 111 M

The lidded cylindrical box is decorated with bold *thuluth* inscriptions interspersed with floral scrolls. The Arabic inscriptions, which radiate from a central rosette on the lid and encircle the body, repeat such typical Mamluk benedictions as "his sublime excellency, the master, the royal, the learned, the efficient," terminating with the phrase, "[the officer] of al-Malik al-Nasir."

Since several fourteenth-century Mamluk sultans used the honorific title al-Malik al-Nasir, it is difficult to identify the ruler mentioned. A number of inlaid brasses bear similar formulaic inscriptions (see **66**), suggesting that these pieces were mass-produced for the court and not commissioned by specific individuals.

STEEL HELMET

68

Made for Sultan al-Ashraf
Turkey, 15th century
Height 32.0 cm (12 ½ in.), diameter 23.0 cm (9 ¹/₁₆ in.)
LNS 145 M

This helmet with a bulbous body tapering toward a high finial is made of steel, which was engraved and overlaid with silver. Called "turban" helmets due to their shape, such helmets were used by the Aq Qoyunlu Turkmens.

The body of the helmet is decorated with faceted fluting to create a honeycomb pattern filled with floral cartouches and wavy lines. Two large panels bearing Arabic inscriptions encircle the edge and crown. The upper panel reads: "Ordered for the arsenal of al-Malik al-Mansur al-Sultan al-Ashraf"; the lower panel contains a series of formulaic good wishes for happiness, well-being, and life "as long as a pigeon coos" (see also **40**). The original owner of this helmet may have been Ashraf ibn Dana Khalil Bayandur (d. 1500), one of the last princes of the Aq Qoyunlu clan.

The helmet bears the mark of the Ottoman arsenal, indicating that it was once in the imperial armory in İstanbul.

Side A   Side B

FILIGREE GOLD ROSETTE

69

Egypt or Syria, 14th century
Diameter 4.2 cm (1 ⁹⁄₁₆ in.)
LNS 21 J

Fabricated entirely of openwork filigree, the piece is constructed of round, flat, and twisted gold wires, which form spiraling foliated patterns on both faces. In the center of one side is a roundel containing an eight-petaled rosette; in the center of the other side is a four-partite interlacing design. Both motifs were formed by flat wires.

Belts composed of similar six-lobed rosettes are represented in fifteenth- and sixteenth-century manuscript illustrations. The two pairs of wire-reinforced openings along the edges of this piece suggest that it was meant to be strung on a cord or a chain and used as part of a belt.

The openwork filigree technique used here may represent an outgrowth of the earlier Fatimid tradition.

CARVED IVORY BOX

70

Spain, 14th century
Height 7.6 cm (3 in.), diameter 8.5 cm (3 ⅜ in.)
LNS 7 I

Spain, which maintained a long tradition of ivory carving, continued to produce a remarkable number of boxes under the Nasrids (see also **22**). Made mostly in the Islamic capital of Granada, Nasrid ivories recall those from the Mamluk lands and employ geometric patterns and inscriptions, as exemplified by this cylindrical box with flat lid.

Carved from a single piece of ivory, the base is decorated with horizontal panels filled with geometric interlaces, roundels, and braids. The same patterns, arranged in concentric bands, appear on the lid.

On the upper panel of the base is an Arabic inscription, which states that "there is no victor but God" and continues with other phrases, including "thank God for all his gifts" and "pride is God's, greatness is God's." The first phrase was frequently used on the art and architecture commissioned by Muhammad I, the founder of the Nasrid dynasty, and his followers.

CARVED WOOD BOX FOR QURAN MANUSCRIPTS

71

Made for Izz al-Din Malik by al-Hasan ibn Qutlubak
Iran, circa 1344
Height 25.0 cm (9 ⅞ in.), length and width 43.2 cm (17 in.)
LNS 35 W

The carved wood box with bronze hinges is grooved, mitered, dovetailed, and painted green. The interior is divided into four rectangular compartments placed around a central square, in which was housed Quran manuscripts as well as writing equipment.

The masterful design, rendered in two planes, relies on *naskhi* calligraphy as its sole decoration. The Arabic inscriptions encircling the central medallion on the lid states that Izz al-Din Malik, son of Nasir Allah Muhammad, endowed it to the tomb of Fakhr al-Din. Those along the edges give the date of the latter's death as Rajab 745 A.H. (November 1344) and mention that the box was made by al-Hasan, son of Qutlubak, son of the deceased Fakhr al-Din. None of the individuals mentioned can be identified, but it appears that the maker was the grandson of the deceased.

Quranic verses from Al-i Imran, the Family of Imran (III:18–19), appear around the sides of the box, placed against a ground of dense floral scrolls.

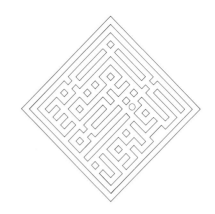

Late Islam
The Age of Empires (1500–1800)

WALTER B. DENNY

During the sixteenth century three great Islamic empires were established in western Asia and India. The oldest and largest of these, the Ottoman Turkish Empire, had been expanding since the late thirteenth century. Ruling from its European capital of İstanbul, the capable sixteenth-century Sunni Ottoman sultans molded a great Mediterranean power that became Islam's frontier with Europe, extending to three continents and surviving to the twentieth century. In the center, the Safavid Empire, founded after 1500 by the charismatic Shiite shah Ismail (r. 1501–24), took shape in the region that today forms parts of Iran, the Caucasus, central Asia, and Afghanistan. The successive capitals of Tabriz (1501–48), Qazvin (1548–98), and Isfahan (1598–1722) became the center of Safavid artistic patronage, commercial development, and political power. Late in the century, building on the accomplishments of his central Asian forebears, Akbar the Great (r. 1556–1605) firmly established the Sunni Mughal Empire in northern India. Over the next several decades the subcontinent was gradually subjugated through a policy of military conquest coupled with religious toleration for the vast Hindu subject population and assimilation of elements of pre-Islamic Indian culture into the creative Mughal synthesis.

The three great dynastic states of late Islam encompassed multi-ethnic empires, and, despite warfare among them based on dynastic, geopolitical, and religious issues, they existed in a world of widespread economic and cultural exchange brought about by their own expansion and that of the European colonial and exploring powers. From conquest, development of efficient bureaucratic systems of taxation and control, and burgeoning long-distance trade, the rulers of the three empires were able to control vast economic resources, enabling them to undertake artistic patronage on an unprecedented scale. In their polyglot, cosmopolitan courts, artists from all over the world worked together. The combination of lavish patronage, efficient organization

Detail of **90**

of artistic production, and cultural cross-fertilization led to one of the most glorious periods in the history of art, in which artists were able not only to build on the developments of previous centuries but create three distinctive new imperial styles.

Royal Patronage and Royal Designers

The focus of imperial patronage in each case involved a palace city—an Islamic capital that served as a royal residence and bureaucratic hub as well as a focus of artistic and economic activity (fig. 25)—and an imperial artistic establishment. Growing out of the Timurid institution of the royal library, the artistic establishments of the three empires focused primarily on the arts of the book: calligraphy, illumination, painting, and binding.[1] But artists trained in the royal libraries were also professional designers in the modern sense, in that they provided designs on paper that were then used to create commissions in other media, often again by artists drawing a salary from the court, in workshops under direct imperial control.

From the art of professional designers working with pen on paper there developed distinctive styles in all media, from architectural decoration to textiles, which are today recognized as characteristic expressions of Ottoman, Safavid, and Mughal royal patronage and artistic commerce.

216

Figure 25. View of Topkapı Palace, detail from a watercolor panorama of İstanbul, made by an anonymous Austrian (?) painter, circa 1580–92. Vienna, Österreichishe en Nationalbibliothek (Cod. 8626).

The traditional tasks of the artists of the book found new frontiers of expression in the three empires. The art of writing, especially the copying of Quran manuscripts, always took precedence over all other arts; sixteenth-century calligraphers in India, Iran, and Turkey brought the classical styles of Islamic calligraphy to new heights (fig. 26), while the bookbinders established the canon of Islamic binding in leather, gilding, papier-mâché, lacquer, and découpage. Book illumination and bindings of the Safavid and Ottoman courts formed the point of genesis of designs for carpets and architectural decoration (fig. 27). The classical Islamic design of an ogival medallion with pendants floating on a field contained within four corner pieces and a decorative border is perhaps the best-known basic design to come from sixteenth-century Islamic courts (72–73).[2]

Islamic manuscript illustration, existing in a limbo between theological damnation and the love of Islamic rulers for beautiful illustrations and album paintings, developed quite distinctively at the three great courts. The Safavid painting style, which grew out of the fifteenth-century Timurid and Turkmen schools, maintained its lyricism and association with the great classic texts of Persian poetry, with their mixture of narrative and mystical overtones.[3] The adventures of legendary kings and heroes from the Persian epic tradition found a place in the literary canon alongside lyric poetry dealing with love, with the world of nature, and even with the pleasures of wine, but patron and artist alike viewed such texts in a mystical as well as a literal sense,

217

Figure 26. Calligraphic exercise by Ahmed Karahisari, Turkey, circa 1540–50. İstanbul, Turkish and Islamic Arts Museum (1443, fol. 2a).

Figure 27. Tile panel from the Mosque of Shah Abbas, Isfahan, Iran, circa 1620.

blending the spiritual and the secular in a mixture that called up the full range of human emotions from stark tragedy to robust satire. Safavid painting from the sixteenth-century royal court of Tabriz is extremely rare (fig. 28). The secondary centers within the orbit of the Safavid royal painting style were Shiraz in southern Iran and Bukhara, the capital of the Uzbek Turks in central Asia; here, lavishly decorated manuscripts incorporated paintings reflecting the innovations of the Safavid royal court at Tabriz (**74–75**) and later at Qazvin and Isfahan.

The distinctive painting style formed in the Ottoman Turkish court atelier in İstanbul benefited from émigré Iranian artists from Herat, Shiraz, and Tabriz, but the primary Ottoman emphasis in imperial patronage of secular manuscripts was always on historical and quasi-historical texts. A multivolume history of the life of the Prophet, for example, concentrated on a direct approach to illustrating the prose narrative, without the poetic lyricism and mystical dimensions of the Safavid style (**76**). The Ottoman sultans were also fascinated with works on geography, contemporary and dynastic history, and genealogy, for which the court atelier developed a style remarkable in its topographical realism and attention to details of architecture, costume, and weaponry (**77–78**).[4] Certainly, the preoccupation of the Ottoman state with military expansion and a consequent regard for the making of maps and writing of military

218

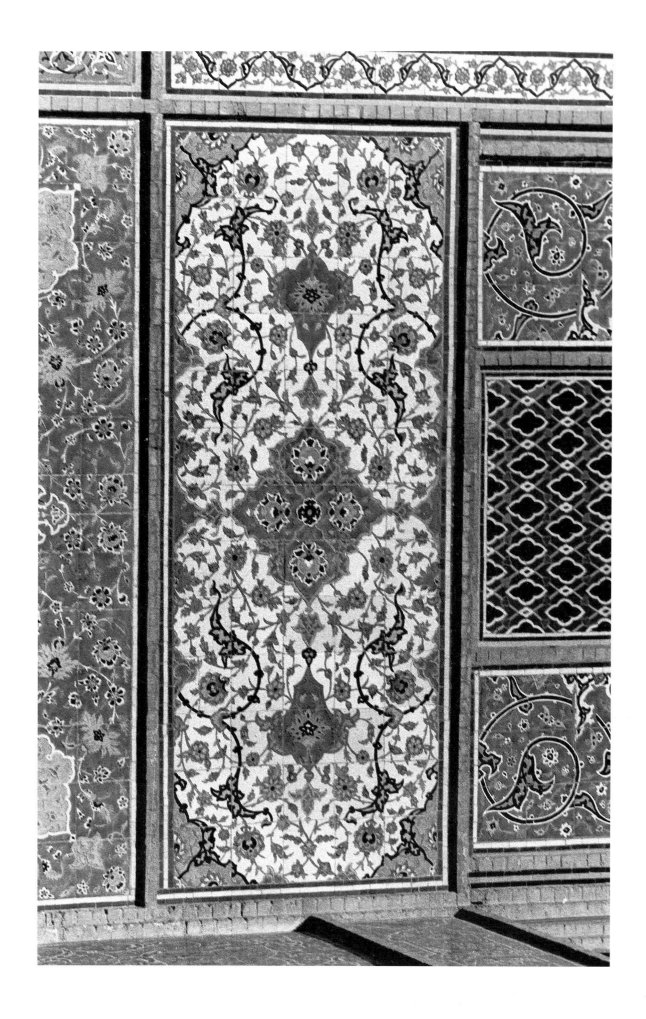

history exercised a major influence on the artists who created such works for their royal patrons at the Ottoman court.

The last of the three imperial painting styles to take form was that of Mughal India. The genesis of the Mughal style is one of the most fascinating stories in the history of Islamic art. The Mughal court atelier was founded by artists from Iran, but from the beginning the Mughal painting style also grew out of indigenous and non-Islamic traditions of pictorial representation. Like the Ottoman rulers, Mughal patrons favored a high degree of practical realism in subject matter. Mughal court artists coupled this interest with a minute attention to detail to create what is the only true portraiture in Islamic art.[5] As with its sister styles in the Ottoman and Safavid realms, Mughal painting not only served to illustrate texts but also existed for its own sake in a more independent sphere, that of the collector's album, where paintings on a variety of subjects were mounted on large folios with lavish margins and sumptuously bound into a kind of portable picture gallery for the delectation of royal and noble patrons. The portrait of an artist (79) is such a work; the accurate depiction of fabrics and the use of perspective together with the individuality of the portrait are typical of the Mughal style at its best.

Royal patronage in India resulted both in illustrated volumes of historical texts—often dealing with the exploits of contemporary Mughal rulers—and in the development of royal themes such as hunting, festivals, and warfare in nonhistorical texts and in ornamental album paintings and drawings as well (80–81).

Patrons and Personalities

In any highly centralized royal system artistic patronage depends to a large degree on the predilections and personalities of the sovereign, his entourage, and immediate family. In Islamic civilization, where the position of works of art, both as figural representations and as luxury items, is theologically and thus legally very tenuous, the dependence of artistic traditions on individual powerful personalities has been even stronger.

The great Islamic patrons of art of the age of empires were in general a remarkable lot. Often motivated by dynastic consciousness and a keen sense of image-making as well as by a sincere appreciation of beauty and creativity, their record of accomplishment is considerable. In the Ottoman realms the sixteenth-century sultan Süleyman the Magnificent typifies the best combination of artistic patronage and political image-making. His great mosque on the heights of İstanbul served at once as a symbol of royal domination and a practical center for charitable community activities, incorporating a hospital, colleges, schools, public baths, an alms kitchen, and other social-service institutions. His patronage of manuscript artists focused on the creation of beautiful copies of Quran codices and on the remarkable dynastic histories of his family. The handsome objects he had created for the court most often focus on the pomp of imperial ritual and public presentation of royal power. Privately, he appears to have avoided extravagance; publicly, his artistic commissions balanced beauty and expense with a keen sense of necessity. The sovereign's pattern was followed by his

Figure 28. The Nightmare of Zahhak by Mir Musavvir, illustration from Firdausi's *Shahnama* made for Shah Tahmasp I, Iran, circa 1530. Private collection.

221

family and court; his wife Hürrem and daughter Mihrimah were among the great patrons of the age both in the creation of social-service buildings and in their patronage of the royal workshops for luxury goods. If Süleyman can be seen as typical of the "wise" use of patronage, his grandson Murad III (r. 1574–95) may be seen as the opposite extreme. The festival that marked the circumcision of his sons in 1582 almost bankrupted the Ottoman treasury, and, like that of the Timurid prince Baysunghur, Murad's patronage of painters and their art was coupled with an embracing of a life-style that disregarded the fundamental tenets of Islamic moderation and puritanism.[6]

The Safavid shah Tahmasp also partook of this pattern of rulers who took painters as boon companions and followed the bohemian life-style of some court artists. The result was lavish private patronage and the creation of some of the most astounding examples of manuscript painting in existence. The tenuous nature of the artistic establishment under centralized patronage is shown by events later in Tahmasp's life, when, growing ever more conscious of his own mortality, he gave up his extravagant and dissolute life-style and withdrew from the patronage of painting, even giving away to the Ottoman sultan Selim II (r. 1566–74) his most beautiful illustrated manuscript. Safavid artists moved to provincial courts in the wake of Tahmasp's change of heart, and many of the most talented emigrated to the Ottoman and Mughal realms. Shah Abbas (r. 1588–1629), perhaps the most famous Safavid royal patron, seems to have combined the energy and image-oriented patronage of Sultan Süleyman with the extravagant life-style of the young Tahmasp; during his reign public and private patronage flourished amid a general atmosphere of enterprise and tolerance, while the excesses of the shah's private behavior became notorious.[7]

Perhaps the most remarkable record of continuous dynastic artistic patronage in the Islamic world is that of the Mughal emperors Akbar, Jahangir (r. 1605–27), and Shah Jahan (r. 1628–58). The religious tolerance of the enlightened Mughal rulers, coupled with their acute personal interest in all aspects of their cultural environment, led to the development of new forms of secular symbolism and religious expression, and the Mughal admiration for remarkable technical accomplishment led in turn to artistic tours-de-force as diverse as the monumental marble Taj Mahal in Agra (1632–43) and carpets with more than twenty-five hundred hand-tied knots in every square inch of fabric.

Royal patronage in the age of empires points out the continuing tensions in the Islamic artistic tradition between art and religion. The strengths of patronage under royal Islamic monarchs were many, and as long as economic resources and religious tolerance struck a balance with conspicuous consumption and love of beautiful things, a succession of gifted and capable rulers brought about remarkable developments in art and architecture.[8]

A Different Hierarchy of Media

The classical repertoire of the Islamic artist and the media most often used by Islamic artists developed in distinctive ways. Strictly speaking, Islamic traditions sanction only one artistic medium: the art of beautiful writing, by which God's revelations to humankind, the Quran, may be enhanced and preserved. Figurative drawing plays a relatively minor role in later Islamic art compared to the artistic traditions of Europe or non-Muslim India; the Islamic artist turned instead to a highly developed repertoire of calligraphy and patterns based on geometric, floral, and vegetal forms generally grouped collectively under the category of "arabesques."[9] Islamic civilization often focuses artistic energy on very rare, costly, or intractable media such as silk, gemstones, gold leaf, or rock crystal. The central focus on technique—the mastery of the skills demanded by the media—as distinct from medium or material, also allows the Islamic artist to create, out of humble materials such as clay or wool, masterpieces of breathtaking artistry. The eloquence of Islamic art—its ability to "speak" to the observer in a purely visual language—is therefore considerably wider in scope than European art with its concentration on narrative and the human form and focus on figural painting and sculpture. Long before European artists developed to a high degree the notion of beauty inherent in abstraction, mathematical order, visual and physical texture, and color, these aspects of artistic imagination were central to the production and patronage of art in Islamic lands. What is relegated to the subsidiary realm of "decorative arts" in the European imagination and academic curriculum is therefore a major focus of artistic energy in the Islamic world.

Two examples, both from the Ottoman court, illustrate this point. A ceramic plate, fabricated from a mixture of crushed flint, potters' clay, and colored glazes (84) in the Turkish ceramic center of İznik in the mid-sixteenth century, may be viewed from several different contexts. Its shape is borrowed from that of near-contemporary Chinese porcelain, much sought after by Islamic collectors of the time. Its technique also developed originally as a response to the collecting mania for porcelain, in a partially successful attempt to duplicate the hardness, strength, whiteness, and translucency of the Chinese mixture of the ingredients kaolin and petuntse. We see in this Turkish plate a very beautiful and expensive object for the serving of food, the domestic response to a taste and a market for expensive "foreign" tableware.

There is, however, another way to look at the Turkish plate. The design has a very clear top and bottom; all the flower stems spring from a single cluster of leaves at the bottom of the composition. Were we to look at a hundred plates in a similar style, we would realize that this plate was executed as a one-of-a-kind object. While paper cartoons were often used by ceramic artists to develop designs, such templates were only rarely reused.[10] Finally, if we look closely, we see that in addition to the mixture of discipline and freehand spontaneity inherent in the firm calligraphic line in black pigment that gives shape and life to the whirling, overlapping forms on this plate, the artist has deliberately chosen to emphasize the feathery brushstrokes of the blue background, giving it a distinctive painterly texture as rich as that of the design itself. While much has been written about the use of Islamic ornament as surface decoration, it is important that we notice that Islamic ornament is always three-dimensional in its conception. Just as the calligrapher's line must always cross over itself, creating a multitude of levels, so the geometric and floral designs of this Turkish plate inevitably imply a surface not only of texture but of three dimensions that is completely coherent spatially without resulting in a deep pictorial or narrative space dictated by the concerns of European figural art.

So what was the true purpose of this plate in the eyes of artist and patron? It was far too fragile and expensive to have been regularly used for eating; the Ottoman nobility seem to have preferred tinned copper and brass ware for such purposes. Rather, a primary function of this plate was to be looked at; it is a tondo painting on ceramic, that, like any painting, dictates its own orientation and distance to the viewer, focus of visual interest, and concerns with elements of line, texture, space, movement, color, balance, and order.

A second work, this time a knotted pile carpet from Ottoman Turkey created at the end of the sixteenth century (106), brings up yet another interesting question in Islamic art, that of representation of religious subjects. In form, this small carpet is what is called a *sejjada,* or prostration rug, intended to be used by a single individual for the act of Islamic prayer, to create the ritually necessary clean place on which a Muslim kneels and touches the forehead to the ground in a simple and beautiful affirmation of humility before the Creator. The border is complex, consisting of the same curved leaves, stems, rosettes, and blossoms seen in the İznik plate but in a much more formal and complicated arrangement. The central field is in the shape of an arch with columns, and a lamp is depicted hanging from three chains in the center of the arch. The fluency of the design—its linear grace—is, in fact, an illusion, created from tens of thousands of tiny dots of wool laboriously knotted on the warp yarns of the carpet. Viewed microscopically, the rug consists only of horizontal, vertical, and forty-five-degree lines. The turning of the insulating hair of the common western Asian sheep into a work of art results from the artistic and technical collaboration of the many individuals who made the yarns and dyestuffs and who designed and wove this rug. The design itself is an equally complex collaboration, not of individuals or materials but of meanings.

The architectural gateway on the Islamic prayer rug first and foremost symbolizes a gateway to paradise, a paradise attainable through a life of prayer and submission to God's will. It also reflects the major architectural element of the traditional Islamic mosque: a hall of columns and arches. It further reflects the form of the mihrab. All these meanings relate directly to the purpose of the rug and to the ultimate purpose of prayer itself.[11]

Strict interpretation of Islamic traditions prohibits the representation of humans in religious art. To be sure, this restriction was often skirted in ingenious ways by illustrators of Islamic religious texts. Sometimes the Prophet and other religious personages were shown veiled, for example; often, the small scale and private and narrative—rather than public and devotional—purpose of the texts allowed for the rationalization of human depictions, even that of the Prophet himself. In the mosque or prayer hall calligraphy was used for representations; in a Sunni mosque the names of God, the divine messenger, and leaders of the community of believers are often present in calligraphic decoration. God—or rather, the presence of God—is represented in the prayer rug by the hanging lamp, referring to the Quranic verse (XXIV:35)

> God is the Light of the heavens and the earth;
> the likeness of His Light is as a niche

wherein is a lamp
(the lamp in a glass,
the glass as it were a glittering star).[12]

In this prayer rug we see a fundamental characteristic of Islamic art that is often the subject of misunderstanding: Islamic art is indeed representational to a high degree, but the representation is often literary (that is, through writing rather than through a pictorial image) or metaphorical rather than literal. There is nothing particularly complex or difficult to understand about this approach to visual creation; it simply involves looking at Islamic art to see what is there, rather than looking for what, from a European perspective, at first appears to be missing.

Transformation and Contradictions

The dazzling mastery of technique that characterizes so much of the art created under royal or noble patronage in later Islamic art is frequently used by artists to make what we might view as creative contradictions between medium and effect. These contradictions can be quite breathtaking. A stone carver may turn a heavy slab of marble into a transparent veil of lace; in the same vein, the skilled worker in metal may take cold steel, one of the hardest and most intractable of metals, and create an object such as the Safavid standard meant to be carried in processions or parades (92). What is remarkable about it is not simply that the artist has created a beautifully planned rendering of interwoven script bearing a religious inscription, but that this script is superimposed conceptually on a minutely delicate background of vine whorls of gossamer texture, all of it cut from steel and brass.

A similar transformation may be seen on the doublure, or inside, of the binding of a mid-sixteenth century Quran manuscript (72), where the technique of découpage has been used to create out of gilded vellum or paper a gold lace of surpassing elegance interposed above compartments of rich colors; the corner pieces and medallions thus created again show that contradictory quality of three dimensions in two, of layering of planes, so essential to the art of surface decoration in Islamic lands.

The ceramic artisan who created a graceful Safavid bottle (89) effected another kind of transformation in medium. In this case, through the use of a venerable technique known as luster painting, involving a special firing of metallic pigments on the surface of a ceramic vessel, the ceramic bottle has been transformed into a richly decorated metallic object glowing with copper red highlights. The graceful, flowing lines of a Mughal bowl (101), more suggestive of blown or molded glass than of the hard rock crystal from which it was carved, again indicate a triumph of art over material, of patience over time, of concept over technique.

Perhaps the ultimate contradiction is that between purpose and product in the case of Islamic arms and armor. To be sure, lavishly decorated military objects, such as the Mughal ceremonial daggers (99–100) or gunpowder flask and battle ax (94–95), are schizophrenic works of art, whose deadly purpose may be subordinated to a practical and symbolic purpose. Ostensibly, their function is obvious: to inflict bodily

225

harm or death on an enemy. Practically, such beautifully decorated objects were items of conspicuous consumption, meant not for use in battle but to be displayed in ceremony as indications of wealth and social position. Symbolically, their use is even more complex; the wearing of a dagger, for example, is a sign of manhood in many traditional Islamic societies, and, therefore, the fact that the dagger's handle (as in **100**) is a beautiful but impractically fragile piece of carved jade is of minor relevance to the object's symbolic purpose. Just as the rite of circumcision marks the coming of age in the life of a young male Muslim, so the wearing of this symbol of adulthood is imbued with the same significance that the wearing of long trousers once had in England or that the possession of a driver's license may indicate today whether or not one has an automobile with which to use it.

Patrons, Artists, and the Creative Challenge

In any culture patrons and artists alike become involved on a playing field of artistic creation that is bounded by two goals, each in its way desirable. On the one hand, there is the goal of originality—the challenge to create an individual and distinctive work, in which the conception or execution marks some new frontier. The distinctiveness of such a work of art confers on patron and artist alike a competitive advantage: a bonus or salary higher than those given to other artists or the possession of a beautiful object acknowledged by one's peers to be the preeminent example of its type, the object of admiration and even of envy.

On the other hand, there is the goal of familiarity—the challenge to create a work of art that has a comfortable context, can be easily compared to other works, fits the general expectations of the patron as to medium, genre, style, or meaning. Islamic societies have a high respect for tradition, which is immediately apparent when one looks at the thousand-year span of Islamic art represented in the present publication. Much of the pleasure that one gets from a work of art involves this combination of newness and familiarity; an exploration of the historical context reveals dimensions that may not be apparent to today's reader living in a cultural and historical remove from the time these works of art took form.[13]

One kind of play on the theme of innovation and familiarity may be seen in the relationship between the Islamic tradition and that of China, stemming from the well-known phenomenon of the collecting of Chinese porcelain by Islamic patrons.[14] An Ottoman ceramic plate from İznik (**82**) and a Safavid example from Iran (**86**) show us this phenomenon. In both cases the inspiration for the shape and various aspects of the decoration comes directly from Chinese porcelain. The Islamic artist has taken many visual cues from the prototypes, calling up the association of Chinese blue-and-white pottery with the prestige of royal collecting along with the wealth and influence necessary to possess the expensive Chinese wares. The results, however, range from a close copy of the original to a dramatic departure from the Chinese repertoire of designs into a new realm of decoration, reflecting both conservative and innovative approaches to the subject on the part of artist and patron alike.

The use of iconographical formulas is one way that artists can convey the comfortable feeling of recognition. In Islamic painting, as the pioneering scholar Eric Schroeder observed, an artist may use a time-honored composition in much the way that a singer accepts the written word and notes of a song.[15] When the Iranian hero-king Bahram Gur visits a series of lovely story-telling women in a succession of colored pavilions, as related in Nizami's famous poem *Haft Paykar* (Seven portraits), the colors of the architectural setting alone quickly give the reader a sense of the familiar (**74**). In other cases, such as the album painting of an artist (**79**), a familiar composition with both Islamic and European antecedents (figs. 29–30) is used by the Mughal painter not because of any specific indication of meaning but because, despite the great differences in details, the general composition had become a well-accepted and comfortable mode of representation of a working artist, probably known to artist and patron alike. The familiar shape of the Islamic candlestick (**39** and **91**) remained constant over the centuries, although the surface decoration, the techniques of fabrication originally dictating the shape, and even the materials used may have changed dramatically.

Art Patronage and Commerce

Recent art-historical scholarship has reminded us, in a salutary if somewhat unsettling fashion, of the fundamental fact that commerce in works of art is often what kept artists fed, clothed, and housed and that many artist-heroes of the European tradition were shameless self-promoters and sharp business people, often quite cavalier about applying their prestigious signatures to works of art created in large part by pupils, assistants, and employees. In the Islamic world the relationship between art and commerce is a more comfortable matter to confront, if only because our peculiar tendency to bestow European easel painting with an aura of quasi-sanctity mercifully does not apply.

A thriving commerce in works of art does not lower the status accorded the beauty, importance, or eloquence of works created to be sold on the marketplace. And in later Islamic art the importance of long-distance trade and emergence of a mercantilist or bullionist economic orientation in the three empires resulted in a broadening and deepening of the traditional links between art and the marketplace. Perhaps the best-known commerce in later Islamic art is the carpet trade between the Ottoman Empire and Europe. From commercial centers in western Turkey, wool carpets in glowing primary colors (**107**) were exported in great numbers to Europe, where they were avidly acquired by wealthy collectors, who included Cardinal Thomas Wolsey, the Medici family, and the Hapsburg rulers of Austria and Spain.[16] The fame of Turkish carpets spread far and wide, and they were so highly prized that imitations were crafted in Spain, England, Poland, and the Balkans. Today the history of earlier Islamic carpets from the three great empires is largely written from the evidence of their appearance in European paintings—where their depiction carried an aura of wealth, power, and sanctity—and from the evidence of European inventories, bills of sale, and customs documents.

The Islamic world did not depend exclusively on European, African, and Asian markets to support its artistic commerce. Thriving domestic markets for ceramics, textiles, metalwork, carpets, armor, and objects of personal adornment existed within

228

and among the three empires. Much of the production of illustrated manuscripts in centers such as Shiraz appears to have been supported by the demands of the domestic marketplace, and popular works in the Persian language, such as illustrated and illuminated copies of the poems of Firdausi, Hafiz, Jami, and Nizami, appear to have been created "on spec" by the industrious calligraphers, illuminators, painters, and binders of Shiraz.

Certain types of artistic goods acquired particularly lustrous reputations. Ottoman velvets from Bursa and pottery from İznik served markets from Moscow to London, and Safavid chinoiserie pottery was exported all over the world from southern Iranian ports. Guild corporations in London commissioned carpets directly from India, and even Iranian seals and gems with carved calligraphic decoration are found in bazaars from Peshawar to Marrakesh. Commerce proved to be the lifeblood of later Islamic art, and the works produced for the marketplace show no less creative energy and artistic eloquence than the admittedly sometimes rare, although often no less beautiful, objects created on specific commission from royal patrons.

Artists and Anonymity

The anonymity that veils the great majority of artists throughout the history of Islamic civilization exists primarily because Islamic societies did not differentiate the role of the artist from that of other artisans. This does not mean that we do not know the names of artists; the meticulous records kept by various Islamic courts give us the names and salaries of artists in great number. The problem emerges when we attempt to relate the individuals named in the documents to the actual works of art themselves. Islamic works of art are quite rarely signed and somewhat less infrequently do they bear written attributions. Significant exceptions to this rule begin to emerge by the time of the three empires, as artists start to acquire important reputations among collectors and the presence of signatures on works of art gradually affects the market. Some media immediately reflected this change, and others did not. A signature or other positive indication of artistic authorship is quite rare on later Islamic textiles and carpets, although some important and unusual examples bear an artist's name. Ceramic wares are almost never signed, although authorship of architectural tiled decoration can sometimes be inferred by stylistic comparison. Islamic weapons, especially swords, are more frequently signed, and certain masters in every age appear to have enjoyed a reputation among the nobility, in this respect closely paralleling the situation of Japanese blade makers.

Figure 29. Portrait of a Turkish Artist, made by an anonymous Italian (?) painter, late fifteenth century. Boston, Isabella Stewart Gardner Museum (P15e 18-3).

Artists of the book, especially calligraphers but also on occasion illuminators, painters, and binders, sometimes left signatures on works, often placed in an inconspicuous location and sometimes ingeniously hidden. When the practice of collecting single-folio paintings in albums became more widespread, the artist's signature appears to have taken on additional significance. Some sixteenth- and seventeenth-century historical texts mention artists by name and give a few pieces of information on their families, training, and in a very vague sense their work as well. Piecing together the oeuvre of an Islamic artist is therefore often a complicated task,

involving collation of meager biographical data, a few signed "benchmark" works, and a vast amount of comparative visual data.[17] The picture is often confused further by attributions to various painters written or even scribbled in the margins of paintings. Names of certain artists, such as the late fifteenth-century Herat painter Behzad, appear with disturbing frequency (**79**), both on first-class works and even in the margins of seventeenth-century hackwork. The evidence from the period of the three empires gives some revealing insights into the artist's status and practice. For example, in Mughal painting artists frequently collaborated on projects, and inscribed examples list the individuals who did the outlines, clothing, faces, landscape, and architecture.[18] Biographies tell us of artists moving from Iran to India or Turkey and chronicle the family dynasties in the world of Safavid painting. In Ottoman painting we encounter the occasional odd character such as a retired naval officer who took up portrait painting. In Iranian painting we are able to infer from biographical sources and from the paintings themselves the stories of artists' midlife crises and nervous breakdowns. So while the extraction of information about artistic personalities under the three empires proceeds with difficulty, it is a process that has advanced notably in recent decades as the result of patient and perceptive scholarship.

The story of Islamic art under the Ottoman, Safavid, and Mughal empires presents us with a continuation of the creative themes, artistic styles, and patterns of patronage existing in earlier Islamic times. The sponsorship of artistic activity was viewed as an essential part of kingship and an appropriate activity for wealthy nobility and merchant patrons. The making of works of art, from the humblest village weavers to the most prestigious court painters, was viewed as a useful social and economic activity. And while certain media flourished even under a shadow of theological disapproval, in a general cultural sense a positive view of the creation and enjoyment of works of beauty has generally marked Islamic societies on all levels in almost all times. In today's Islamic world this pattern persists, taking new forms in response to new challenges in a changing world.

Figure 30. Portrait of a Turkish Artist, Turkey, late fifteenth century. Washington, D.C., Freer Gallery of Art (32.28).

72

STAMPED AND GILDED LEATHER BOOKBINDING

Iran, mid-16th century
Height 35.6 cm (14 in.), width 24.9 cm (9 ¹³/₁₆ in.)
LNS 10 L

This binding protects sixteen folios with the fourteenth *juz,* which contains verses from chapters XV–XVI of the Quran. The central medallion, axial pendants, corner quadrants, and entire field of the exterior are covered with a profusion of floral scrolls. Half the field was stamped with a large mold, reversed and repeated on the other half to create a symmetrical composition. The line between the two impressions is clearly visible. The wide borders are inscribed with Quranic verses placed in cartouches (XVII:45–46, 82, 106; LXXV:17). The doublures, or inner faces of the covers, are decorated with central medallions and corner quadrants rendered in paper filigree.

Filigree bindings reached an epitome of technical and aesthetic perfection in the fifteenth century under the Mamluks and Timurids. Patterns were originally cut out of leather, but in later Safavid examples paper was used because it was less expensive and easier to handle. In this period stamping with large molds replaced tooling and gilding by hand.

233

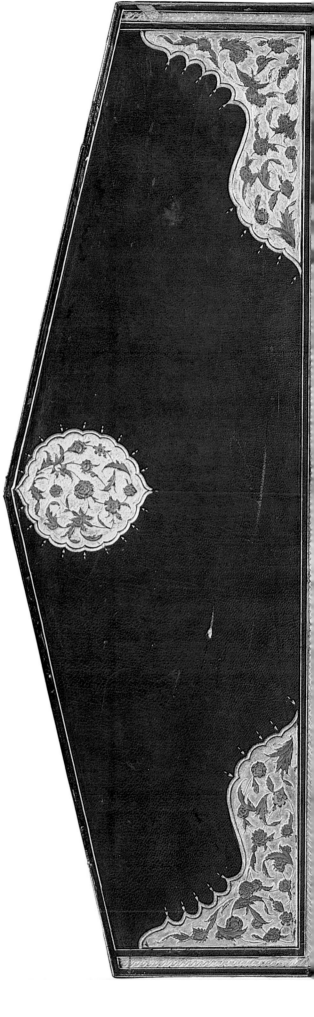

73

STAMPED AND GILDED LEATHER BOOKBINDING

Turkey, mid-16th century
Height 50.0 cm (19 ⅝ in.), width 39.5 cm (15 ½ in.)
LNS 17 L

This brown leather binding separated from its text follows the traditional layout of a central medallion with pendants and corner quadrants enclosed by a border. The central medallion is ovoid, its shape repeated on the flap and cartouches in the border. The axial pendants and corner elements are larger and the border is wider than earlier examples, following the Ottoman style of the sixteenth and seventeenth centuries.

The flat field is devoid of embellishment, in contrast to the gold-stamped components decorated in high relief with floral scrolls and cloud bands. Parts of the border design are painted deep red on a gold ground, thus adding a touch of color. The same layout is applied to the interior, which is made of reddish brown leather, its gold-stamped units decorated in reserve with floral scrolls.

234

236

BAHRAM GUR WITH TWO PRINCESSES

74

Illustrations from the *Khamsa* of Nizami
Iran, dated January 1537
Each folio: height 30.5 cm (12 in.), width 18.0 cm (7 in.)
LNS 4 MS (a, f)

These two paintings belong to a copy of Nizami's *Khamsa,* which consists of 357 folios with twenty-two paintings. They illustrate two scenes from the section entitled *Haft Paykar* (Seven portraits). This poem narrates the romance of Bahram Gur with the seven princesses he installed in separate pavilions, symbolizing the progress of the soul through seven stages combined with seven days, colors, planets, climates, and regions.

On the right, the king is visiting the princess of the Maghrib, or North Africa, in the turquoise pavilion on Wednesday; and on the left, he is with the princess of Iran in the white pavilion on Friday.

The painting style indicates that the manuscript was made in Shiraz, a renowned center for book production during the sixteenth century (see also **53**).

Illustrated on the preceding pages

SUFI WATCHING THE POET SADI IN ECSTACY

75

Illustration from the *Subhat al-Abrar* of Jami, dated 1496/97
Made for Abd Allah Bahadur Khan
Uzbekistan, second quarter 16th century
Height 28.0 cm (11 in.), width 17.0 cm (6 ¹¹⁄₁₆ in.)
LNS 16 MS (c)

The *Subhat al-Abrar* (Rosary of the pious) was composed by the Persian poet and mystic Jami toward the end of the fifteenth century at the Timurid court in Herat. Transcribed in 1496/97, most likely in Herat, this manuscript with 128 folios contains two paintings made in Bukhara, Uzbekistan.

One of the illustrations represents the ecstacy of Sadi, the famous thirteenth-century poet, as envisioned by a mystic, who stands at lower left, observing the whirling figure. The angels above carry trays of light as a gift from heaven to Sadi for composing a couplet in praise of God. The inscription on the structure indicates that the painting was ordered for the library of Abd Allah Bahadur Khan, a descendant of the Uzbek ruler Muhammad Khan (r. 1500–1510), who overthrew the Timurids in 1507 and gathered the artists of Herat in his court at Bukhara. This manuscript must have been part of his booty and passed on to Abd Allah Bahadur Khan, who commissioned the two paintings inserted into the text.

أول ارادندنیه دوندلر انا مکه جریسیدنه ایکی کیشیی
قاجدلر مسلمانانغه قوسندلر مسلماند اولمشلردی جری ایله

جقدو قلری اول مصلحت ایچون زاده یولیولار مسلمانانغه
قجالر بریسی مقداد بن عمرو ادی البنهاذ بریسی عقبه بن غزون

MIQDAD AND UTBAH JOINING THE MUSLIMS

76

Illustration from the *Siyar-ı Nabi* of Darir
Turkey, dated 1595
Height 37.5 cm (14 ¾ in.), width 27.0 cm (10 ⁹⁄₁₆ in.)
LNS 205 MS

The *Siyar-ı Nabi* (Journey of the Prophet), which narrates the life of Muhammad and his followers, was written in 1388 in Turkish by Darir of Erzurum, a city in northeastern Turkey. An illustrated six-volume copy was commissioned by the Ottoman sultan Murad III and completed in 1595. This folio, together with another in the collection, belongs to the fourth volume, the bulk of which is now in the Chester Beatty Library in Dublin.

The painting illustrates a battle that took place in 622/23, during which Miqdad and Utbah (in the foreground) deserted the non-Muslims and took refuge with the followers of the Prophet Muhammad.

The Ottoman artists have treated this episode in the same manner as the battle scenes illustrated in contemporary histories, with the figures arranged in confronting groups and bearing late sixteenth-century arms and armor. Even the white banner is inscribed with the Quranic verse (LXI:13) often employed by the Ottomans.

PORTRAITS OF OTTOMAN SULTANS

77

Illustration from the *Silsilename* of Yusuf ibn Abd al-Hadi
Iraq (?), circa 1600
Height 24.4 cm (9 ⁹/₁₆ in.), width 16.7 cm (6 ½ in.)
LNS 66 MS (fol. 14b)

Historical texts with portraits of the sultans were popularly produced in the Ottoman world. One of these, known as the *Silsilename* (Book of genealogy), traces the genealogy of the Turkish dynasties, beginning with Adam and Eve, continuing with the ancient prophets and patriarchs, and terminating with the Ottomans. Several copies of this Turkish work were made in the Ottoman capital, İstanbul, as well as in such major provincial centers as Baghdad and Cairo during the late sixteenth and early seventeenth centuries.

This version of the *Silsilename* with twenty-one folios is attributed to Baghdad. As in other copies, the figures, set in small medallions against a gold ground, are identified in red and surrounded by explanatory texts and roundels bearing the names of their descendants.

The sultans illustrated here are Orhan (r. ca. 1324–ca. 1362), Murad I (r. ca. 1362–1389), and Bayezid I, the first three descendants of Osman (r. ca. 1299–ca. 1324), founder of the Ottoman dynasty.

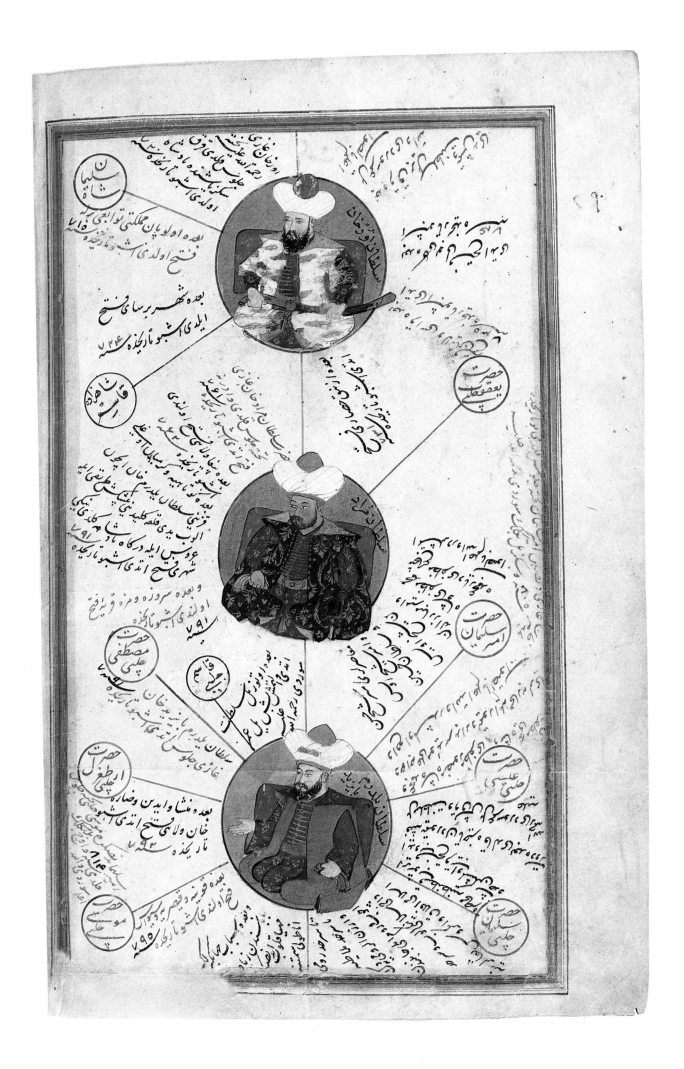

244

VIEW OF VENICE

78

Illustration from the *Kitab-ı Bahriye* of Piri Reis
Turkey, dated 1688/89
Height 31.7 cm (12 ½ in.), width 21.2 cm (8 ⅜ in.)
LNS 75 MS (fol. 82a)

The *Kitab-ı Bahriye* (Book of the mariner), a naval guide to the Mediterranean, was written in 1525 by Piri Reis (ca. 1465–1554), a captain in the Ottoman admiralty, and dedicated to Sultan Süleyman the Magnificent. The work was very popular and copied many times. This version, containing 192 folios with 131 illustrations depicting various ports and harbors, was transcribed in 1688/89.

The illustrations in almost all the copies follow those in the original volume, showing the coastal cities with their geographic peculiarities as well as identifiable landmarks and buildings. The view of Venice, one of the most elaborate paintings in the manuscript, depicts the circular inner harbor with the city proper and its auxiliary islands densely filled with religious, secular, and defensive structures.

PORTRAIT OF A PAINTER

79

Illustration from an album
India, first quarter 17th century
Painting: height 20.0 cm (7 ¹³⁄₁₆ in.), width 14.3 cm (5 ⁹⁄₁₆ in.)
Folio: height 33.3 cm (13 ⅛ in.), width 27.3 cm (10 ¾ in.)
LNS 57 MS

Attired in courtly garments and wearing an elaborate turban, the painter is seated on the ground while working on a full-length figure. His outer robe is embellished with a gold-embroidered cloud collar. The portrait is mounted on an album page, its margins decorated with figures and animals in a landscape executed in gold.

This portrait is a mirror image of a painting made in the Ottoman court during the 1480s, which itself was based on a painting made by a European artist, presumably during a visit to İstanbul around the same time (see figs. 29–30). The Ottoman version must have been in the Mughal court during the seventeenth century to serve as the model. Both the Ottoman and Mughal copies contain the spurious attribution to "Behzad" placed at the lower left.

SLAYING OF AN ELEPHANT-HEADED CREATURE

80

Illustration from an album
India, late 16th century
Painting: height 18.0 cm (7 ¹/₁₆ in.), width 11.0 cm (4 ⁵/₁₆ in.)
Folio: height 46.9 cm (18 ½ in.), width 33.5 cm (13 ³/₁₆ in.)
LNS 105 MS

The album painting depicts a mythical hunt set within a spacious landscape. The hero dominates the scene, highlighted by his colorful outfit and energetic movement.

The painting reveals the stylistic features of early Mughal art and a blend of several traditions. The decorative landscape is Iranian; the naturalism, volume, and vitality of the figures is Indian; and the receding planes with a diminutive city in the background point to European influences. The same features appear in the paintings produced during the second half of the sixteenth century in the court of Akbar, where artists of diverse traditions were gathered.

LION HUNT

81

Illustration from an album
India, 17th century
Drawing: height 15.8 cm (6 ³/₁₆ in.), width 11.6 cm (4 ½ in.)
Folio: height 39.1 cm (15 ⁵/₁₆ in.), width 27.9 cm (11 in.)
LNS 106 MS

A royal preoccupation since time immemorial and used as a symbol of a monarch's courage and power, hunting was frequently represented in Islamic art.

This tinted album drawing is representative of the style favored in the Mughal court, particularly during the first quarter of the seventeenth century under the patronage of Jahangir. The diagonal composition and energetic movement of the hunters and their prey create a vitality that contrasts to the subtle palette and sparse details rendered in color.

CERAMIC PLATE WITH SPIRAL SCROLL

82

Turkey, second quarter 16th century
Height 7.5 cm (2 ¹⁵⁄₁₆ in.), diameter 44.0 cm (17 ⁵⁄₁₆ in.)
LNS 231 C

Underglaze painted in blue with touches of turquoise, this plate represents a type of Ottoman pottery decorated with spiral scrolls. The design—found on manuscript illuminations and *tuğras,* or imperial monograms, of Süleyman the Magnificent, produced after the 1520s—appears to have originated in the court studios and transmitted to the potters of İznik.

The central medallion contains circular formations created by spiral scrolls with trefoil cartouches placed at the points of intersection; the cavetto (curved sides) bears cloud bands and the foliated rim repeats the scroll used in the center. The shape of the plate and decorative layout divided into three concentric zones reflect the influence of blue-and-white Chinese porcelains collected by the Ottoman court.

CERAMIC BOTTLE WITH TULIPS AND TRIPLE BALLS

83

Turkey, second quarter 16th century
Height 27.6 cm (10 ⅞ in.), diameter 18.5 cm (7 ¼ in.)
LNS 327 C

The decorative repertoire of İznik, the most renowned center for Ottoman pottery, underwent a number of changes, abandoning some colors and motifs and assimilating others. For instance, around the second quarter of the sixteenth century turquoise was added to the earlier blue-and-white palette and naturalistic themes were incorporated into ceramic designs.

These features are represented by this bottle, which has white tulips, painted in reserve on a blue ground, growing from clusters of turquoise balls. Both the tulip and clusters of triple balls were popular Turkish motifs, especially during the sixteenth century.

CERAMIC PLATE WITH FLORAL SPRAY

84

Turkey, second quarter 16th century
Height 6.0 cm (2 5/16 in.), diameter 36.2 cm (14 1/4 in.)
LNS 325 C

İznik wares painted sage green, pale purple, and greenish black in addition to blue
and turquoise were frequently decorated with a combination of naturalistic and
fantastic flowers, as in this example.

Blossoms and buds with large serrated leaves grow from a central source and
extend into the walls. The flat lobed rim bears stylized tulips alternating with
rounded flowers. Directional compositions with undulating and overlapping
branches, blossoms, and leaves that create a lively movement became a distinct
feature of Ottoman ceramics.

CERAMIC JUG WITH FLORAL DESIGN

85

Turkey, second half 16th century
Height 27.6 cm (10 ⅞ in.), diameter 20.2 cm (7 ¹⁵⁄₁₆ in.)
LNS 99 C

The final development in İznik ceramics is the appearance of a bright and thick red, first employed in the tiles of the Süleymaniye Mosque in İstanbul completed in 1557. Together with an emerald green, it was applied to a variety of objects, including single-handle jugs, such as this example.

Sinuous branches bearing large blossoms and buds alternating with elegantly twisting serrated leaves decorate the body and neck. The elements are freely drawn and naturalistically rendered, creating a harmony of design and movement.

CERAMIC PLATE WITH INCISED DECORATION

86

Iran, 17th century
Height 6.4 cm (2 ½ in.), diameter 41.1 cm (16 ³/₁₆ in.)
LNS 369 C

The decoration of this large plate, which employs incised designs alternating with those underglaze painted in varying shades of blue, was inspired by Ming dynasty (1368–1644) porcelains. The painted and incised areas create a most striking contrast. This type of seventeenth-century ware is attributed to Kerman and Mashhad, two renowned pottery centers in eastern Iran.

In the center of the plate is a square with a figure seated in a landscape, recalling the scenes depicted on late Ming dynasty wares with contemplating monks or ascetics. Enclosing it are four pairs of lobed triangular panels filled with incised scales or blue scrolls revolving around a central lotus blossom. Additional incised floral elements appear in the voids along the rim. Under the base is a sketchy motif painted blue, imitating Chinese reign marks.

CERAMIC PLATE WITH CONCENTRIC DESIGN

87

Iran, 17th century
Height 6.3 cm (2 ½ in.), diameter 42.0 cm (16 ½ in.)
LNS 101 C

With a low foot, curving walls, and lobed rim, this large blue-and-white plate is representative of the fine wares produced in Kerman and Mashhad during the sixteenth and seventeenth centuries.

The finely potted white body is underglaze painted in various intensities of blue outlined with black. The floral designs are reserved in white, except for those on the rim.

The interior is divided into concentric zones, in the center of which is a medallion bearing a sunflower surrounded by five pairs of leaves. Around it is a wide zone with floral sprays overlaid by a pale blue cloud band dividing it into six large trefoils. The cavetto has a scrolling branch with thick leaves and six lotus blossoms, while a simpler scroll appears on the rim.

The undulating vine with leaves and bunches of grapes on the exterior walls and the mark imitating a tassel on the base reflect Chinese influences.

CERAMIC BOWL WITH FACETED SIDES

88

Iran, 17th century
Height 9.1 cm (3 ½ in.), diameter 18.4 cm (7 ¼ in.)
LNS 130 C

The potters of Kerman also produced polychrome-painted wares, as represented by this faceted bowl. Divided into eight panels, the walls curve out from the low foot and flare toward the rim.

   The panels are alternately decorated with trefoil cartouches painted in mustard yellow or brownish red slips. The former is surrounded by blue floral scrolls, while the latter creates a reciprocal pattern, flanked by white cloud bands reserved on blue. The interior is painted with blue florals; the base has a four-petaled blossom amid other foliage and along the rim are floral sprays and blossoms.

LUSTER-PAINTED CERAMIC BOTTLE

89

Iran, second half 17th century
Height 26.9 cm (10 ½ in.), diameter 14.5 cm (5 ¾ in.)
LNS 321 C

Despite the popularity of underglaze-painted blue-and-white wares, a revival of luster painting occurred in Iranian ceramics during the second half of the seventeenth century.

The neck of this graceful bottle with a low foot and ovoid body has a thick ring to provide support while liquid is poured out of the bottle; the mouth is shaped as a spout to control the flow of the contents. The white body was covered with a dark blue slip and coated with a transparent glaze, above which the design was painted in deep copper red luster. The decoration follows the repertoire of the age and employs floral sprays, tufts of grass, cypress trees, flying birds, vases, and lobed cartouches in an overall design.

Lobed cartouches were commonly used on ceramics (see **88**) as well as metalwork. Landscape elements, however, are derived from manuscript decoration and recall the marginal drawings executed in gold.

ENAMELED AND GILDED GLASS WATER PIPE BOWL

90

India, 18th century
Height 14.4 cm (5 ⁹/₁₆ in.), diameter 15.0 cm (6 in.)
LNS 10 G

This free-blown spherical bowl of transparent colorless glass has a short neck and thick rim to secure the long tube used with a water pipe.

The body is embellished with staggered rows of peacock feathers made of applied glass studs painted blue and gold and enclosed by wide, gold feathery bands. A gold scroll bearing blue and green blossoms, also executed as applied studs, encircles the shoulder. The clear glass with gold scrolls and raised enameled elements resembles rock crystal vessels encrusted with gems (see **101**).

BRASS CANDLESTICK

91

Iran, late 16th century
Height 24.5 cm (9 ⁹/₁₆ in.), diameter 19.7 cm (7 ¾ in.)
LNS 121 M

The cast brass candlestick with a projecting foot and shoulder and concave body is decorated with chased and engraved scrolls and linked cartouches, creating an overall pattern rendered in horizontal registers.

Lobed medallions and oblongs, filled with slender split-leaves, lotus blossoms, and four- or five-petaled flowers, appear on the foot, body, and shoulder. The edge of the shoulder, neck, and socket bear scrolls with split-leaves, four-petaled blossoms, or reciprocal trefoils.

The traditional shape employed by this example was rarely produced in the Safavid period, the more popular type being the tall, cylindrical "pillar" candlestick.

STEEL STANDARD

92

Iran, dated 1712/13
Height 73.3 cm (28 ⅞ in.), width 38.5 cm (15 ⅛ in.)
LNS 52 M

This ogival ceremonial standard was made of pierced metal plates joined by rounded bands and affixed to a solid axial rod. At the pinnacle is a spherical socket for the banner; projecting from the upper sides are four pairs of dragon heads cast in the round (one of the heads is missing).

The brass plate at the core of the standard is pierced with scrolls bearing split-leaves and five-petaled blossoms. The same pierced scroll appears in the next unit, fabricated in steel. Pierced steel was also used for the widest component, which contains majestic epigraphy placed against a floral scroll. The inscription contains all four verses of the Quranic chapter Ikhlas (CXII), terminating with the date, 1124 A.H. (1712/13), rendered in numerals.

The axial rod bears engraved floral scrolls; written on its base is an invocation to Ali (r. 656–61), the first Shiite imam, fourth caliph, and husband of Fatima, daughter of the Prophet.

IRON (?) BELL

93

Iran, 17th–18th century
Height 21.0 cm (8 ¼ in.), diameter 13.5 cm (5 ⁵⁄₁₆ in.)
LNS 56 M

Revealing a high degree of sophistication, this spherical cage bell made of hammered and cut iron (or steel) is decorated with engraved, incised, and gold-overlaid designs. Its immediate aesthetic appeal results from the bold, organic form, enhanced by fluting.

The upper hemisphere bears swirling, rounded flutes and the lower hemisphere has open, vertical flutes that curve under to form the base. The vertical design of the lower half stabilizes the piece and counteracts the diagonal movement of the upper half. Between the two sections is a band of gold scrolls with four-petaled blossoms and split-leaves. The apex and heart-shaped handle are also decorated with gold overlays.

STEEL GUNPOWDER FLASK

94

India, 17th century
Height 18.9 cm (7 ½ in.), diameter 8.5 cm (3 ⅜ in.)
LNS 141 M

This steel flask was hammered in two halves from a sheet of metal and affixed with a cast neck and spout. The front is decorated with gold-overlaid floral scrolls enclosing an inscribed cartouche, the lateral extensions of which curve up and terminate in bird heads. The Persian text placed in the cartouche is from a poem by Sadi: "What remains in life is what we achieve because our existence is transient."

Made of metal, wood, leather, and shell as well as horn, flasks for carrying gunpowder were common wherever muzzle-loading guns were used. Since the earliest examples were made of horn, the term *powder horn* was popularly used. These early flasks were large because of the sizable amounts of ammunition powder required to fire the guns.

STEEL AX

95

India, dated 1734/35
Length 55.8 cm (22 in.), width of head 15.4 cm (6 ¹/₁₆ in.)
LNS 100 M

This type of ceremonial ax with curved head attached to a long shaft was popular in Iran as well as India. The head is made from finely watered steel (so named because the surface pattern resembles waves or ripples of water). The handle is decorated with a floral latticework overlaid with gold and inlaid with silver.

One side of the head bears inscriptions rendered in both Arabic and Persian. The Arabic begins with the *basmala*, a pious invocation, and continues with: "There is no brave man other than Ali and no sword other than the Zulfiqar." The sword mentioned is the one with double blades associated with Caliph Ali (see also **92**). The date 1147 A.H. (1734/35) appears at the flat top of the head. A pair of animals or birds in combat decorates both sides of the section that attaches the head to the shaft, reinforcing the theme of victorious battle.

JADE PENDANT

96

Made for Shah Jahan
India, dated 1637/38
Length 4.5 cm (1 ¾ in.), width 3.8 cm (1 ½ in.)
LNS 120 J

Made of cut and polished white nephrite, this pendant is shaped like a five-lobed leaf, with each lobe further embellished with scallops. Both sides bear engraved and gold-inlaid Persian inscriptions written in *nastaliq*, a small trilobed motif on the bail at the top, and a line that follows the contours of the edges. The gold inlays are recessed and lie flush with the surface. The jade is set into a lobed gold frame that has two heavy rings for suspension at the top.

The inscriptions contain benedictions and praises, include the date 1047 A.H. (1637/38), and terminate with Shah Jahan's name.

The gold frame around the pendant was not part of the original conception as the piece has its own transversely pierced bail. Furthermore, the frame partly covers the gold-inlaid border along the edges. The high quality of the frame suggests that it may be contemporary with the pendant, added to enhance the importance of the piece or made on the demand of the wearer who wanted a more impressive ornament.

GOLD NECKLACE SET WITH DIAMONDS

97

India, 18th century
Length 38.9 cm (15 5/16 in.), width of pendant 4.1 cm (1 9/16 in.)
LNS 16 J

The graduated necklace is composed of sixty-six hinged, circular elements, each enameled on the back in transparent green and set on the front with a large flat diamond. Attached to the two central elements is a floral pendant composed of ten large and six smaller flat diamonds with green, red, and white enamel backing. Suspended from the pendant is a large teardrop-shaped emerald.

The enameling technique used was champlevé in which vitreous compounds are applied to recesses made in the metal base by chasing or engraving.

Although the necklace has a typically Mughal shape, it is possible that the emerald originally belonged to an earlier piece. Such a long necklace would have been worn with other neck ornaments, such as chokers and strings of pearls.

Back of pendant

Back

GOLD PENDANT SET WITH GEMS

98

India, 18th century
Height 9.3 cm (3 ⁹/₁₆ in.), width 5.6 cm (2 ¼ in.)
LNS 28 J

Shaped as a bird of prey, the pendant is set with rubies, emeralds, diamonds, and rock crystal (in the area around the eyes); the back of the wings and tail is engraved and niello inlaid with floral designs. The beak was carved from two solid pieces of ruby and the feet were formed of thick gold wire. Large pearls are suspended from the beak and tail; similar pearls were once attached to the tips of the wings as well. The gems were set in the typically Indian fashion backed by a filling of hard thermoplastic material, here a red lac or hard wax.

Pendants shaped as eagles with outspread wings were commonly produced in Spain, North Africa, and India. This example may have been part of an imperial regalia, such as a throne, or conceived as the centerpiece of a necklace.

Detail of chape

STEEL DAGGER WITH GOLD HILT AND SCABBARD

99

India, first quarter 17th century
Length 35.5 cm (14 in.), width 11.6 cm (4 ⅝ in.)
LNS 25 J

This exquisite dagger with a steel blade, solid gold hilt, and wood scabbard sheathed with gold is entirely covered with floral designs, birds, and animals. The front of the scabbard and its chape and hilt are engraved and set with diamonds, rubies, and emeralds as well as with pieces of green and blue glass. Originally, more than twenty-four hundred stones were used; ten to twenty are now missing, including a large one on the pommel. All the stones, except the diamonds, were cut and polished. The diamonds were left in their natural state and affixed according to size; those on the edges of the chape, quillon, and knuckle guard are natural octahedrals set in graduated order. The back of the scabbard is worked in repoussé and devoid of gems.

The dagger might have been worn by Jahangir himself or his son and future heir, Shah Jahan. It could also have been made as a gift from the ruler to a person of high rank as such royal generosity was common in the Mughal court. Although similar jeweled items appear in paintings of the period, this dagger is the finest extant example.

Detail of hilt

STEEL DAGGER WITH JADE HILT SET WITH GEMS

100

India, mid-17th century
Length 38.5 cm (15 ⅛ in.), width 7.5 cm (3 in.)
LNS 12 HS

The hilt of the dagger as well as the chape and locket of the scabbard are made of off-white jade that was grooved, inlaid with gold, and set with diamonds, emeralds, and rubies. The scabbard has a wood core covered with a brocaded fabric.

Although gem-encrusted hardstone items were popularly produced during the sixteenth century in Ottoman Turkey and to a lesser extent in Safavid Iran, no examples dating from this period have been identified as Indian. It is thought that the tradition was imported from Iran; but once established, the Indian school matched and even exceeded the quality of its western predecessors.

This princely dagger with original scabbard and mounts is representative of the opulence, refinement, and technical perfection that characterize seventeenth-century Mughal artistry.

ROCK CRYSTAL BOWL SET WITH GEMS

101

India, 18th–19th century
Height 4.6 cm (1 ¾ in.), diameter 9.2 cm (3 ½ in.)
LNS 8 HS

With its exterior of twelve curving facets, this hemispherical bowl was carved from a block of rock crystal. Inlaid with gold and set with diamonds and rubies, the exterior displays a grid pattern with quatrefoils of alternating rubies and diamonds connected by a pair of curving gold lines. Additional stone-inlaid elements placed at the top join the quatrefoil lattice to the gold band encircling the lip.

The Mughal school of inlaid hardstones was established during the seventeenth century and continued for the next two hundred years. Its high-quality products reflect the virtuosity of the artists as well as the aesthetics of the patrons.

Although of fairly late date, the piece exhibits flawless execution of shape and decoration. Even if it lacks the grandeur and verve of the seventeenth-century pieces, it is a remarkably fine object.

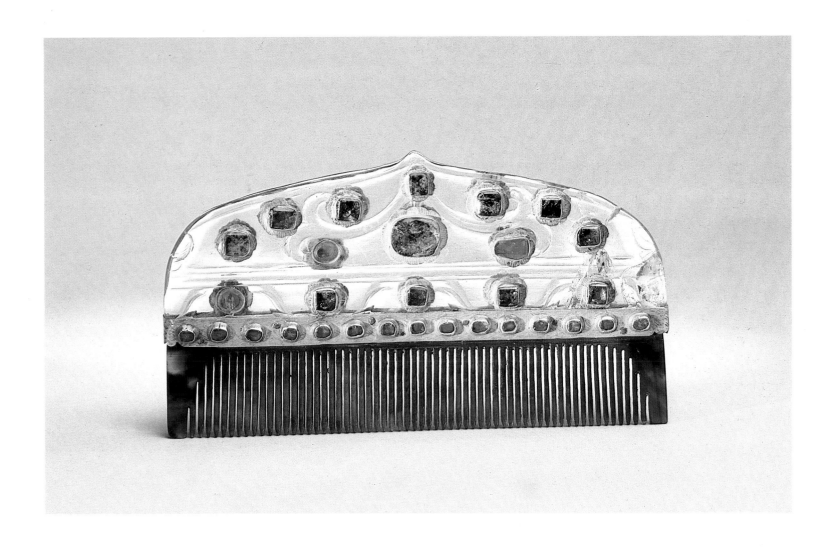

COMB WITH ROCK CRYSTAL HANDLE

102

Turkey, late 16th–early 17th century
Height 6.8 cm (2¹¹⁄₁₆ in.), width 12.7 cm (5 in.)
LNS 7 HS

The handle of this horn or tortoiseshell comb was cut from a block of rock crystal and carved in relief. The gold settings for the emeralds and rubies are inlaid into deeply recessed sockets; the gold ferrule at the juncture of the handle and comb is encrusted with gems.

Many Ottoman items were made of carved hardstones, inlaid with gold, and often set with precious stones. Most pieces date from the sixteenth and seventeenth centuries and are preserved in the Treasury of the Topkapı Palace, the residence of the sultans, in İstanbul. Ottoman artistry is distinguished by the use of multipetaled gold mounts, with the gems forming the cores of the blossoms, as in this example.

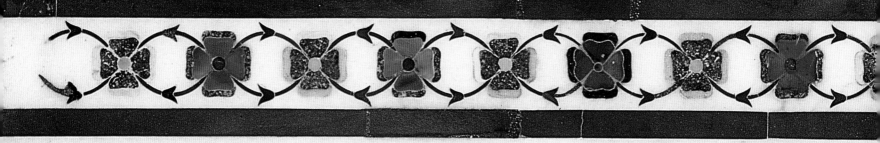

INLAID MARBLE PANEL

103

India, 17th–18th century
Height 47.5 cm (18 ¾ in.), width 99.0 cm (39 in.)
LNS 70 S (d)

Carved and inlaid with multicolored stones, such as lapis lazuli, malachite, jasper, and agate, this marble panel belongs to a set of six similar examples in the collection. Representing three symmetrically arranged floral compositions divided by cypress trees, the panels are decorated in the technique known as *pietre dure*, a kind of mosaic work in which colored stones are used to imitate the effect of painting. The florals evolve from a vase or cluster of leaves and are surrounded by birds, butterflies, and insects. Continuous bands with strapwork, beading, and floral scrolls appear above and below the panels.

The tradition of facing the interiors and sometimes the exteriors of buildings with marble revetments inlaid with semiprecious stones became a characteristic of imperial Mughal architecture, particularly after the mid-seventeenth century.

Detail illustrated on the preceding pages

EMBROIDERED TENT HANGING

104

India, 17th century
Length 170.0 cm (66 ¹⁵⁄₁₆ in.), width 140.0 cm (55 ⅛ in.)
LNS 115 T (a)

Tent hangings, such as this example, were usually made of woven cotton and decorated with embroidered, painted, or printed designs. Grouped together around a tent to form a protective wall, they were held up by poles inserted through pockets between the panels. Most were decorated with floral motifs surmounted by arches, suggesting a garden seen through an arcade.

The lobed ogival arch used in this silk-embroidered cotton hanging is a characteristic feature of Mughal architecture. Growing from a vase placed in a field, stylized floral arrangements became the hallmark of Mughal decorative vocabulary by the mid-seventeenth century and were used on rugs, textiles, metalwork, jade, woodwork, bookbindings, and architectural decoration (see **103**).

In the al-Sabah Collection is another piece from the same fabric enclosure.

293

294

RUG WITH OVERALL PATTERN

105

Iran or Afghanistan, 16th century
Length 200.0 cm (78 ¾ in.), width 150.0 cm (59 in.)
LNS 7 R

The city of Herat, a famous center of artistic activities under the Timurids, became renowned for the high quality and intricate floral designs of its rugs during the sixteenth and seventeenth centuries.

The red ground of this example is densely covered with lotus blossoms, peonies, and other flowers connected by fine scrolls. In the center is a small lozenge flanked by two pairs of large lotus blossoms, suggesting a larger lozenge. This pattern, repeated throughout the rug and extending beyond the border, is almost camouflaged by the lush vegetation. Other elements, such as cloud bands and split-leaves, appear in the linked reciprocal cartouches forming the border.

This type of rug, although identified with the city of Herat, was also produced in a number of other centers in Afghanistan and eastern Iran.

296

PRAYER RUG

106

Turkey, second half 16th century
Length 172.0 cm (67 ¾ in.), width 130.0 cm (51 ³⁄₁₆ in.)
LNS 29 R

Decorated with a profusion of naturalistic and stylized floral motifs, the finest Turkish rugs were made of cotton, silk, and wool. Woven in the imperial workshops during the sixteenth and seventeenth centuries and known as "court-style" rugs, they include a group of small prayer carpets distinguished by mihrabs framed by wide floral borders.

The mihrab in this example is formed by an arch resting on slender columns; suspended in the center is a mosque lamp. The plain red field is contrasted with the blue border filled with scrolls bearing tulips, carnations, and hyacinths as well as stylized blossoms and long, serrated leaves. These decorative themes, employed on all imperial Ottoman arts, ranging from tiles to textiles, were created in the royal studios and first applied to manuscript illuminations.

STAR-PATTERN UŞAK RUG

107

Turkey, 17th century
Length 290.0 cm (114 ½ in.), width 167.0 cm (65 ¾ in.)
LNS 17 R

Uşak, a city in western Anatolia, has been famous for its rugs since the fifteenth century. Turkish weavers produced a variety of patterns, including overall designs with small and large stars, octagons, and squares as well as those with central medallions. These patterns continued through the seventeenth century.

This example represents the all-wool Uşak type with star pattern. It has a red ground and large eight-pointed starlike motifs alternating with smaller lozenges, rendered in blue and filled with symmetrically arranged stylized florals. The design is conceived as a repeat pattern that can be multiplied infinitely and used for carpets of any size. The interstices between the medallions and lozenges are filled with floral scrolls.

Illustrated on the following pages

Notes

Patronage in Islamic Art

To not overburden the notes and unless otherwise specified, all monuments constructed before 1250 are assumed to be available through Richard Ettinghausen and Oleg Grabar, *The Art and Architecture of Islam, 650–1250* (Harmondsworth: Penguin, 1987).

1. Francis Haskell, *Patrons and Painters: A Study in the Relations between Italian Art and Society in the Art of the Baroque* (New Haven: Yale University Press, 1980).

2. Issam El-Said and Ayşe Parman, *Geometric Concepts in Islamic Art* (London: World of Islam Festival, 1976); and Annemarie Schimmel, *Calligraphy and Islamic Culture* (New York: New York University Press, 1984).

3. Three striking examples illustrating different states and types of research are Ömer Lütfi Barkan, *Süleymaniye Cami ve İmareti İnşaatı (1550–1557)* (The construction of the Süleymaniye mosque and alms kitchen) (Ankara: Türk Tarih Kurumu, 1972–79); Muhammad Amin, *Fihrist Wathaiq al-Qahirah Nihayat as-Salatin al-Mamalik* (Catalogue of Mamluk documents from Cairo) (Cairo, 1981); and I. Afshar and M. Minovi, *Waqf-nāma-yi Rab'-i Rāshidi* (The endowment of the Rab-i Rashidi) (Tehran, 1978).

4. Jonathan M. Bloom, "The Mosque of al-Ḥākim in Cairo," *Muqarnas* 1 (1983): 15–36. For the treasures see Paul Kahle, "Die Schätze der Fāṭimiden," *Zeitschrift der deutschen Morgenländgesellschaft* 89 (1935): 329–62; Zaky Mohammed Hassan, *Kunūz al-Fāṭimīyin: The Treasures of the Fāṭimids* (Cairo: Egyptian Library Press, 1937); and Ibn al-Zubayr, *Kitāb al-Dhakhā'ir wa al-Tuḥaf* (Kuwait, 1959), 249ff.

5. Oleg Grabar, "Imperial and Urban Art in Islam: The Subject-Matter of Fatimid Art," 173–90, in *Colloque internationale sur l'histoire du Caire* (Cairo: Ministry of Culture of the Arab Republic of Egypt, 1972).

6. Masudi, *Muruj al-Dhahab* (Golden meadows), ed. M. Muhi al-Din Abd al-Hamid (Cairo, 1948), 4:86–87. The first to have noted this passage is, to my knowledge, Dominique Sourdel, "Questions de cérémonial 'abbaside," *Revue des études islamiques* 28 (1960): 128. See also Oleg Grabar, "Reflections on the Study of Islamic Art," *Muqarnas* 1 (1983): 1–14. A new interpretation of the architectural references has been proposed by Hazem Sayyed, "The Rab in Cairo" (thesis, Massachusetts Institute of Technology, 1987).

7. There is no comprehensive or analytic survey of appropriate Quranic passages with their commentaries nor of the *hadiths*, or traditions, dealing with or appropriate to the arts. For preliminary statements and selections of sources see Thomas Walker Arnold, *Painting in Islam: A Study of the Place of Pictorial Art in Islam* (Oxford: Clarendon, 1928), chap. 1; Oleg Grabar, *The Formation of Islamic Art* (New Haven: Yale University Press, 1987), 72–98, 195–214; and Bishr Farès, *Essai sur l'esprit de la décoration islamique* (Cairo: Institut français d'archéologie orientale, 1952).

8. Saleh A. al-Hathloul, "Tradition, Continuity, and Change in the Physical Environment: The Muslim City" (Ph.D. diss., Massachusetts Institute of Technology, 1981). Some of al-Hathloul's themes were developed in an entirely different context by Jamel Akbar, *Crisis in the Built Environment: The Case of the Muslim City* (Singapore: Concept Media, 1988).

9. I wonder whether this absence of legal opinion about the arts applied to the very contemporary period, as remarkable and controversial buildings had been erected all over the Muslim world and as many movements of contemporary art were bought or sponsored by clients in the Muslim world or made there.

10. Ibn Khaldun, *The Muqaddimah: An Introduction to History*, trans. Franz Rosenthal (Princeton: Princeton University Press, 1967). Since then much has been written about Ibn Khaldun. For a bibliographical survey see Aziz al-Azmeh, *Ibn Khaldun in Modern Scholarship: A Study in Orientalism* (London: Third World Centre for Research, 1981).

11. Main passages used are 1:449ff., 2:69–72, 249–66, and 357ff.

12. For a series of striking examples see Yoshiaki Shimizu and John M. Rosenfield, *Masters of Japanese Calligraphy: Eighth through Nineteenth Centuries* (New York: Asia Society Galleries and Japan House Gallery, 1984), nos. 56ff. For Testa see Elizabeth Cropper, *The Ideal of Painting: Pietro Testa's Düsseldorf Notebook* (Princeton: Princeton University Press, 1984).

13. Charles K. Wilkinson, *Nishapur: Pottery of the Early Islamic Period* (New York: Metropolitan Museum of Art, 1973), colorpls. 6–9 and pls. 36, 40, 47. Nearly every stylistic or technical subgroup possesses a range of forms that includes the "eccentric" (Ettinghausen and Grabar, *Art and Architecture of Islam*, 114–15 and 230–31).

14. Mazhar S. İpşiroğlu, *Masterpieces from the Topkapi Museum: Paintings and Miniatures* (London: Thames & Hudson, 1980); *Islamic Art* 1 (1981); and Martin Dickson and Stuart Cary Welch, *The Houghton Shahnameh* (Cambridge, Mass.: Fogg Art Museum, 1981), 51ff.

15. Among many examples see *Calligraphie islamique* (Geneva: Musée d'art et d'histoire, 1988), no. 158.

16. *Calligraphers and Painters: A Treatise by Qāḍi Aḥmad, Son of Mīr-Munshī (circa A.H. 1015/A.D. 1606)*, trans. V. Minorsky, Freer Gallery of Art Occasional Papers 3, no. 2 (Washington, D.C.: Freer Gallery of Art, 1959), 101.

17. Anthony Welch, *Artists for the Shah: Late Sixteenth-Century Painting at the Imperial Court of Iran* (New Haven: Yale University Press, 1976). For the full texts of Sadiqi's statement on painting and passim for accounts of painters see Dickson and Welch, *Houghton Shahnameh*, 259ff.

18. I do not know the exact source of the story. One of its versions is Galina Anatolevna Pugachenkova, *Samarkand—Bukhara* (Moscow: State Museum of Art, 1961), 56.

19. There are, to my knowledge, no studies of legendary personages from the point of view I am developing. For that matter, several of the great "heroes" of pan-Islamic literature like Antar, Layla, Majnun, Shirin, and, of course, Farhad, have aesthetic connotations with the visual arts that derive from their work. In the meantime the article "Farhād wa-Shīrīn" in the *Encyclopaedia of Islam*, 2d ed., 2:793–95, may serve as a beginning.

20. *Calligraphers and Painters*, 64.

21. For the mosque of Ibn Tulun see K. A. C. Creswell, *Early Muslim Architecture: Umayyads, 'Abbāsids, and Ṭūlūnids* (1932; New York:

Hacker, 1979), 2:332–59; and Ettinghausen and Grabar, *Art and Architecture of Islam*, 92–94. The competition, based on a text found in Maqrizi, is discussed, among many other places, in Richard Ettinghausen, *Arab Painting* (Geneva: Skira, 1962), 54–56.

22. Nizami, *The Haft Paikar* (Seven portraits), trans. C. E. Wilson (London: Probsthain, 1924), 1:110–11. *The Thousand and One Nights* is replete with such passages, but the forthcoming research by Muhsin Mahdi is bringing to light so many new interpretations of the text that the identification of these, which are valid as documents for the Muslim Middle Ages rather than European orientalism, has to wait for the publication of his findings.

23. Dickson and Welch, *Houghton Shahnameh*. Marianna Shreve Simpson, "The Production and Patronage of the *Haft Aurang* by Jāmī in the Freer Gallery of Art," *Ars Orientalis* 13 (1983): 93–119.

24. To older bibliographies add a reinterpretation by Oleg Grabar, "The Meaning of the Dome of the Rock," 1–10, in *The Medieval Mediterranean: Cross-Cultural Contacts*, ed. Marilyn J. Chiat and Kathryn L. Reyerson, Medieval Studies at Minnesota 3 (Saint Cloud, Minn.: North Star Press, 1988).

25. Esin Atıl, *Renaissance of Islam: Art of the Mamluks* (Washington, D.C.: Smithsonian Institution Press, 1981), no. 21.

26. For instance, Qadi Ahmad (*Calligraphers and Painters*) and Dost Muhammad (translated and discussed in Dickson and Welch, *Houghton Shahnameh*). The latter's text, a miniaturized Vasari, has been used by all historians of Iranian painting, but a comprehensive textual investigation remains to be made.

27. I owe most of my understanding of Timurid painting to working with Thomas W. Lentz on his doctoral thesis, "Painting at Herat under Baysunghur ibn Shahrukh" (Ph.D. diss., Harvard University, 1985). Some of his ideas appear in Thomas W. Lentz and Glenn D. Lowry, *Timur and the Princely Vision: Persian Art and Culture in the Fifteenth Century* (Los Angeles: Los Angeles County Museum of Art, 1989).

28. For the buildings see K. A. C. Creswell, *The Muslim Architecture of Egypt* (1952–59; New York: Hacker, 1978), vol. 2. For the interpretation of the mosque of Baybars see Jonathan M. Bloom, "The Mosque of Baybars al-Brunduqdari in Cairo," *Annales islamologiques* 18 (1982): 45–78.

29. For information and further studies see Eva Baer, *Metalwork in Medieval Islamic Art* (Albany: State University of New York Press, 1983); and Ettinghausen and Grabar, *Art and Architecture of Islam*, last chapter. For a very peculiar group still not fully explained from the point of view of patronage see the excellent new book by Eva Baer, *Ayyubid Metalwork with Christian Images* (Leiden: Brill, 1989).

30. For the best introduction to the subject see Schimmel, *Calligraphy and Islamic Culture*.

31. Among recently published examples see Marianna Shreve Simpson, "The Narrative Structure of a Medieval Iranian Beaker," *Ars Orientalis* 12 (1981): 15–24.

32. The most recent survey of ceramics is Jean Soustiel, *La céramique islamique* (Fribourg, Switzerland: Office du livre; Paris: Vilo, 1985); see review by Oleg Grabar in *Muqarnas* 5 (1989): 1–8.

33. For an imaginative study see Veronika Gervers, "An Early Christian Curtain in the Royal Ontario Museum," 56–81; and Lisa Golombek and Veronika Gervers, "Tiraz Fabrics in the Royal Ontario Museum," 82–125, both in *Studies in Textile History*, ed. Veronika Gervers (Toronto: Royal Ontario Museum, 1977).

Early Islam: Emerging Patterns

1. The discussion here is based largely on Michael L. Bates, "History, Geography, and Numismatics in the First Century of Islamic Coinage," *Revue suisse de numismatique* 65 (1986): 231–62.

2. *Encyclopaedia of Islam*, 1st ed., and supplement, s.v. "Ṭirāz"; R. B. Serjeant, "Material for a History of Islamic Textiles up to the Mongol Conquest," *Ars Islamica* 9 (1942): 57–80; 15–16 (1951): 29–40; Maurice Lombard, *Les textiles dans le monde musulmane du VIIᵉ au XIIᵉ siècle*, vol. 3 of *Etudes d'économie médiévale* (Paris: Mouton, 1978), 207–22; and Lisa Golombek and Veronika Gervers, "Tiraz Fabrics in the Royal Ontario Museum," 82–125, in *Studies in Textile History*, ed. Veronika Gervers (Toronto: Royal Ontario Museum, 1977).

3. Serjeant, "Islamic Textiles," 68, supplementary notes; and Florence E. Day, "The Ṭirāz Silk of Marwān," 39–61, in *Archaeologia orientalia in memoriam Ernst Herzfeld*, ed. George Carpenter Miles (Locust Valley, N.Y.: Augustin, 1952).

4. Ibn Khaldun, *The Muqaddimah: An Introduction to History*, trans. Franz Rosenthal (Princeton: Princeton University Press, 1967), 2:66.

5. For this interpretation see Oleg Grabar, "The Umayyad Dome of the Rock in Jerusalem," *Ars Orientalis* 3 (1959): 33–62.

6. On the composition of the work force see Jean Sauvaget, *La mosquée omeyyade de Médine* (Paris: Editions d'art et d'histoire, 1947), 114–16.

7. *The Fihrist of al-Nadīm: A Tenth-Century Survey of Muslim Culture*, ed. and trans. Bayard Dodge (New York: Columbia University Press, 1970), 1:11.

8. For the circumstances under which this labor force was assembled see Jacob Lassner, *The Topography of Baghdad in the Early Middle Ages: Text and Studies* (Detroit: Wayne State University Press, 1970), 231–32 n. 4 and 237 n. 11.

9. Rhuvon Guest, translated from the ninth-century author Yaqubi, in K. A. C. Creswell, *Early Muslim Architecture: Umayyads, 'Abbāsids, and Ṭūlūnids* (1932; New York: Hacker, 1979), 2:228–31.

10. Makers of *arandīb* also came from Kufa; Guest interpreted this term to mean "kinds of paint," which, if correct, suggests that Kufa may have been a center for painting. The word has, however, also been translated as "ointments" (Florence E. Day, "A Review of 'The Ceramic Arts: A History' in *A Survey of Persian Art*," *Ars Islamica* 8 [1941]: 26–28).

11. Serjeant, "Islamic Textiles," 73.

12. Georges Marçais, *Les faïences à reflets métalliques de la grande mosquée de Kairouan* (Paris: Libraire orientaliste Paul Geuthner, 1928), 9–10; and Day, "Review," 28.

13. Serjeant, "Islamic Textiles," 76.

14. *A Survey of Persian Art from Prehistoric Times to the Present*, ed. Arthur Upham Pope and Phyllis Ackerman (London: Oxford University Press, 1938–39), 6: pl. 981.

15. Ricardo Velázquez Bosco, *Medina Azzahra y Alamiriya* (Madrid: Blass, 1912), pls. XLIX–LII.

16. Dorothea Duda, "Die frühe spanisch-islamische Keramik von Almería," *Madrider Mitteilungen* 13 (1972): 348, 377, 409; and Florence E. Day, "The Inscription of the Boston 'Baghdad' Silk: A Note on Method in Epigraphy," *Ars Orientalis* 1 (1954): 191–94.

17. John Beckwith, *Caskets from Cordoba* (London: Victoria and Albert Museum, 1960), 6, 16, 21, 29; Ernst Kühnel, *Die islamischen Elfenbeinskulpturen, VIII.–XIII. Jahrhunderts* (Berlin: Deutscher Verlag für Kunstwissenschaft, 1971), 4–5.

18. Lassner, *Baghdad*, 86–91.

19. Paul Kahle, ''Die Schätze der Fātimiden,'' *Zeitschrift der deutschen Morgenländgesellschaft* 89 (1935): 329–62.

20. *Encyclopaedia of Islam,* 2d ed., s.v. ''Billawr.''

21. Barbara Finster, ''Die Reiseroute Kufa, Sa'ūdī-Arabien in frühislamischer Zeit: Bericht über den Survey vom 9.–14. Mai 1976 auf den westeuphratischen Wüstenstreifen,'' *Baghdader Mitteilungen* 9 (1978): 57–67, 77–78; see also *Encyclopaedia of Islam,* 1st ed., s.v. ''Zubaida.''

22. On the Zirids see, for example, Lucien Golvin, *Le Magrib central à l'époque des Zirides: Recherches d'archéologie et d'histoire* (Paris: Arts et métiers graphiques, [1957]), 179.

23. The term *Habashiyya* literally means ''Abyssinian,'' that is, ''Ethiopian.'' Whether this woman was in fact an Ethiopian or whether her name was simply an approximation of the sound of an originally Greek name cannot be determined. See *Incipient Decline,* vol. 34 of *The History of al-Ṭabarī,* trans. Joel L. Kraemer (Albany: State University of New York Press, 1989), 223; and Creswell, *Early Muslim Architecture* 2:282–85.

24. Oleg Grabar, ''The Earliest Islamic Commemorative Structures: Notes and Documents,'' *Ars Orientalis* 6 (1966): 14–15.

25. Charles K. Wilkinson, *Nishapur: Pottery of the Early Islamic Period* (New York: Metropolitan Museum of Art, 1973), 179–83; Rudolph Schnyder, ''Tulunidische Lüsterfayence,'' *Ars Orientalis* 5 (1963): 49–78; George T. Scanlon, ''Fatimid Underglaze Painted Wares: A Chronological Readjustment,'' 194 n. 1, in *A Way Prepared: Essays on Islamic Culture in Honor of Richard Bayly Winder,* ed. Farhad Kazemi and Robert D. McChesney (New York: New York University Press, 1988).

26. Jonathan M. Bloom, ''The Mosque of al-Ḥakim in Cairo,'' *Muqarnas* 1 (1983): 24.

27. For example, Ibn Durustuyah, *Kitab al-Kuttab,* ed. Louis Cheikho (Beirut: Matbaat al-Aba al-Yusuiyin, 1921); and Franz Rosenthal, ''Abū Ḥaiyān al-Tawḥīdī on Penmanship,'' *Ars Islamica* 13–14 (1948): 1–30.

28. David Storm Rice, *The Unique Ibn al-Bawwāb Manuscript in the Chester Beatty Library* (Dublin: Emery Walker, 1955), 5–10; and idem, *The Unique Ibn al-Bawwāb Manuscript: Complete Facsimile Edition of the Earliest Surviving Naskhī Qur'ān* (Graz: Akademische Druck- und Verlagsanstalt, 1983).

29. The term *Quran,* literally ''recitation,'' originally referred to the Word of God as transmitted and disseminated orally. The text was first written down in codex (*mushaf;* plural, *masahif*) form, and Quran manuscripts thus came to be designated as Masahif.

30. For a more detailed discussion of the issues presented here see Estelle Whelan, ''Writing the Word of God: Some Early Qur'ān Manuscripts and Their Milieux, Part I,'' *Ars Orientalis* 20 (forthcoming).

31. Ralph Pinder-Wilson, ''The Illuminations in the Cairo Moshe-b.-Asher Codex of the Prophets Completed in Tiberias in 895 A.D.,'' 1–21, in *Studies in Islamic Art,* ed. Ralph Pinder-Wilson (London: Pindar Press, 1985); and John Williams, *Early Spanish Manuscript Illumination* (New York: Braziller, 1977), pl. 5.

32. François Déroche, ''Collection de manuscrits anciens du Coran à Istanbul: Rapport préliminaire,'' 158–60, in *Etudes médiévales et patrimoine turc: Volume publié à l'occasion du centième anniversaire de la naissance de Kemal Atatürk,* ed. Oktay Aslanapa (Paris: Centre national de la recherche scientifique, 1983).

33. Wilkinson, *Nishapur,* 90–157; see also Lisa Volov, ''Plaited Kufic on Samanid Epigraphic Pottery,'' *Ars Orientalis* 6 (1966): 107–33.

34. Youssef Eche [Yūsuf 'Ishsh], *Les bibliothèques arabes publiques et semi-publiques en Mésopotamie, en Syrie, et en Egypte au Moyen Age* (Damascus: Institut français de Damas, 1967), 273–74, 279–80; and Paul Kahle, ''Chinese Porcelain in the Lands of Islam,'' 342, in *Opera Minora* (Leiden: Brill, 1956).

The Classical Period

1. For a general introduction to the period see Marshall G. S. Hodgson, *The Expansion of Islam in the Middle Period,* vol. 2 of *Venture of Islam* (Chicago: University of Chicago Press, 1974).

2. Hansjörg Schmidt, *Die Madrasa des Kalifen al-Mustansir in Baghdad* (Mainz: Von Zabern, 1980); and K. A. C. Creswell, *The Muslim Architecture of Egypt* (1952–59; New York: Hacker, 1978), 1:254–57.

3. K. A. C. Creswell, *Early Muslim Architecture: Umayyads, 'Abbāsids, and Ṭūlūnids* (1932; New York: Hacker, 1979), 1:167; and Creswell, *Muslim Architecture of Egypt* 1:161–217.

4. Etienne Combe, Jean Sauvaget, and Gaston Wiet, *Répertoire chronologique d'épigraphie arabe* (Cairo: Institut français d'archéologie orientale, 1931–), nos. 2734–37 and 2762 (hereafter cited as *RCEA*).

5. *RCEA,* no. 2775.

6. For the pen box and brasses of Najm al-Din see Esin Atıl, W. T. Chase, and Paul Jett, *Islamic Metalwork in the Freer Gallery of Art* (Washington, D.C.: Freer Gallery of Art, 1985), 102–10 and 137–47; for those of Badr al-Din Lulu see David Storm Rice, ''The Brasses of Badr al-Dīn Lu'lu','' *Bulletin of the School of Oriental and African Studies* 13, no. 3 (1950): 627–34.

7. *RCEA,* no. 2931.

8. Grace D. Guest and Richard Ettinghausen, ''The Iconography of a Kāshān Luster Plate,'' *Ars Orientalis* 4 (1961): 25–64.

9. Ernst Herzfeld, *Syrie du nord: Inscriptions et monuments d'Alep,* 2d pt. of *Matériaux pour un Corpus inscriptionum Arabicarum* (Cairo: Institut français d'archéologie orientale, 1955), 1:150–64.

10. *RCEA,* no. 2792.

11. *RCEA,* no. 3076.

12. Richard Ettinghausen, ''The Bobrinski 'Kettle': Patron and Style of an Islamic Bronze,'' *Gazette des beaux-arts,* 6th ser., 24 (October 1943): 193–208.

13. *RCEA,* no. 2968.

14. *RCEA,* nos. 3049, 3154, 3224, and 3238.

15. *RCEA,* no. 3775.

16. *RCEA,* nos. 2942 and 2977.

17. *RCEA,* no. 3078.

18. *Encyclopaedia of Islam,* 2d ed., s.v. ''Marrākush.''

19. Creswell, *Muslim Architecture of Egypt* 1:161–217 and 2:1–63.

20. Oleg Grabar, ''The Architecture of Power: Palaces, Citadels, and Fortifications,'' 48–79, in *Architecture of the Islamic World: Its History and Social Meaning, with a Complete Survey of Key Monuments,* ed. George Michell (New York: Thames & Hudson, 1978).

21. For these buildings see Aptullah Kuran, ''Anatolian-Seljuk Architecture,'' 83–35, in *The Art and Architecture of Turkey,* ed. Ekrem Akurgal (New York: Rizzoli, 1980).

22. This mosque and its splendid minbar were destroyed in 1982.

23. *Isfahān: Masğid-i Ğum'a,* ed. Eugenio Galdieri (Rome: Istituto per il medio et estremo oriente, 1972–73), vol. 2. The date has recently been established by Sheila S. Blair, *A Corpus of Arabic Inscriptions from the Eastern Islamic World* (Leiden, forthcoming).

24. *RCEA,* nos. 3234 and 3238.

25. Henri Terrasse, *La Mosquée al-Qaraouiyin à Fès* (Paris: Klincksieck, 1968), 17–21.

26. Jonathan M. Bloom, *Minaret: Symbol of Islam* (Oxford: Oxford University Press, 1989).

27. Janine Sourdel-Thomine, "Deux minarets d'époque seljoukide en Afghanistan," *Syria* 30 (1953): 108–36.

28. Chahryar Adle and Assadullah Souren Melikian-Chirvani, "Les monuments du XIe siècle du Damqan," *Studia Iranica* 1 (1972): 229–97.

29. *Encyclopaedia of Islam,* 2d ed., s.v. "Madrasa [III. Architecture]."

30. David Stronach and T. Cuyler Young, Jr., "Three Octagonal Tomb Towers from Iran," *Iran* 4 (1960): 1–20.

31. Richard Ettinghausen and Oleg Grabar, *The Art and Architecture of Islam, 650–1250* (Harmondsworth: Penquin, 1987), 270–71.

32. Kurt Erdmann and Hanna Erdmann, *Das anatolische Karavansaray des 13. Jahrhunderts* (Berlin: Verlag Gebr. Mann, 1961–76).

33. Alessio Bombaci, *The Kūfic Inscription in Persian Verses in the Court of the Royal Palace of Mas'ud III at Ghazni* (Rome: Istituto italiano per il medio et estremo oriente, 1966); and Daniel Schlumberger, Janine Sourdel-Thomine, and Jean-Claude Gardin, *Lashkari Bazar: Une résidence royale ghaznévide et ghoride* (Paris: Klincksieck, 1963–78).

34. André Godard, "Khorasan," *Athar-é Iran* 4 (1949): 7–68.

35. Turkish Ministry of Culture and Tourism, *The Anatolian Civilisations. III: Seljuk/Ottoman* (İstanbul: Topkapı Palace Museum, 1983), 21–45.

36. S. M. Stern, "A Manuscript from the Library of the Ghaznawid Amīr 'Abd al-Rashid," 7–31, in *Paintings from Islamic Lands,* ed. Ralph Pinder-Wilson (Oxford: Cassirer, 1969).

37. Kurt Holter, "Die Galen-Handschrift und die Makamen des Hariri der wiener Nationalbibliothek," *Jahrbuch der kunsthistorischen Sammlungen in Wien,* n.s. 11 (1937): 1–48.

38. S. M. Stern, "A New Volume of the Illustrated Aghānī Manuscript," *Ars Orientalis* 2 (1957): 501–3.

39. Richard Ettinghausen, *Arab Painting* (Geneva: Skira, 1962), 87ff.

40. Oleg Grabar, *The Illustrations of the Maqamat* (Chicago: University of Chicago Press, 1984).

41. *Kalila and Dimna:* Paris, Bibliothèque Nationale, MS Arabe 3465; *Maqamat:* Paris, Bibliothèque Nationale, MS Arabe 5847.

42. East Berlin, Islamisches Museum; and Arthur Lane, *Early Islamic Pottery: Mesopotamia, Egypt, and Persia* (London: Faber & Faber, 1947), pl. 66.

43. Oliver Watson, *Persian Lustre Ware* (London: Faber & Faber, 1985), 189; and Madrassi Tabataba'i, *Turbat-i Pākān* (The pure tombs) (Qum, 1976), 1: pl. 9.

44. Guest and Ettinghausen, "Iconography of a Kashan Luster Plate."

45. Turkish Ministry of Culture and Tourism, *Anatolian Civilisations,* 26–34.

46. Ettinghausen, "Bobrinski Kettle."

47. Ettinghausen and Grabar, *Art and Architecture of Islam,* 340; and Atıl, Chase, and Jett, *Islamic Metalwork,* 102–10.

48. Assadullah Souren Melikian-Chirvani, "Silver in Islamic Iran: The Evidence from Literature and Epigraphy," 89–106, in *Pots and Pans: A Colloquium on Precious Metals and Ceramics in the Muslim, Chinese, and Graeco-Roman World,* ed. Michael Vickers (Oxford: Oxford University Press, 1986).

49. Ettinghausen and Grabar, *Art and Architecture of Islam,* 334–36.

50. Ibid., 367–70.

51. Richard W. Bulliet, *Conversion to Islam in the Medieval Period: An Essay in Quantitative History* (Cambridge, Mass.: Harvard University Press, 1979).

52. Oleg Grabar, "Imperial and Urban Art in Islam: The Subject-Matter of Fatimid Art," 173–90, in *Colloque internationale sur l'histoire du Caire* (Cairo: Ministry of Culture of the Arab Republic of Egypt, 1972).

The Postclassical Period

1. A convenient introduction to the history of the period is Marshall G. S. Hodgson, *The Expansion of Islam in the Middle Periods,* vol. 2 of *Venture of Islam* (Chicago: University of Chicago Press, 1974), 2:369–574.

2. The basic reference for architecture from fifteenth-century Iran and central Asia, containing a complete bibliography of primary and secondary sources, is Lisa Golombek and Donald N. Wilber, *The Timurid Architecture of Iran and Turan* (Princeton: Princeton University Press, 1988).

3. The basic work for Egyptian architecture of the period is K. A. C. Creswell, *The Muslim Architecture of Egypt* (1952–59; New York: Hacker, 1978), vol. 2.

4. Shihāb al-Dīn 'Abd Allāh ibn Faḍl Allāh al-Shīrāzī, *Taḥrīr-i Tārīkh-i Wassāf* (Edition of the history of Wassaf), ed. Abd al-Muhammad Ayatī (Tehran: Intishārāt-i Bunyād-i Farhang-i Irān, 1968).

5. References to all these sources can be found in Golombek and Wilber, *Timurid Architecture;* one of the most readable is Ruy Gonzáles de Clavijo, *Embassy to Tamerlane, 1403–1406,* trans. Guy Le Strange (London: Routledge; New York: Harper, 1928).

6. George Makdisi, *The Rise of Colleges: Institutions of Learning in Islam and the East* (Edinburgh: Edinburgh University Press, 1981), 37–38.

7. Thomas W. Lentz and Glenn D. Lowry, *Timur and the Princely Vision: Persian Art and Culture in the Fifteenth Century* (Los Angeles: Los Angeles County Museum of Art, 1989), supplies information on the arts from the Timurid period.

8. Sheila S. Blair, "Ilkhanid Architecture and Society: An Analysis of the Endowment Deed of the Rab'-i Rashidi," *Iran* 22 (1984): 67–90.

9. In addition to Golombek and Wilber, *Timurid Architecture,* 62–63, see Bernard O'Kane, *Timurid Architecture in Khurasan* (Costa Mesa, Calif.: Mazda in association with Undena, 1987), 85–87.

10. Donald N. Wilber, *The Architecture of Islamic Iran: The Il Khānid Period* (Princeton: Princeton University Press, 1955), no. 39; and Sheila S. Blair, *The Ilkhanid Shrine Complex at Natanz, Iran* (Cambridge, Mass.: Center for Middle Eastern Studies, Harvard University, 1986).

11. David Storm Rice, *Le Baptistère de Saint Louis: A Masterpiece of Islamic Metalwork* (Paris: Editions du chêne, 1953).

12. For Mamluk objects see Esin Atıl, *Renaissance of Islam: Art of the Mamluks* (Washington, D.C.: Smithsonian Institution Press, 1981).

13. *Maqamat:* London, British Library, Add. 7293; Oleg Grabar, *The Illustrations of the Maqamat* (Chicago: University of Chicago Press, 1984), 14–15, and no. 9.

14. Bowl: Christian Décorbert and Roland-Pierre Gayraud, "Une céramique d'époque mamelouke trouvée à Tōd," *Annales islamoloqiques* 18 (1982): 95–104.

15. Creswell, *Muslim Architecture of Egypt* 2:135–6.

16. West Berlin, Staatsbibliothek, Orientabteilung, Tubinger Dept., Diez album, fol. 70.S.22; and *Saray-Alben: Diez'sche Klebebände aus den berliner Sammlungen,* ed. Mazhar S. İpşiroğlu, vol. 8 of *Verzeichnis der orientalischen Handschriften in Deutschland,* ed. Wolfgang Voight (Wiesbaden: Franz Steiner Verlag, 1964), pl. VII, fig. 11.

17. Oleg Grabar and Sheila Blair, *Epic Images and Contemporary History: The Illustrations of the Great Mongol Shahnama* (Chicago: University of Chicago Press, 1980).

18. Washington, D.C., Arthur M. Sackler Gallery, S86.0106.

19. Golombek and Wilber, *Timurid Architecture,* 62 and nos. 11–24.

20. Ibid., 62, and nos. 69–70 and 90; and O'Kane, *Timurid Architecture in Khurasan,* 83–84 and nos. 2–3 and 13.

21. Sheila S. Blair, "The Mongol Capital of Sultaniyya, 'The Imperial,' " *Iran* 24 (1986): 139–51.

22. Anthony Welch and Howard Crane, "The Tughluqs: Master Builders of the Delhi Sultanate," *Muqarnas* 1 (1983): 123–66.

23. Golombek and Wilber, *Timurid Architecture,* no. 36; and O'Kane, *Timurid Architecture in Khurasan,* 103–4.

24. Leonid S. Bretanitsky, "The Shirvanshah Palace in Baku, Azerbaijan," *Archaeology* 26 (1973): 162–69.

25. Oleg Grabar, *The Alhambra* (Cambridge, Mass.: Harvard University Press, 1978).

26. Wilber, *Architecture of Islamic Iran,* no. 47; and Blair, "Mongol Capital of Sultaniyya."

27. See note 20 above.

28. Creswell, *Muslim Architecture of Egypt* 2:190–212; and John D. Hoag, *Islamic Architecture* (New York: Abrams, 1977), 162–77.

29. Godfrey Goodwin, *A History of Ottoman Architecture* (Baltimore: Johns Hopkins University Press, 1971), 46–51.

30. Renata Holod-Tretiak, "The Monuments of Yazd, 1300–1450: Patronage and Setting" (Ph.D. diss., Harvard University, 1972).

31. Creswell, *Muslim Architecture of Egypt* 2:242–48.

32. Sheila S. Blair, "Sufi Saints and Shrine Architecture in the Early Fourteenth Century," *Muqarnas* 7 (forthcoming).

33. Golombek and Wilber, *Timurid Architecture,* no. 53.

34. Lisa Golombek, *The Timurid Shrine at Gazur Gah* (Toronto: Royal Ontario Museum, 1969).

35. K. A. C. Creswell, "A Brief Chronology of the Muhammadan Monuments of Egypt to A.D. 1517," *Bulletin de l'Institut français d'archéologie orientale* 16 (1919): 120–21; Rachid Bourouiba, *L'art religieux musulman en Algerie* (Algiers: SNED, 1973), 1590–89; and Wilber, *Architecture of Islamic Iran,* no. 64.

36. Goodwin, *History of Ottoman Architecture,* 46–51, 96–101.

37. Hoag, *Islamic Architecture,* 119–22.

38. Golombek and Wilber, *Timurid Architecture,* no. 30.

39. Ibid., no. 31.

40. Cairo, National Library, 72; David James, *Qur'āns of the Mamlūks,* (New York: Thames & Hudson, 1989), no. 45; Eleanor Sims, "The Internal Decoration of the Mausoleum of Oljeitü Khudābanda: A Preliminary Re-examination," *Quaderni del Seminario di iranistica, uralo-altaistica, e caucasologia dell'Università degli studi di Venezia* 9 (1982): 89–123; and idem, "The 'Iconography' of the Internal Decoration in the Mausoleum of Uljāytā at Sultaniyya," 193–218, in *Content and Context of Visual Arts in the Islamic World: Papers from a Colloquium in Memory of Richard Ettinghausen,* ed. Priscilla P. Soucek (University Park: Pennsylvania State University Press, 1988).

41. Esin Atıl, *The Age of Sultan Süleyman the Magnificent* (Washington, D.C.: National Gallery of Art; New York: Abrams, 1987), 29–33.

42. Atıl, *Renaissance of Islam,* no. 52.

43. Elisabeth Naumann and Rudolf Naumann, "Ein Kösk im Sommerpalast des Abaqa Chan auf dem Tacht-i Sulaiman und seine Dekoration," 35–65, in *Forschungen zur Kunst asiens: In memoriam Kurt Erdmann* (İstanbul: İstanbul Üniversitesi, 1969); Assadullah Souren Melikian-Chirvani, "Le *Shāh-nāme:* La gnose soufie et le pouvoir mongol," *Journal asiatique* 222 (1984): 249–338; and Blair, *Ilkhanid Shrine Complex at Natanz, Iran,* chap. 3.

44. Assadullah Souren Melikian-Chirvani, *Islamic Metalwork from the Iranian World, Eighth–Eighteenth Centuries* (London: Victoria and Albert Museum, 1982), chap. 3.

45. İstanbul, Topkapı Palace Museum, MS Hazine 841; and Assadullah Souren Melikian-Chirvani, "Le Roman de Varqe et Golšah," *Arts asiatiques* 22 (1970).

46. Edinburgh, University Library, MS Arab 20; Geneva, Rashidiyya Foundation, ex-Royal Asiatic Society; İstanbul, Topkapı Palace Museum, MS Hazine 1653 and 1654; Richard Ettinghausen, "An Illuminated Manuscript of Hāfiz-i Abrū in Istanbul," *Kunst des Orients* 2 (1955): 30–44; Güner Inal, "Some Miniatures of the *Jāmi' al-Tavārīkh* in Istanbul, Topkapi Museum, Hazine Library No. 1654," *Ars Orientalis* 5 (1963): 165–75; idem, "Artistic Relationship between the Far and Near East as Reflected in the Miniatures of the *Ğāmi' at-Tawārīḫ,*" *Kunst des Orients* 10 (1975): 108–43; David Talbot Rice, *The Illustrations to the 'World History' of Rashīd al-Dīn,* ed. Basil Gray (Edinburgh: Edinburgh University Press, 1976); and Basil Gray, *The World History of Rashid al-Din: A Study of the Royal Asiatic Society Manuscript* (London: Faber & Faber, 1978).

47. Baltimore, Johns Hopkins University, Milton S. Eisenhower Library, John Work Garrett Collection, 1467–68; Eleanor Sims, "The Garrett Manuscript of the *Zafer-name:* A Study in Fifteenth-Century Timurid Patronage" (Ph.D. diss., Institute of Fine Arts, New York University, 1973); and Lentz and Lowry, *Timur,* no. 147.

48. See note 17 above.

49. Geneva, Musée d'art et d'historie, 1971-107/1A.

50. Tehran, Gulistan Library, no. 61; and Basil Gray, *An Album of Miniatures and Illuminations from the Baysonghori Manuscript of the Shahnameh of Ferdowsi . . . Preserved in the Imperial Library, Tehran* (Tehran, 1971).

51. Blair, "Ilkhanid Architecture and Society."

52. İstanbul, Topkapı Palace Museum, MS Hazine 2153, fol. 98a; translated in Lentz and Lowry, *Timur,* app. 1.

53. Cairo, National Library, Adab Farsi 908; Lentz and Lowry, *Timur,* no. 146.

54. Maria Eva Subtelny, "Socioeconomic Bases of Cultural Patronage under the Later Timurids," *International Journal of Middle East Studies* 20, no. 4 (1988): 479–505. Under the Hanafi system of law in practice at the time conditions were favorable for the endowment of immovable and movable property and for family endowments.

55. Glenn D. Lowry and Milo C. Beach, *An Annotated and Illustrated Checklist of the Vever Collection* (Washington, D.C.: Arthur M. Sackler Gallery, 1988), nos. 74–85; on the school of Shiraz see Basil Gray, *Persian Painting* (Geneva: Skira, 1961), 57–64.

56. İstanbul, Turkish and Islamic Arts Museum, MS 1978, İstanbul, University Library, Yildiz 7954/310, and dispersed; and Lowry and Beach, *Vever Collection,* nos. 104–10.

57. Marianna Shreve Simpson, *The Illustration of an Epic: The Earliest Shahnama Manuscripts* (New York: Garland, 1979).

58. Basil W. Robinson, "The Turkman School to 1503," 243–44, in *The Arts of the Book in Central Asia: Fourteenth–Sixteenth Centuries,* ed. Basil Gray (Boulder, Colo.: Shambala, 1979); Grace D. Guest, *Shiraz Painting in the Sixteenth Century* (Washington, D.C.: Freer Gallery of Art, 1949).

Late Islam: The Age of Empires

1. On the formation of the royal library see Thomas W. Lentz and Glenn D. Lowry, *Timur and the Princely Vision: Persian Art and Culture in the Fifteenth Century* (Los Angeles: Los Angeles County Museum of Art, 1989), especially chap. 3. For a general description of the workings of the royal library in the making of a major book see Stuart Cary Welch, *A King's Book of Kings: The Shah-Nameh of Shah Tahmasp* (New York: Metropolitan Museum of Art, 1972).

2. On Islamic bookbinding of the period see Emil Gratzl, "Book Covers," 5:1975–94, in *A Survey of Persian Art from Prehistoric Times to the Present,* ed. Arthur Upham Pope and Phyllis Ackerman (1938–39; London: Oxford University Press, 1965); Jeremiah P. Losty, *The Art of the Book in India* (London: British Library, 1982); and Kemal Çığ, *Türk Kitap Kapları* (Turkish book covers) (İstanbul: Yapı ve Kredi Bankası, 1971). Among the many useful introductions to Islamic calligraphy see Yasin Hamid Safadi, *Islamic Calligraphy* (Boulder, Colo.: Shambhala, 1979); Annemarie Schimmel, *Calligraphy and Islamic Culture* (New York: New York University Press, 1984); and Anthony Welch, *Calligraphy in the Arts of the Muslim World* (New York: Asia Society; Austin: University of Texas Press, 1979).

3. Among the many excellent works on Safavid painting see the Stuart Cary Welch volume mentioned in note 1 above; and the same author's exhibition catalogue *Wonders of the Age: Masterpieces of Early Safavid Painting, 1501–1576* (Cambridge, Mass.: Fogg Art Museum, 1979); also the earlier catalogue by Basil W. Robinson, *Persian Miniature Painting from Collections in the British Isles* (London: Victoria and Albert Museum, 1967).

4. See Nurhan Atasoy and Filiz Çağman, *Turkish Miniature Painting* (İstanbul: R. C. C. Cultural Institute, 1980); Esin Atıl, "The Art of the Book," 137–238, in *Turkish Art,* ed. Esin Atıl (Washington, D.C.: Smithsonian Institution Press; New York: Abrams, 1980).

5. On Mughal painting see Milo Cleveland Beach, *The Grand Mogul: Imperial Painting in India, 1600–1660* (Williamstown, Mass.: Sterling and Francine Clark Art Institute, 1978); and Stuart Cary Welch, *Imperial Mughal Painting* (New York: Braziller, 1978).

6. On Süleyman see Esin Atıl, *The Age of Sultan Süleyman the Magnificent* (Washington, D.C.: National Gallery of Art; New York: Abrams, 1987).

7. On later Safavid patronage after Shah Tahmasp see Anthony Welch, *Artists for the Shah: Late Sixteenth-Century Painting at the Imperial Court of Iran* (New Haven: Yale University Press, 1976); and on that of Shah Abbas, the same author's *Shah 'Abbas and the Arts of Isfahan* (New York: Asia Society, 1973).

8. On Mughal patronage see the catalogue for the exhibition held at the Victoria and Albert Museum, *The Indian Heritage: Court Life and Arts under Mughal Rule* (London: Victoria and Albert Museum, 1982). On some of the problems inherent in Islamic royal patronage see Walter B. Denny, "Contradiction and Consistency in Islamic Art," 137–73, in *The Islamic Impact,* ed. Yvonne Yazabeck Haddad, Byron Haines, and Ellison Findly (Syracuse: Syracuse University Press, 1984).

9. The formation of an Islamic artistic vocabulary is discussed in Oleg Grabar, *The Formation of Islamic Art* (1973; New Haven: Yale University Press, 1987); among many general works on Islamic patterns and the arabesque, an introduction is Ernst Kühnel, *The Arabesque,* trans. Richard Ettinghausen (Graz: Verlag für Sammler, 1976).

10. On İznik ceramics see Walter B. Denny, "Ceramics," 239–97, in Atıl, *Turkish Art.*

11. On Islamic prayer rugs see *Prayer Rugs* (Washington, D.C.: Textile Museum, 1974); and Walter B. Denny, "Saff and Sejjadeh," in *Oriental Carpet and Textile Studies* (London, forthcoming).

12. Arthur J. Arberry, *The Koran Interpreted* (New York: Macmillan, 1955), 50–51.

13. Denny, "Contradiction and Consistency."

14. See John Carswell, *Blue and White: Chinese Porcelain and Its Impact on the Western World* (Chicago: David and Alfred Smart Gallery, University of Chicago, 1985).

15. See Schroeder quoted in Basil W. Robinson, "Preliminary Symposium," 13–18, in Robinson, *Persian Miniature Painting.*

16. See Donald King and David Sylvester, *The Eastern Carpet in the Western World from the Fifteenth to the Seventeenth Century* (London: Arts Council of Great Britain, 1983); and *Carpets of the Mediterranean Countries, 1400–1600,* vol. 2 of *Oriental Carpet and Textile Studies,* ed. Robert Pinner and Walter B. Denny (London: Hali, 1986).

17. An important contribution to the scholarship of Islamic painting, using a full range of visual and documentary data, is the two-volume study by Martin Dickson and Stuart Cary Welch, *The Houghton Shanameh* (Cambridge, Mass.: Fogg Art Museum, 1981). The manuscript is the major monument of Safavid painting, created in the early sixteenth century for Shah Tahmasp I at Tabriz; the eponymous Mr. Houghton, by contrast, presided over the breaking up of the manuscript and the sale and dispersal of its paintings.

18. For numerous examples of multiple-signature works see Beach, *Grand Mogul,* for example.

Dynastic Tables

By Geographic Location

Spain and North Africa
  Umayyads of Spain   756–1031
  Aghlabids (Tunisia, Algeria, Sicily)   800–909
  Muluk al-Tawaif (Spain)   ca. 1010–ca.1090
  Almoravids (North Africa and Spain)   1056–1147
  Almohads (North Africa and Spain)   1130–1269
  Marinids (Morocco)   1196–1465
  Nasrids (Granada)   1230–1492

Egypt, Syria, Iraq
  Tulunids (Egypt and Syria)   868–905
  Fatimids (North Africa, then Egypt and Syria) 909–1171
  Seljuks of Syria   1078–1117
  Zangids (Syria and northern Iraq)   1127–1222
  Ayyubids (Egypt, Syria, southeastern Turkey,
    Yemen)   1169–1260
  Mamluks (Egypt, Syria, the Hijaz)   1250–1517

Turkey
  Seljuks of Rum, or Anatolia   1077–1307
  Artuqids (southeastern Turkey)   1102–1408
  Ottomans (Turkey, eastern Europe, Arab lands,
    North Africa)   1281–1924

Iran, Caucasus, Transoxiana
  Khwarazmshahs (eastern Iran and Transoxiana) ca. 305–1231
  Samanids (eastern Iran and Transoxiana)   819–1005
  Ziyarids (northern Iran)   926–ca. 1090
  Buyids (Iran and Iraq)   932–1062
  Seljuks (Iran and Iraq)   1038–1194
  Ilkhanids (Iran)   1256–1353
  Muzaffarids (southern Iran)   1314–1393
  Jalayirids (western Iran and Iraq)   1336–1432
  Timurids (Iran and Transoxiana)   1370–1506
  Aq Qoyunlus (eastern Turkey and western Iran) 1378–1508
  Qara Qoyunlus (western Iran and Iraq) 1380–1468
  Uzbeks or Shaybanids (Transoxiana)   1500–1598
  Safavids (Iran)   1501–1732

Afganistan and India
  Ghaznavids (eastern Iran, Afganistan,
    northern India)   977–1186
  Ghurids (eastern Iran, Afganistan, northern India) ca. 1000–1215
  Tughluqids (Delhi)   1320–1414
  Mughals (India)   1526–1858

In Alphabetical Sequence

Abbasids of Baghdad   750–1258
Abbasids of Cairo   1261–1517
Aghlabids (Tunisia, Algeria, Sicily)   800–909
Almohads (North Africa and Spain)   1130–1269
Aq Qoyunlus (eastern Turkey and western Iran) 1378–1508
Artuqids (southeastern Turkey)   1102–1408
Ayyubids (Egypt, Syria, southeastern Turkey,
    Yemen)   1169–1260
Buyids (Iran and Iraq)   932–1062
Fatimids (North Africa, then Egypt and Syria 909–1171
Ghaznavids (eastern Iran, Afganistan,
    northern India)   977–1186
Ghurids (eastern Iran, Afganistan, northern India) ca. 1000–1215
Ilkhanids (Iran)   1256–1353
Jalayirids (western Iran and Iraq)   1336–1432
Khwarazmshahs (eastern Iran and Transoxiana) ca. 305–1231
Mamluks (Egypt, Syria, the Hijaz)   1250–1517
Marinids (Morocco)   1196–1465
Mughals (India)   1526–1858
Muluk al-Tawaif (Spain)   ca. 1010–ca.1090
Muzaffarids (southern Iran)   1314–1393
Nasrids (Granada)   1230–1492
Ottomans (Turkey, eastern Europe, Arab lands,
    North Africa)   1281–1924
Qara Qoyunlus (western Iran and Iraq) 1380–1468
Safavids (Iran)   1501–1732
Samanids (eastern Iran and Transoxiana)   819–1005
Seljuks (Iran and Iraq)   1038–1194
Seljuks of Rum, or Anatolia   1077–1307
Seljuks of Syria   1078–1117
Timurids (Iran and Transoxiana)   1370–1506
Tughluqids (Delhi)   1320–1414
Tulunids (Egypt and Syria)   868–905
Umayyads   661–750
Umayyads of Spain   756–1031
Uzbeks or Shaybanids (Transoxiana)   1500–1598
Zangids (Syria and northern Iraq)   1127–1222
Ziyarids (northern Iran)   926–ca. 1090

Concordance

Each accession number is preceded by the initials LNS. Following the accession number is a letter indicating the media of the object, for instance, in the accession number LNS 7 C, the letter *C* signifies ceramic.

Accession Number		Catalogue Number
C [ceramic]	7	60
	24	33
	55	54
	56	54
	58	54
	90	9
	98	8
	99	85
	101	87
	110	6
	119	10
	128	5
	130	88
	160	11
	167	30
	173	57
	187	59
	190	61
	207	28
	210	32
	218	58
	231	82
	278	7
	279	27
	295	31
	306	34
	316	56
	321	89
	325	84
	327	83
	350	29
	363	55
	369	86
CA [calligraphy]	2 (a)	3
G [glass]	8	36
	10	90
	34	62
	48	63

	63	13
	69	64
	85	12
	88	15
	113	37
	124	35
	127	14
HS [hardstone]	3	21
	7	102
	8	101
	12	100
	43	20
I [ivory]	7	70
	12	45
	19	22
J [jewelry]	7 (a–b)	43
	16	97
	21	69
	25	99
	28	98
	30 (a–b)	44
	55	16
	120	96
L [leather]	10	72
	17	73
M [metalwork]	3	38
	17	40
	36	19
	52	92
	56	93
	81	39
	85	17
	100	95
	102	41
	104	42

	110	66
	111	67
	116	65
	121	91
	132	18
	141	94
	145	68
MS [manuscript]	4 (a, f)	74
	6 (fols. 2b–3a)	24
	16 (c)	75
	17 (m)	49
	28 (f)	53
	33	52
	44 (fols. 2b–3a)	48
	57	79
	59	51
	63 (b)	25
	65 (a, g)	4
	66 (fol. 14b)	77
	67 (fol. 68b)	26
	74 (a–b)	47
	75 (fol. 82a)	78
	101 (b)	2
	104	50
	105	80
	106	81
	203	1
	205	76
R [rug]	7	105
	17	107
	29	106
S [stone]	2	23
	70 (d)	103
T [textile]	115 (a)	104
W [woodwork]	35	71
	55	46

Suggested Readings

Publications of Dar al-Athar al-Islamiyyah

Jenkins, Marilyn, ed. *Islamic Art in the Kuwait National Museum: The al-Sabah Collection*. London: Sotheby, 1983.

Keene, Manuel. *Selected Recent Acquisitions, 1404 A.H. (A.D. 1984): Dar al-Athar al-Islamiyyah, Kuwait National Museum*. Kuwait, 1984.

Qaddumi, Ghada Hijjawi. *Variety in Unity: A Special Exhibition on the Occasion of the Fifth Islamic Summit in Kuwait*. Kuwait, 1987.

Science in Islam. Kuwait, 1984.

General

Allan, J. W. "The Survival of Precious and Base Metal Objects from the Medieval Islamic World," 57–70. In *Pots and Pans*. See Vickers.

Atıl, Esin. *Ceramics from the World of Islam*. Washington, D.C.: Freer Gallery of Art, 1973.

_____. *Renaissance of Islam: Art of the Mamluks*. Washington, D.C.: The Smithsonian Institution Press; 1981.

_____. *The Age of Sultan Süleyman the Magnificent*. Washington, D.C.: National Gallery of Art; New York: Abrams, 1987.

_____, ed. *Turkish Art*. Washington, D.C.: Smithsonian Institution Press; New York: Abrams, 1980.

Atıl, Esin, W. T. Chase, and Paul Jett, *Islamic Metalwork in the Freer Gallery of Art*. Washington, D.C.: Freer Gallery of Art, 1985.

Beach, Milo Cleveland. *The Grand Mogul: Imperial Painting in India, 1600–1660*. Williamstown, Mass.: Sterling and Francine Clark Art Institute, 1978.

Blair, Sheila S. *The Ilkhanid Shrine Complex at Natanz, Iran*. Cambridge, Mass.: Center for Middle Eastern Studies, Harvard Uniersity, 1986.

Bloom, Jonathan M. *Minaret: Symbol of Islam*. Oxford: Oxford University Press, 1989.

Creswell, K. A. C. *The Muslim Architecture of Egypt*. 2 vols. 1952–59. Reprint. New York: Hacker, 1978.

_____. *Early Muslim Architecture: Umayyads, 'Abbāsids, and Tūlūnids*. 2 vols. Oxford: Clarendon, 1932. 2d ed. of volume 1 only. Oxford: Clarendon, 1968. Reprint. New York: Hacker, 1979.

_____. *A Short Account of Early Muslim Architecture*. 1958. Rev. ed. and suppl. by James W. Allan. Aldershot: Scolar, 1989.

Dickson, Martin, and Stuart Cary Welch. *The Houghton Shahnameh*. Cambridge, Mass.: Fogg Art Museum, 1981.

The Encyclopaedia of Islam. 1908–38. 2d ed. Leiden: Brill, 1954–.

Ettinghausen, Richard. "The Bobrinski 'Kettle': Patron and Style of an Islamic Bronze." *Gazette des beaux-arts*, 6th ser., 24 (October 1943): 193–208.

_____. *Arab Painting*. Geneva: Skira, 1962.

Ettinghausen, Richard, and Oleg Grabar. *The Art and Architecture of Islam, 650–1250*. Harmondsworth: Penguin, 1987.

Golombek, Lisa. *The Timurid Shrine at Gazur Gah*. Toronto: Royal Ontario Museum, 1969.

Golombek, Lisa, and Donald N. Wilber. *The Timurid Architecture of Iran and Turan*. Princeton: Princeton University Press, 1988.

Grabar, Oleg. "The Visual Arts, 1050–1350," 5:636–58. In *The Saljuk and Mongol Periods*. Vol. 5 of *The Cambridge History of Iran*. Cambridge: University Press, 1968–70.

_____. "Imperial and Urban Art in Islam: The Subject-Matter of Fatimid Art," 173–90. In *Colloque internationale sur l'histoire du Caire*. Cairo: Ministry of Culture of the Arab Republic of Egypt, 1972.

_____. *The Alhambra*. Cambridge, Mass.: Harvard University Press, 1978.

_____. *The Illustrations of the Maqamat*. Chicago: University of Chicago Press, 1984.

_____. *The Formation of Islamic Art*. 1973. Rev. ed. New Haven: Yale University Press, 1987.

Grabar, Oleg, and Sheila Blair. *Epic Images and Contemporary History: The Illustrations of the Great Mongol Shahnama*. Chicago: University of Chicago Press, 1980.

Guest, Grace D., and Richard Ettinghausen. " The Iconography of a Kāshān Luster Plate." *Ars Orientalis* 4 (1961): 25–64.

Herzfeld, Ernst. *Die Malereien von Samarra*. Berlin: Reimer, 1927.

Hoag, John D. *Islamic Architecture*. New York: Abrams, 1977.

Hodgson, Marshall G. S. *The Expansion of Islam in the Middle Periods*. Vol. 2 of *Venture of Islam*. Chicago: University of Chicago Press, 1974.

James, David. *Qur'āns of the Mamlūks*. New York: Thames & Hudson, 1989.

Lentz, Thomas W., and Glenn D. Lowry. *Timur and the Princely Vision: Persian Art and Culture in the Fifteenth Century*. Los Angeles: Los Angeles County Museum of Art, 1989.

Melikian-Chirvani, Assadullah Souren. *Islamic Metalwork from the Iranian World, Eighth–Eighteenth Centuries*. London: Victoria and Albert Museum, 1982.

_____. "Silver in Islamic Iran: The Evidence from Literature and Epigraphy," 89–106. In *Pots and Pans*. See Vickers.

Rice, David Storm. *Le Baptistère de Saint Louis: A Masterpiece of Islamic Metalwork*. Paris: Editions du chêne, 1953.

Schimmel, Annemarie. *Calligraphy and Islamic Culture*. New York: New York University Press, 1984.

Simpson, Marianna Shreve. *The Illustration of an Epic: The Earliest Shahnama Manuscripts*. New York: Garland, 1979.

Talbot David, Rice. *The Illustrations to the 'World History' of Rashīd al-Dīn*. Edited by Basil Gray. Edinburgh University Press, 1976.

Terrasse, Henri. *La Mosquée al-Qaraouiyin à Fès*. Paris: Klincksieck, 1968.

Vickers, Michael, ed. *Pots and Pans: A Colloquium on Precious Metals and Ceramics in the Muslim, Chinese, and Graeco-Roman World*. Oxford: Oxford University Press, 1986.

Watson, Oliver. *Persian Lustre Ware*. London: Faber & Faber, 1985.

Welch, Anthony. *Shah 'Abbas and the Arts of Isfahan*. New York: Asia Society, 1973.

_____. *Artists for the Shah: Late Sixteenth-Century Painting at the Imperial Court of Iran*. New Haven: Yale University Press, 1976.

Welch, Stuart Cary. *A King's Book of Kings: The Shah-Nameh of Shah Tahmasp*. New York: Metropolitan Museum of Art, 1972.

_____. *Wonders of the Age: Masterpieces of Early Safavid Painting, 1501–1576*. Cambridge, Mass.: Fogg Art Museum, 1979.

Wilber, Donald N. *The Architecture of Islamic Iran: The Il Khānid Period*. Princeton: Princeton University Press, 1955.

Appendix

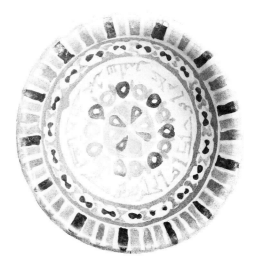

CERAMIC BOWL WITH POLYCHROME LUSTER PAINTING

Iraq, 9th century
Diameter 23.5 cm (9 1/4 in.), height 6.5 cm (2 1/2 in.)
LNS 6 C

Among the most characteristic and important types of early Islamic ceramics are those decorated overglaze with metallic pigments, the technique being known as luster painting. Although a strong metallic sheen was commonly achieved in the ninth century wares, this piece belongs to a group characterized by a much softer effect. Its extensive inscription is worthy of quoting in full: "The work of Sulayman, disciple of Abu Khallikan. Forbearance is a virtue. Blessing to its owner."

CERAMIC JAR WITH INCISED DECORATION

Iran, 12th century
Height 28.5 cm (11 3/4 in.), diameter 18 cm (7 1/16 in.)
LNS 71 C

Storage jars of this type and other vessels in twelfth century Iran were commonly produced with incised decoration under monochrome glazes. Glazes were turquoise, cobalt or, more rarely, aubergine colored manganese glaze as with this example.

The incised decoration of wide vertical bands may have been derived from the shafts of a Kufic inscription which, as here, frequently appear against a scrolling foliate ground.

LUSTER PAINTED CERAMIC JAR

Spain, perhaps Granada, 15th century
Height 30.5 cm (12 in.), diameter 13.5 cm (5 1/4 in.)
LNS 91 C

The technique of painting in luster on ceramic glazes first flowered in the ninth century in the Abbasid heartlands, whence it spread to Egypt, Syria, Iran and finally Spain. The application of luster to colored (especially blue) glazes was also on occasion practiced in eleventh and twelfth century Egypt, as well as twelfth and thirteenth century Iran and thirteenth and fourteenth century Syria. The kind of decoration seen here with its oak leaves and other suggestions of temperate forest is, however, characteristically Spanish.

This form of storage jar with its slightly concave sides is best known under its Italian name, *albarello*. The form is, however, likely to be of Iranian origin and made its way to Europe from Syria, probably as part of the trade in sweetmeats, dried fruits, etc./, from eastern Mediterranean shores.

CERAMIC AQUAMANILE IN THE FORM OF A LADY HOLDING A WATERSKIN

Iran, 13th century
Height 26 cm (10 1/4 in.), base 11 x 12 cm (4 3/8 x 4 3/4 in.)
LNS 305 C

There was in thirteenth century Iran a vogue for such anthropomorphic and zoomorphic ceramic aquamanile. Numerous examples are known, among which this is one of the finest.

The precise significance attached to the present piece is not certain, but it could represent the piety of a member of a royal family, because of the high virtue in Islamic society of providing water to the thirsty. A well-known form in which this value is expressed is the establishment in every neighborhood of *sabils* or public fountains, often elaborately and beautifully decorated.

ENAMELED GLASS BOTTLE

Syria or Egypt, 14th century
Height 30.5 cm (12 in.), diameter 17.7 cm (7 in.)
LNS 6 G

Enameling on glass is another among numerous techniques of Islamic origin which were bequeathed to western European craftsmen. It likely has its origins in the enameling over ceramic glazes of twelfth and thirteenth century Iran (*minai* — No **34** in this exhibition), which may have been stimulated by the overglaze luster technique, which in turn relied upon the earlier tradition of luster-painting on glass.

This robust example is typical of the Mamluk school of glass enameling which supplied a princely clientele, both for their private use and, for example, in making sumptuous lamps for the mosques, mausolea and religious schools founded and endowed by the Mamluk *amirs*. The lotus blossoms incorporated into its decoration represent elements of widespread Chinese influence in the arts of the period.

ROCK CRYSTAL BOTTLE

Region uncertain, probably 10th century
Height 4.5 cm (1 3/4 in.), diameter 3 cm (1 3/16 in.)
LNS 4 HS

The early Islamic hardstone industry was widespread and prolific. It favored rock crystal as a material and often produced objects of great quality. Aside from the well-established school of Fatimid (10th–11th century) rock crystal working, it is extremely likely that rock crustal objects were produced, among other places, in Iraq and eastern Iran. Due to its abstract sculptural qualities, it is possible that the present piece was made in one of the more eastern areas.

There exists the possibility that the top of the bottle was broken and ground down in ancient times and that the present bronze or silver lid replaces an original gold one. The corroded-in-place nature of this lid, however, assures that it has been on the piece during its centuries of burial.

LARGE CARVED ROCK CRYSTAL BOWL

Mughal India, 17th century
Height 9 cm (3 9/16 in.), length 24.2 cm (9 9/16 in.), width 16.7 cm (6 9/16 in.)
LNS 48 HS

The Mughals were among the world's great patrons of hardstone carving, the ateliers patronized by them producing a wide range of objects including some of the most exquisite vessels ever executed. The present example is one of the largest and finest Mughal rock crystal pieces which have come down to us. The rosette and lotus leaf foot, as well as the acanthus leaf and lotus bud handles, are marvelously designed and modeled. The subtle but sharp lobing of the bowl exhibits a precise correspondence between exterior and interior, the wall thickness diminishing with great precision as it rises.

The gold mounts were added later, perhaps in the eighteenth century, in Nepal or Tibet, to disguise breakage which had occurred.

PAINTED AND GILDED IVORY CASKET

Sicily, 12th century
Height 8 cm (3 1/8 in.), length 17.8 cm (7 in.), width 11 cm (4 3/8 in.)
LNS 5 I

Ivory has since time immemorial been an important artistic material in large parts of
the ancient and medieval world. Sicily, which was under strong Islamic influence
from the ninth to the thirteenth centuries, is well represented by a sizeable corpus of
ivory objects, one type of which is represented by this casket with gilded bronze
mounts.

The iconography and style of its animal representations, as might be expected,
exhibit a combination of Islamic and Byzantine elements.

GOLD PENDANT SET WITH GARNETS AND EMERALD

Probably Anatolia, second half 12th–first half 13th century
Height 5.4 cm (2 1/8 in.), width 3.25 cm (1 9/32 in.)
LNS 20 J

Filigree constructed box-like gold jewelry was widely made and much in favor in a
variety of Islamic lands between the tenth and fourteenth centuries, the different
schools exhibiting characteristic forms and workmanship. This piece is of a very rare
type, although it employs some particular features of both earlier Egypto-Syrian and
Iranian work of the eleventh century (e.g. the figure eight borders) and of later,
thirteenth to fourteenth century Syro-Egyptian and South Russian schools (e.g. the
densely-set backing strips).

It is unclear whether any of the stones are the originals. The piece would have
been outlined by small pearls held by means of a wire or string running through the
edge loops.

BIRD

Himalayan Blue-throated Barbet (*Cyanops asiatica*) perched on a branch
Opaque watercolor on paper by Ustad Mansur
India, c. 1620
Height 33.9 cm, width 22.3 cm
LNS 29 MS

This painting is inscribed: *amal-i nadir al-asri jahangir shahi* 'The work of the Wonder
of the Age (in the service of) King Jahangir'. Mansur had gained the title Ustad
(Master) during the reign of Akbar and had already received the title Nadir al-Asr by
1612. The form Nadir al-Asri is more usually found attached to the name of Farrukh
Beg, to whom Jahangir gave the title 'Wonder of the Age' in 1609. However, this
form of the title appears in Jahangir's handwriting together with the name Mansur
on a painting of a Zebra in the Victoria and Albert Museum and a Bengal Florican in
the Indian Museum, Calcutta. Another painting of a blue throated barbet by Mansur
is in the Victoria and Albert Museum.

THREE BIRDS IN A TREE

Illustrated page from "The Usefulnesses of Animals" by Ibn Bakhtishu
Iran, early 14th century
Height 26.5 cm (10 1/2 in.), width 20.8 cm (8 1/4 in.)
LNS 30 MS

The manuscript of which this page forms a part, like so many others of the period,
embodies the blend that was Iranian Islamic culture at the time.

Most notably in this connection we may point out its Persian text written in
Arabic script (including the archaizing "Kufic" line in the lower half) and its
painting, exhibiting strong Chinese influence but executed in an unmistakably
Islamic spirit.

PRINCELY MANUSCRIPT OF THE QUR'AN

Egypt, completed 25 Ramadan 746 AH/19 January 1346 AD
Individual pages 51.5 cm x 38 cm (20 1/4 x 15 in.)
LNS 47 MS

Such large and noble Mamluk Qur'an manuscripts are extremely rare outside the collection of the Egyptian National Library. They were usually commissioned for one of the grand mausolea, religious schools or mosques with which the Mamluk *amirs* so enriched Cairo, and which are largely responsible for the city's unique architectural heritage.

The fine paper and calligraphy, along with the sumptuous floral and geometric decoration, executed in colors and gold leaf, combine to embody the finest type of Qur'an manuscript production in one of its great classic aspects.

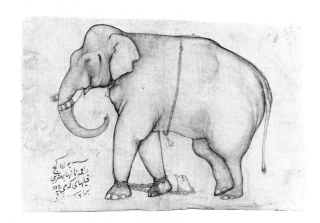

SAYINGS OF THE PROPHET MUHAMMAD

Manuscript of the 28th part of al-Bukhari's "True Collection" of the *Hadith*
Egypt, 14th century
Individual page, 26.7 cm. x 18 cm (10 1/2 x 7 1/8 in.)
LNS 73 MS

Whereas for Muslim's the Qur'an is the pure word of God as revealed to and pronounced by the Prophet Muhammad, the *Hadith* is constituted by various collections of his sayings as a wise and divinely guided man, which were expressed for the further guidance of the community of believers.

Among these collections, that of al-Bukhari (born 810, died 870 AD) is perhaps the most well-known, and as we see here, was sufficiently revered to be executed in an opulent edition for the edification of refined readers.

THE EMPEROR JAHANGIR'S ROYAL ELEPHANT PAVAN GAJ

Corrected brush drawing on paper
Mughal India, 1615
Height 20.3 cm (8 in.), width 31.1 cm (12 1/4 in.)
LNS 76 MS

The drawing is inscribed in the lower left hand corner in the Emperor's own hand: 'Likeness of Pavan Gaj drawn by Nanha, the best of the elephants which runs like an Iraqi horse'.

The elephant's Hindi name Pavan is that of the Vedic Wind God Vayu (pavana), alias the wind, an allusion to its speed. The choice of name may indicate that the elephant was a gift to Jahangir from one of the Rajput princes in his service. Other inscriptions on the reverse include librarian's notes recording its inspection by the Emperors Shah Jahan and Aurangzeb and transfers of its custody.

The artist Nanha was the uncle of Jahangir's celebrated portraitist Bishandas. He was already employed in Akbar's royal library c. 1585 working on the Timur Nama (started by 1584) and contributed miniatures to other royal manuscripts during Akbar's reign and portraits under Jahangir.

BRONZE ASTROLABE

Iran, Isfahan, dated 571 AH/1175–76 AD
Height overall 14.3 cm (5 5/8 in.), width 8.9 cm (3 1/2 in.)
LNS 34 M

The making of fine scientific instruments was a highly developed handicraft industry in Islam, and the making of planispheric astrolabes (which required extensive astronomical tables) was one of the most important of these. Somewhat analogous to the sextant, it allowed navigation and the determination of directions from the heavenly bodies.

This astrolabe has the *qibla* (directions of Mecca, for prayer) from Isfahan marked on its back, inside a niche-shaped compartment. This is consistent with the fact that the maker, who is represented by two other known astrolabes, signs himself "Muhammad, son of Hamid al-Isfahani".

STEEL POWDER FLASK

India, Deccan, perhaps Hyderabad, later 16th–first half 17th century
Length 14.1 cm (5 3/4 in.), width 8.9 cm (3 1/2 in.)
LNS 142 M

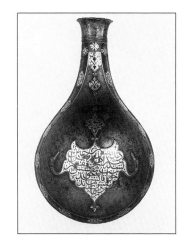

Firearms were an important factor in warfare in India from the first half of the sixteenth century onwards, and they are prominently depicted in miniature paintings in the second half of the century.

Such a flask as this, which is relief cut and overlaid with gold but missing its upper spout, would have served an important musketeer in filling his powder chamber, and was perfectly functional, aside from its beautiful form and decoration.

PARCEL GILT BRONZE DIVINING BOWL

India, Deccan, dated 956 AH/1549–50 AD
Height 7.5 cm (3 in.), diameter 22.8 (9 in.)
LNS 293 M

Large numbers of bowls of this form and function are known from the later (18th–19th) centuries, but this must rank as one of the earliest, finest and most important examples in existence. Although it exhibits aspects of the continuation of the Timurid traditions, this is unquestionably an Indian object, making it perhaps the earliest firmly dated example of Indian Islamic metalwork. Considering its finesse, we understand the large and bold signature inside the foot ring "The work of Husayn Shakani".

The piece is missing the central post and its whirling element which was spun around in divining. There was also a further element attached on one side near the lip, where there is a rather large hole through the side wall.

CARVED LIMESTONE NICHE

Greater Syria, probably second quarter 8th century
Height 125 cm (49 1/4 in.), width 62.5 cm (24 5/8 in.)
LNS 65 S d

This panel comes from the palace and administration center in the Citadel of 'Amman, an important member of a rather extensive series of Umayyad palaces in various parts of Greater Syria.

The use of such colonnette-flanked niches, as well as the denticulate borders and the stylized grape scrolls, form part of the Umayyad repertory of ornament, although all have pre-Islamic backgrounds. Horseshoe arches are also to be encountered in other monuments of the Umayyad period, whereas they are often thought of as typical of later *Maghribi* (Spanish and North African) architecture.

PAIR OF CARVED WOOD DOORS

Iran, Khurasan, 12th century
Height 182.5 cm (71 7/8 in.)
LNS 3 W a-c

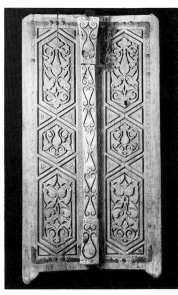

This fine and extremely rare example of twelfth-century Iranian wood carving affords us the opportunity to witness the close consonances between the woodwork and other elements of architectural decoration of the period. The hexagon and elongated hexagon layout of the door leaves was a popular one for stucco and terracotta, particularly borders and frames of large architectural units and areas. The style of the floral and foliate decoration of the doors and the central post offer the closest kind of parallels for two different styles of stucco decoration of twelfth-century Iran, both derived ultimately from the "bevelled style" of the ninth century.

Index